OTHER BOOKS BY *Jim Bishop*

THE GLASS CRUTCH

THE MARK HELLINGER STORY

PARISH PRIEST

THE GIRL IN POISON COTTAGE

THE MAKING OF A PRIEST

THE DAY LINCOLN WAS SHOT

THE GOLDEN HAM

THE DAY CHRIST DIED

GO WITH GOD

THE DAY CHRIST WAS BORN

SOME OF MY VERY BEST

THE MURDER TRIAL OF JUDGE PEEL

HONEYMOON DIARY

A DAY IN THE LIFE OF PRESIDENT KENNEDY

JIM BISHOP: REPORTER

A DAY IN THE LIFE OF
PRESIDENT JOHNSON

RANDOM HOUSE  NEW YORK

A DAY IN THE

LIFE OF

PRESIDENT

JOHNSON

JIM BISHOP

Dedicated to my Daughters
Karen and Kathleen;
Old enough to read,
And young enough to think
Their father is the best

FOR THE RECORD:

It is doubtful that the scope of the office of President of the United States is fully understood. Most Americans think of it as one leg in a governmental triad, the other two being the Congress and the United States Supreme Court. In a constitutional sense, this is almost true. The founding fathers of the United States of America designed a system of balance so that the Congress would enact the laws; the President would implement them and comport himself as the head of the nation; the Supreme Court would be empowered to negate the actions of the other two if such actions were not sanctioned by the Constitution and the Bill of Rights.

In practice, the three legs of government are uneven in strength. The only time in history one might find triangular balance would be in a period of political calm, such as the early part of the Calvin Coolidge administration. No action produces no contest. When political turbulence stirs, either within or outside the country, a struggle for power begins between the President and the Congress. With a few exceptions, these have been won by Congress, which in its sectional loyalties could halt progress by refusing to pass such legisla-

: vii

tion as the Chief Executive desired, or pass legislation he might be reluctant to sign into law.

The road to presidential power runs through the committee rooms of Congress. Lyndon B. Johnson knows this road better than any of his predecessors. His detractors say that he doesn't know any other. History already shows that this man has made greater strides with more legislation in one year than most Presidents achieve in a full term of office.

He has more power, and has kept it on a tighter leash, than any President in American history. This is not to re-emphasize that he leads the most favored nation in the most favored century, because this honor has accrued to several Presidents. Johnson's scope of power is broader because he has made it so. He leads a military organization more powerful than any other in history; he leads a country which, economically, is so affluent that it boasts the largest middle class in the world; he uses technological advances for the welfare of the people as well as a measure of might; he initiates more legislation than Congress does; he executes what were only the dreams of former Presidents; he helps troubled nations economically, orders others policed, protected, or defended—and, withal, has managed to alienate the press and incur the suspicion of jaded intellectuals who see Lyndon Johnson as an ornery Texan falling downstairs to success.

The elusive truth lies somewhere in the confusion of all this activity. To find it, I asked Jack Valenti, then a presidential assistant, to obtain permission for me to spend a few days in the White House—as I had done with other Presidents. Mr. Johnson wasn't sure that he could afford to have me around day and night for any length of time. Much of his work involves national security and some of it reveals the President's personal opinions of politicians here and abroad.

I, on the other hand, needed complete co-operation in order to follow a story wherever it might lead. And after further negotiations with the White House, I was told, to my satisfaction, that President Johnson was prepared to open everything —closets too, if necessary—to get an accurate picture of his day and his personality. I was granted the freedom of the Executive Mansion, to see whatever I pleased and to interview secretaries, servants and executives. It was understood, of course, that I was not to walk into Mr. Johnson's office unannounced or when he was engaged in a confidential discussion.

The President, once committed, was more expansive and more generous with his time than any other I had known. He was not only available to me, but several times had men looking for me even late at night when I had quit working. Mrs. Bishop, who has been my assistant for five years, accompanied me, and we spent eleven days with President and Mrs. Johnson, eight at the White House and three at their Texas ranch. We observed, took notes, listened and asked questions of assistants and cooks and presidential pilots and ranch foremen, friends and enemies, those who regard Lyndon Johnson as a genius and those, on the nether end of the scale, who fear and distrust him.

President Johnson did not try to present his "best side" for me, nor did any of the family, except Mrs. Johnson, who has no other. The President was, in turn, informative, discerning, hospitable, impatient, sarcastic, considerate, and never pulled rank. He walked too fast, wore his forbidding expression, worked too many hours, constantly consulted with his team of advisers, made decisions as Harry Truman once did—quietly and irrevocably—and, at home, turned out to be a kissing husband and father.

A Day in the Life of President Johnson

He is not easy to approach or to know. President Johnson gives his confidence slowly and completely. The roars of rage are reserved for those for whom he feels affection. The rest are castigated with icicles of formality. As a man, he has no hobbies and abhors cocktail parties; he scans newspapers and television newcasts all day and averages about thirteen hours a day at work.

This book is not political. It is a portrait of a President at home and at work.

Jim Bishop
Hallandale, Florida

A DAY IN THE LIFE OF PRESIDENT JOHNSON

7:00 A.M.

A finger of breeze comes out of the South, spinning the leaves of poplars and oaks and red maples, dimpling the Potomac River and lifting the American flag on top of the White House to a tired salute. It is warm, but not hot, and the front of the Executive Mansion holds a cast of blue behind the colonnades.

Some of Washington is up. On Pennsylvania Avenue, taxis cross bands of pink and yellow light at the side streets, carrying lounging newspaper readers to the Department of Justice, the Capitol, the Post Office, cafeterias, the Government Printing Office. The broad band of concrete coming up out of Virginia channels a ribbon of automobiles toward the city. The express highway out of Baltimore spins a thin line of speeding cars, and the roads out of Silver Springs and Bethesda pour hot engines and cool drivers into the huge pinwheel of streets which spoke the nation's capital.

In the Pentagon, men on bicycles wheel slowly along the corridors of the huge doughnut, dropping mail here and there. Some clerks park their cars on the east plaza of the Capitol and walk slowly through the revolving doors. In the Washington

: 3

Hotel, the Speaker of the House lifts his white head off the pillow and studies the little clock on the night table. Up Connecticut Avenue, along Embassy Row, a few of the older men take their morning walks while the young sleep.

School buses begin the cheerful businesss of stopping at curbs to pick up chattering children. In Lafayette Park, brazen bluejays chase the larks from the grass. Gifted machines hammer words onto paper in dozens of offices and in nearby Georgetown; lilacs and budding roses fight a losing battle for a square inch of sunshine.

On the east side of the White House, a shaft of light stands tight and narrow on a corridor rug. Table lamps are lit the length of the second-floor hall. The oil portraits stare solemnly from the walls, as they do in darkness as well as in light, and no one pauses to think of what some of them have seen in this historic house.

The paintings have kept these secrets, and many more. They have seen kings and queens and princes in their finery; wedding parties and the grief of Presidents' families; the trill of laughter and stifled sobs; most of all, they have seen august men come and go, and some were precisely right for the time, and some were not, but all were bigger men than they had been, and each departed with a great deal of work yet to be done.

Two men are in the corridor. Marshall Gaddis is finishing a tour of night duty, and he pauses a moment with Paul Glynn, the day man, at the desk which stands between the elevator and the President's bedroom. Glynn, slender and thirty-five, a veteran Air Force sergeant, nods at the routine news: an usher has stacked the morning newspapers against the President's bedroom door; no phone calls of importance are on the log; no

message marked with the little red tab of urgency has arrived
from the West Wing. Gaddis leaves and Glynn sits at the desk,
doodling with a pencil on a pad.

He glances at the newspapers leaning against the door, and
walks west toward the presidential living room. Glynn shoves a
swinging door on the right side and says good morning to one
of the butlers. Three members of the kitchen personnel have
been on duty since 5:30 A.M. He looks for Zephyr Wright,
but she is not in the kitchen.

Glynn, as the President's personal man, knows every inch of
the second-floor living quarters. He knew it even when he
served aboard *Air Force Two,* the Vice-President's plane: now
and then Glynn had accompanied Vice-President Lyndon
Johnson to the White House before a flight to a faraway place.
He knew Johnson too, but not as well as he thought.

When John F. Kennedy died, Lyndon Johnson moved up to
Air Force One, and Sergeant Glynn was transferred back to
Andrews Air Force Base. Six days later he was told that the
White House was on the phone. "That you, Paul?" the Presi-
dent said. "What happened? Why did you leave me?" Sergeant
Glynn was embarrassed. He explained that the transfer was
routine. "Well," the President had said, "don't you want to be
with me? I need you now more than ever."

It was personal talk between the Commander in Chief and a
sergeant. So Paul Glynn is back. He works two days on and
two off, and he stands in the living room—which is the last
thirty feet of the corridor, closed off by double doors—and he
wonders where he will take his three children tomorrow. The
room in which he stands has been changed since the Kennedy
family left. Mrs. Johnson put some yellow into it, and the color
picks up the daylight in the cathedral west window and makes

: 5

the room more cheerful, as judicious use of make-up will do for a wan face.

Mrs. Johnson kept some of the furniture which had endured through several Presidents, and added some pieces from her home in Texas. On a chest of drawers, there are two photographs of John F. Kennedy. An inscription reads: "We want Tex to feel as at home here as on the ranch. Jackie." She referred to a gift pony. A Kennedy liquor wagon has been replaced by a card table and four chairs. There are few other changes. Mrs. Kennedy redecorated the White House, and Lady Bird Johnson is a person who can admire another's work without envy.

Paul Glynn walks back to his desk. He is half seated when he sees that the newspapers have disappeared. At once he walks to the door with the President's seal and stoops. There is light underneath. He turns the knob and opens the door. Inside, the foyer light is on. The sergeant stands. He says, "Good morning, Mr. President. You ready for breakfast now, sir?"

"Morning, Paul," the President says. "How's the weather?" Glynn steps into the bedroom. "Sunny, sir," he says. "Not too hot." President Lyndon Baines Johnson reclines on a couple of pillows in a four-poster bed. The newspapers are spread across his stomach. In his hand is a television remote control. The room is high-ceilinged, and he looks across it and up to three television sets. The control in his hand maintains three separate images, while depressing the sound on two as he listens to one.

He wears his glasses and switches from station to station to pick up the morning news. Sergeant Glynn lifts some papers from a table and a few from the floor and assembles them in a folder. "Where are the boys?" the President says. The boys are W. Marvin Watson, his appointments secretary, and Jake

Jacobsen, his legislative counsel. Usually they are in the presidential bedroom with news of the latest developments, domestic and foreign, before Lyndon Johnson is out of bed.

"They'll be up soon, sir," Glynn says.

The remote control is set on the night table and the President of the United States swings upright and flicks his hair back. His feet seek no slippers. He stands upright in plain striped cotton pajamas and picks up a robe and the newspapers.

"Some melon balls and a little chipped beef," the President says. Paul Glynn nods. "Tea, sir?" he says. The President doesn't answer. He is on his way to the bathroom, a big man with a strong frame, brown sun-squinted eyes, lips which appear to be compressed with bitterness, and the heavy stride of an overage athlete.

The bathroom door closes. Glynn walks fast, out of the bedroom, across the hall, and into the kitchen. "Melon balls, chipped beef in cream, and tea," he says. Mrs. Zephyr Wright, a middle-aged Negro who has worked as a cook for the Johnsons for twenty-five years, is a lady of poise. She is unimpressed with the Presidency, and is probably the only person who if a President is late for a meal can tell him, "Go sit in the kitchen until I fix you something."

Glynn is back in a moment. He opens and closes doors as quietly as a frightened burglar. He stands in the center of the bedroom to see what has to be cleaned up before breakfast. There is nothing. He looks across the beige rug for remnants of the President's night work; he moves a floor humidifier and pulls back the drapes facing the south lawn of the White House. The blue eyes dart from point to point.

From a closet near the door to Mrs. Johnson's bedroom come a blue suit, several ties from which the wearer can make a choice, and black shoes. A white shirt and black socks and underwear are drawn from a chest. President Johnson doesn't have a big wardrobe. Recent Presidents have averaged three dozen suits of clothes; Johnson has twenty suits, two pairs of black shoes, two of brown, two pairs of lounging shoes, and two pairs of Texas boots which he never wears.

The clothes are folded carefully across a chair. The sergeant stands at ease, but his eyes still dart. The painting over the fireplace of a Negro sewing flags is straight; the photos of the President's wife and two daughters stand pensive on the mantel, where the President wants them; a crucifix hangs over the mantel; beneath the mantel, inscribed in marble, are words put there by Mrs. John F. Kennedy before she left: "Occupied by John Fitzgerald Kennedy during his Two Years, Ten Months and Two Days as President of the United States. Jan. 20, 1961–Nov. 22, 1963."

On the side of the bed nearest the bathroom is a night table with some notes and a pen. A matching night table on the other side supports cold cream and other feminine lotions. The President's telephone reposes on his notes. It is a yellow instrument with sixteen square buttons which make instantaneous connections with his assistants and his most important Cabinet secretaries. When he presses one of them, the phone at the other end does not pause in its ring.

In the bathroom, the President does not dawdle. The morning ablutions are observed in orderly arrangement. He scans the newspapers with little appreciation of the interpretation of news by the White House correspondents. He feels that he knows what has happened and how it happened, and sometimes why. The superior and prior knowledge of most Chief Executives about world events imbues in them a rancor for news writers.

Mr. Johnson tosses the papers aside, brushes his teeth, and begins the morning shave. He uses a magnifying mirror which exposes every pore in his big face. This is the only time of the day he is on the receiving end of the stern and forbidding presidential face. The electric shaver moves up and down and crosswise with swift strokes. His free hand feels the skin to see if it is clear of stubble. The robe is taken off, draped on a towel rack, and the pajamas come off.

He turns the shower on, feels the warmth of water, pushes the drape aside and steps in. He is still there, soaping himself with the vigor he applies to all of his duties, when Dr. George Burkley is admitted to the bedroom by Glynn. Burkley was also President Kennedy's physician. The new President asked him to stay, and to show his appreciation, sent an order to the Department of Defense, promoting Dr. Burkley from Rear Admiral, U. S. Navy, to Vice-Admiral.

Dr. Burkley is a quiet man with a deep concern for ethics. He rarely discusses his relationship with his patient. A week after the promotion request, Johnson passed the doctor's office on the ground floor of the White House and saw him standing in the doorway. "Hello," he said. "Did you get your promotion, Doctor?" The doctor hesitated. "They haven't got around to it yet, Mr. President," he said.

President Johnson stopped walking. His head began to incline downward and the forehead contracted into the familiar wrinkles of annoyance. He turned to an aide. "Get me Cy Vance at the Pentagon," he said. In a moment the President was on the phone demanding to know why it required a week to obey an order. Two hours later the certificate of promotion was on Dr. Burkley's desk.

The doctor is graying, a Catholic of deep faith and few words. He waits for the President to come out of the bathroom. Mr. Johnson seems surprised. The doctor asks him to sit for a moment. Softly he says that he has been following Mr. Johnson's work schedule, and some days the President has not left his office before 10:20 P.M. "It's a long workday," he says. "I'm not going to forbid you to keep going at this pace, but I certainly am going to keep checking you while you're doing it."

President Johnson sits like an obedient boy. The rubber cuff is placed on his arm. He opens his mouth on command (he gave up smoking in 1955 when he sustained a myocardial infarction), sits patiently as the doctor listens to the solid thump of the most important heart in the country, bends forward as the doctor taps his back percussively, and stands buttoning his pajama coat as Dr. Burkley replaces instruments in a bag. "Well?" the President says, and hops back into bed. Burkley zips the bag. "Everything is okay, Mr. President," he says. "No problems. I don't know how you do it, but you do it. A blood pressure of one hundred and twenty over seventy is a steady thing with you." Dr. Burkley returns to his office on the ground floor.

The President makes some phone calls. Between them he says to Paul Glynn, "See if Mrs. Johnson wants to come in." Some of the people he phones are at home. Others are already in their offices. In each case he asks no preface and no epilogue, just the unprefabricated facts. "How about that housing bill? Did you get to the Hill yet and see the committee? I told you to get there because it's never going to get out of committee until you fellows learn to go over there and talk for what you want. If you have a good case, they'll listen.

"What's this in the paper about a trip to Chicago? No, I don't want any advance notice and you know it. I don't care who leaked it, I want it stopped . . . You fellows did a good job on the hospital Medicare section and I want you to know that I appreciate it. It wasn't easy to get everybody in line . . . Paul, where's that breakfast? I'm hungry."

Glynn goes to the door. A Negro waiter is there with a tray. The sergeant precedes him back into the bedroom and goes on into the bathroom, where he picks up the wrinkled *Baltimore Sun*, the *Wall Street Journal*, the *Washington Post* and the *New York Times*. The day has begun.

At 7:25 A.M. the White House police at the west gate pass a car through. In it is Walt Whitman Rostow, Special Assistant to the President for National Security, a Rhodes Scholar who taught economic history at the Massachusetts Institute of Technology. He has an ageless and pleasant face. Mr. Rostow gets out of the car with a briefcase and strides through the big reception room and down the steps to his office in the basement. The hour is early, but Rostow has already seen the previous night's summary of world events and has distilled it and sent it up to the President's bedroom.

He drops the briefcase in his office, checks the coffee to make certain that it is steamy and black, looks on his desk for new papers. The phone rings. It is a scrambler type, so that whatever is said at either end of a conversation is garbled in the transmitter and reassembled into words in the receiver. The caller is a military operator who wants to test the phone. "I hear you loud and clear," Mr. Rostow says.

He walks down to the first level of the Situation Room, which is in the basement, chatting with his assistant, Arthur McCafferty. The question is always the same: "What's new?" McCafferty looks like a Latin in mid-siesta. He shakes his head. In a world of chronic tension, the question is relative. What's new depends upon what is happening in the world. A bombing in Viet Nam. A statement by Foreign Minister de Courville that France will find her destiny independently of East or West. A threat from China. Silence in Moscow. A copy of a confidential memo to the President from Arthur Goldberg at the United Nations.

The pulse of the world is counted here. It is always arhythmic, but it keeps beating. Chattering machines spew out news and intelligence. They are marked Associated Press, United Press International, Reuters, F.B.I. Service, Foreign Broadcast Service. There are pneumatic tubes for messages, and there is a "hot line" to Moscow which runs through the Pentagon to the Kremlin. A few steps down lead to the Situation Room itself.

This is a windowless room in the basement where on some occasions the President of the United States is summoned in the late hours to face a crisis which will not hold until morning. There is a conference table, an assortment of telephones, and neutral wall drapes which hide unneutral wall maps. It is an instantaneous reaction room. Within a few minutes of any ominous news, the Secretaries of State and Defense, the Joint Chiefs of Staff, the President and Walt Rostow will assemble here to discuss, debate, decide. The enormous power of President Lyndon Johnson is most apparent in this room.

Intelligence from the State Department, from the Central Intelligence Agency, from the Army, Navy, and Air Force hangs on clipboards. There are three "secure phones"—private lines policed by the military—in the Situation Room. There is a direct line to the Prime Minister of Great Britain. Others reach out from the White House to embassies abroad.

Back in his office, Walt Whitman Rostow removes his jacket

and sits over a cup of coffee to begin the routine work with a staff of eight intelligence officers and five communications men. All of them fight the big second hand on the wall clock, because no matter what happens anywhere in the world, they want to know at once and they must know accurately. They smother panic with smiles; imminent threats to world peace with confidential whispers.

The philosophy of Mr. Rostow's office is that there will be no great war because the price is too high for the victor. Only an accidental miscalculation can trigger a universal holocaust. There is also a long-range feeling for pendulum history—that the Soviet Union swings slowly from left toward center, that the United States swings from right toward center, and that the two nations have more common interests than either has with, say, China. This is an oversimplification, because in the tide of history there are rips and currents crossing the main stream, and momentary but disturbing political winds and squalls.

The wealth and might of the United States make it mandatory that foreign policy should always steer toward peace and away from conflict because nothing can be gained, and much lost, in an international death struggle. Fifty years ago a crisis between two such nations as Albania and Greece would be of small moment at the White House. Today the alarm bells ring all over the world, and as strong nations express partisan feelings, the question in the White House becomes: "Who struck the match and how quickly can we put out the fire?"

The so-called small crisis is gone. Any tipping of the international boat is noted everywhere, and some nations automatically try to tip it further, while others attempt to restore its balance. Everything is of concern to President Johnson. He wants to know at once. Mr. Rostow, who worked for Kennedy as well as Johnson, found that the difference between the two was not a superior knowledge of foreign affairs on the part of Kennedy versus a disinterest in Johnson, but that Kennedy wanted every bit of news spelled out and interpreted (he once said, "Rostow is the only man who can write faster than I can read"), while Johnson wants the memo cut to the irreducible facts.

Johnson's schooling in foreign affairs was achieved as majority leader of the United States Senate and as Vice-President of the United States. Rostow, an expert in the field, thinks of Johnson as "immensely knowledgeable." If it were not so, Rostow knows his work would entail the additional drudgery of explaining and re-explaining the checks and balances of world events to the President. To the contrary, all Mr. Johnson asks is a terse statement of what has happened.

"Is the President awake?" Mr. Rostow asks. An assistant nods. The word has been passed through the switchboard that he is working, as he usually does, in his bedroom. The "word" goes out in the White House no matter what Mr. Johnson does: "The President has just left his office for the Rose Garden"; "The President is now in his private quarters"; "The President just left through the southwest gate to keep a dental appointment"; "The President just entered his office."

Rostow does not plan to see Mr. Johnson. There is nothing of consequence to be discussed on this particular morning. However, it is possible that the President may ask to see Mr. Rostow. These are the "at once" calls. "Walt, can you see me right away? I'm upstairs." This is the irritant, and also the joy, of the Johnson administration. Everything is accomplished instantaneously or as close to now as presidential impatience will permit.

The Cabinet and the White House assistants accept it as

part of Mr. Johnson's personality. The trait is not new. He has been an "at once" man all of his life. He didn't like schoolwork in Texas, so he did it at once and studied perhaps fifty percent harder than any other student to make good grades. Also, he aspired to be the "good boy" in his mother's eyes, and this required unremitting labor and house chores. In this, as in all the work of his life, the boy drove himself hard to mow lawns, run errands, clean his room, and thus win approval, when his spirit yearned to be two blocks away pitching a winning game.

As a representative from Texas, he worked so hard that the joke among members of his party was that Lyndon Johnson would be lost in Washington if he was taken anywhere except the House Office Building, his apartment, and the Capitol itself. The jest was bitter. On the floor at high noon he would present a completed bill with the snide comment: "While you guys were out partying all night, I was up in the office getting this thing straightened out." As a United States senator, he worked so hard and understood the aims of his party so well that he was elected as the youngest majority leader in history, and the most junior of senators to achieve the post.

He works harder because he yearns for approval. The President bruises easily, so, to kill criticism, he aspires to permanent perfection. If one of the scores of thousands of employees in scores of departments under the Chief Executive makes a mistake, Mr. Johnson takes personal umbrage. It amounts to an affront. This applies to the Secretary of State as well as to a freshman clerk.

When Johnson won the approval of the American people in a commanding election, he felt such joy that he sounded like a Texas braggart. It was the boy again, displaying a report card with lots of A's. Still, it was interpreted as hillbilly crowing.

But there is no one among the men close to Johnson who believes that he is boastful. His goal is to leave a record of accomplishment unmatched by any other President, and if this happens, he expects the country to know it and appreciate it. If he lacks the charm of Kennedy, the brilliance of Franklin Roosevelt, the philosophy of Wilson, it must be admitted that they lacked the Johnsonian capacity to work aggressively on every problem to come to the presidential attention, and also to work longer hours and to consult more before reaching a decision.

Since Franklin D. Roosevelt's tenure, Presidents have drawn attention to themselves with summit meetings. In his first three years, Johnson asked for none. He has not risked rebuff, as Eisenhower did in Paris. He has had no Vienna spanking, such as Kennedy sustained at the hands of Khrushchev. No Bay of Pigs disaster stains his record. No Berlin impasse has left him in the untenable position Roosevelt faced in 1945. But Johnson's administration is not yet close to the smooth silent operation for which he yearns. He applies unguents to the chronic sores of the nation—Viet Nam, Cuba, Peking, Moscow, inflation—but they do not heal, and he wonders why men of good will cannot see that peace and relaxation of tension is as good for their countries as it is for his. International bluff and belligerence are beyond his understanding, and when they occur, the thin mouth becomes more compressed and he works harder at preaching unity and understanding.

Two men are with him in the bedroom. Both are Texans, both have his confidence. Paul Glynn is again in the corridor at his desk, flashing the word: "Mr. Watson and Mr. Jacobsen are with the President upstairs." Watson sits at the foot of the bed. Jacobsen is on a chair near the end table. Mr. Johnson still has all three television sets on, but the sound has been shut off.

7:00 A.M.

He is going over his night reading with them. The catalyst for this sheaf of papers is Mrs. Juanita Roberts, the President's personal secretary. Anyone who has a special memorandum, or a terse report, or something pleasant but unimportant, or a suggestion for the President, gives it to Mrs. Roberts. She tries to keep the number of papers to fifty per night, but she averages ninety.

Each paper now carries a decision in the presidential hand. "Good man for the position. Too bad we already have two men from his state." "Approved." "Carry this out at once." "Disapproved." "This should be State's decision. See Ball." In Congressional matters, he often writes a notation that he wants to call Speaker John McCormick, Senator Mike Mansfield or Smathers; sometimes Congressman Albert or Boggs.

He goes over these items, and his reasons for his decisions, with his two aides. Jacobsen, tall and gray and courtly, a man with a deep voice and compassionate eyes, presents the morning *Congressional Record* to the President. Jacobsen has read it, and has paper clips to mark the places he thinks the President should read.

The *Record* is like a mine assaying a dollar of gold per ton of rock. It is oratorical, crammed with flattering adjectives, and is printed on cheap paper in dull type. To locate the legislative ore, it is necessary for the courageous reader to wet his finger and turn many pages. The last quarter of most issues usually consists of reprints of articles which support the sponsoring Congressman's point of view, or with accolades and favors. Jacobsen reads it every morning to find the thin vein of gold. The President follows the clipped pages, reading quickly, making comments.

"Jake" is a lawyer with a facility for working with the Texas delegation in Congress. He also knows a great deal about the

President's personal affairs, his ranch, businesses, investments. He wears gold cuff links which carry the President's seal—a mark of friendship. Jacobsen is one of the dedicated followers of Johnson who sees him as one of the great men of history. His faith is implicit, and like some of the other assistants, he does not need this fatiguing job. The job needs him. He has neglected a thriving law practice in Austin to remain at the side of Johnson. He is immaculate, meticulous, and he draws the papers from his morning folder with a sentence or two to explain each one. They are returned in the same order.

When the President is irritable or unreasonable, Jake smiles and reminds himself that this is the man who air-conditioned the First Christian Church of Johnson City, Texas, without permitting it to be mentioned. This is the man who discovered a farmer with four children living in squalor on a remote part of a ranch. Johnson seemed merely to glance at the situation, then grunted, put his hands in his trouser pockets, and walked away.

Jake remembers the orders given that night. "Rebuild that house. Send the bill to me." Johnson bought furniture, an automatic washer, asked his aides for adult and children's clothing, and gave the father a job. It worked out well. But Jake knows that Johnson is not a do-gooder or a sucker. He will help people, and do it happily, but in business matters he and Mrs. Johnson seldom permit sentiment to stand in the way of a profit. They have built a fortune through shrewd investments in real estate, television, and securities, and with time, these will be enhanced. Starting with the administration of Dwight D. Eisenhower, Presidents have placed their investments in irrevocable trusts, so that they cannot profit by early knowledge of government purchases and favored corporations. The Johnson fortune, intended in large measure for their daughters,

7:00 A.M.

is now administered by Texas trustees Waddy Bouillion, A. W. Moursund, and Jesse Kellem.

Current business, such as legal contracts and the purchase and sale of cattle and land, runs through Mr. Jacobsen's hands. In most cases, Jake does not bring details to his boss's notice. He consults only when a problem has an optional solution, or if he has bad news. "Then," Jake says, "duck." Today there is nothing of consequence to discuss, and the President turns to Marvin Watson.

Watson hands a typed calendar of the day's appointments to Johnson, who yawns and looks through the bottom of his glasses at it. Watson is a square-built man with a bright face and freshly scrubbed skin. He has been a municipal judge in Texas, a college teacher, and is a Baptist deacon. He is so firm in his admiration that if he was discharged from his duties, he would leave Washington still thinking that Lyndon Johnson is the greatest President in history. He is a man who requires time to reach a firm opinion, but once he stakes a claim to it, his position is unalterable.

The sheet of paper in the President's hand looks like this:

THE PRESIDENT'S SCHEDULE

10:30 Meeting with the Assistant Secretaries of Defense

11:00 Cabinet Meeting

12:30 Honorable Ted Heath, Leader of the British Conservative Party

12:45 George Meany
(off the record)

1:00 P.M. Board of Governors Meeting

1:30 Richard Strout and Seville Davis of the *Christian Science Monitor*
(off the record)

2:00 J. E. Wolfe, Secretary Wirtz and Bill Moyers

: 19

A Day in the Life of President Johnson

(off the record)

5:30 Congressman Tom Curtis

(off the record)

6:00 Charles Schultze, Sam Hughes and Sam Cohn

On the calendar, it doesn't look like a busy day. There is a good avenue of time for lunch and a nap between 2:30 and 5:30. However, the official White House calendar is only a jump-off point for Mr. Johnson. There is a second, unofficial, calendar which doubles the appointments. These are persons whom the President would like to see today to discuss matters which have arisen since the first calendar was designed the day before. Then there is a third calendar—made up later—which is never publicized; it details all the additional people the President saw during his day, including his assistants. This list usually covers three sheets of typing paper.

Watson watches the President's reaction from his chair near the bed. A lazy President is difficult for an appointments secretary, but a diligent man who runs all day is equally impossible. He wants to see more people than can be slotted into waking hours, and Watson must keep the President on time, no matter how heavy the schedule. He must also allow an extra few minutes for each person, and hope that it will not be used. In addition, he must know how many minutes it will take the President to ride to the State Department, or Arlington National Cemetery, or any nearby place, and how long it will take to get back. The President does not want to arrive anywhere five minutes ahead of time, and wait.

"All right, fellows," the President says. He hands the appointment sheet to Watson. Jacobsen has a small white pad in his breast pocket in case the President has additional instructions for him. There are none today. Both men get up. If either has any additional news—not part of the record—he states it now. It might be family news, or something amusing. They leave and the servant approaches the bed with the breakfast tray.

Mr. Johnson waves him away, and gets out of bed. He strides barefooted to a door between closets, and opens it and looks in. "Bird," he says loudly, "You coming in to have breakfast with me?" Mrs. Johnson says that she will be right in. The President is a full-time husband. Without Mrs. Johnson, he would be half a man and less. She is a tempering influence, a lady of modesty and good taste, a person who has the ultimate in consideration when he has none left; a pacifier, a reader of her husband's mind—a petite person who thinks of the White House as a temporary abode and who still selects her dresses from a rack in a shop and makes an appointment at a local hairdresser rather than have the beautician come to the First Lady of the Land.

8:00 A.M.

The West Wing begins to light up. Here is the power and the pulse of the Presidency. There are no sinecures. Everybody works. The muted electric typewriters speak an encyclopedia of opinions, decisions, speeches, responses, executive dogma, and hopes, while the brains behind them absorb, read, research, study, and try to maintain a steady course down the middle of Lyndon B. Johnson's mind.

The offices are white and lush. The corridors are narrow and curving. A blizzard of paper settles here and, in time, is swept into file cabinets to be resurrected again if and when someone challenges a judgment. Some of the workers arrive at seven. More at eight. Many at nine. The cars pause at the sentry box in the west gate. The police stoop to study the faces. Sometimes they ask for a look at passes. At other times they wave the occupants through.

Along the sidewalk in front of 1600 Pennsylvania Avenue, a few pickets shoulder signs and begin a march. This morning it is "Let's Pull Out of Viet Nam." Yesterday it was "Black Power Will Dominate." Tomorrow it will be "Send Our Communist

8:00 A.M.

President Back to Texas." The pickets appear to be young and unhappy and poorly nourished. Their feet drag slowly along the smooth sidewalk under a burnished sun. No one looks as indignant as the signs. They stroll in long ellipses, waiting for the cameramen to come. As the sun pauses behind Lafayette Park, they will depart for coffee and conversation; their signs, broken and abused, will be in the gutter.

The White House police patrol the grounds, the mansion, and the corridors. In the big reception room, one of them sits at a desk opposite the shabby press room, examining passes and invitations, nodding good morning to old hands, sending word through Negro ushers that someone is here to see the press secretary, the special assistants, the assistant assistants, the attractive secretaries who walk the halls with important papers and petulant expressions, and the President.

Secret Service agents stand at strategic posts throughout the mansion, the West Wing, the East Wing, and on the grounds. They look like ordinary young men, not Secret Service men, and they guard this particular life more assiduously because they lost one. Two are in the President's office now. They examine everything, lifting blotters, disassembling the Johnson desk phone to see that a transistor set hasn't been put in it overnight. They use Geiger counters on radiators and other metal objects to make certain that active nuclear products have not been introduced into the furnace boilers or drilled into tiny holes in letter openers. They examine the President's watch too.

Bernard West, the urbane chief usher, reports to his small office between floors and goes about the business of supervising public rooms and state dinners. At 8:15 the first mail arrives from the White House Annex—the old State Department

Building—and Juanita Roberts, wearing a small smile, riffles through it. She yanks envelopes from the pile like a magician doing a card trick.

Like a few others who have been with Lyndon Johnson a long time, she knows her man. She knows that when he phones and merely says, "Get me . . ." without the word "please," it is not that Lyndon Johnson is not cordial and polite—"please" represents an extra word. Mrs. Roberts is a middle-aged Southerner with charm and green eye shadow and she presides over an office adjoining the President's. She has three young stenographers to assist her, and their wall desks leave an aisle, but not much more.

They know that the President works late, so they have a schedule allowing the "late" stenographer to report for duty at 1 P.M. Mrs. Yolanda Boozer is the late worker today, and if Mr. Johnson remains in his office until 10:20 P.M., she too will remain. The early workers are Victoria McCammon, a pretty brunette, and Marie Fehmer, a slender girl with blondish hair and pale blue eyes. They assist with the mail. Marvin Watson, on his way back to his office, drops the President's night work off at Mrs. Roberts' desk. She has called a White House messenger to take the early mail upstairs.

Across the hall behind the Fish Room, Harry McPherson enters his office and, like the others, studies the top of the desk before removing his jacket. He is thirty-six, a big brown-haired man, one more Texan. He comes from Tyler and has experience working with the Democratic National Committee. He is the legal expert of the Johnson team, and no bill is passed by Congress before crossing his desk for scrutiny.

The Bureau of the Budget sends McPherson a summary of all Congressional bills and writes notes to the President about each of them. Also, he is Mr. Johnson's strong man in civil

8:00 A.M.

rights matters, and this alone is full-time work. Two lawyers assist him, but McPherson is responsible for this department, and is also charged with recommending federal paroles and pardons to the President. But this is not enough. Arts and Humanities was thrust upon McPherson and so was the White House relationship to the Civil Aeronautics Bureau, in addition to Housing and Urban Affairs.

The desk looks like a stationery store hit by a twister. The big placid Texan sits down behind it and is pleased to find that he can still see a stenographer sitting on the other side. At the moment he is dictating a first draft of a speech for Mr. Johnson. He does his best and is not worried about the echo which will undoubtedly come back this afternoon. It may read: "I'm not satisfied with this. See me."

The most difficult lesson which White House employees have had to learn is that none of the presidential critiques is deadly. Mr. Johnson, an old-line schoolteacher, is blunt and often crude with opinions. Sometimes, when his people react with shock or tears or even threats to resign, it is the President's turn to be shocked. He grew up in a tough school of politics in which Sam Rayburn, Alben Barkley, Harry Hopkins, and John Nance Garner viewed matters as being either good or bad, intelligent or stupid, and there was no such thing as mediocrity or passivity. A man was a party regular who could be trusted to do as he was told, or he was a maverick not worth party confidence.

President Johnson has many of the attributes of the "boss." His actions and his proposals are almost always positive, and like John F. Kennedy, he insists that the team follow his dictates with enthusiasm. The time to differ with Johnson is before the decision. He listens with the wary glance and the restive attitude of a man who mutters, "Talk. It's your nickel," but he listens. Sometimes, when his assistants disagree and become flamboyant in their speeches, he will cut in to say, "All right. Get to the point." When the argument is concluded, the President makes the final decision and the entire West Wing of the White House points in the direction the boss has indicated.

He is less of a committee President than either of the two before him. Eisenhower enjoyed a consensus before making a move; Kennedy had a "bang-board" every evening before dinner, at which time the Kenny O'Donnells, the Larry O'Briens and McGeorge Bundys and Pierre Salingers were expected to be pitted against each other on public questions, in the same way in which an old-time Irish priest pits his curates against each other at dinner. John F. Kennedy listened and made the ultimate decision, of course; but Lyndon Johnson is not only a listener, he's a participant who has studied the question and knows the statistics and the risks.

The choice bedroom on the second floor is Mrs. Johnson's. It has an adjoining room overlooking the West Wing. The President's room has one exposure—windows facing the south grounds. His wife's has windows to the south and the west. The First Ladies almost invariably selected these rooms for themselves. General Eisenhower gave it to his Mamie without a struggle (her mother, Mrs. Doud, a constant guest, had a room on the far side of a corridor which First Families call a living room). Treasury Secretary Anderson and Press Secretary Hagerty said goodnight at the door of Eisenhower's bedroom for three years before they realized that he never slept in his room. He prepared for bed, took his glass of water, and pit-patted through the small connecting closet into his wife's room. In the morning he greeted the early birds back in his own bedroom.

Kennedy gave the choice suite to Jacqueline, but she slept in the four-poster with him. At 7 A.M. or a little later, when George Thomas, his valet, knocked to awaken the President, Thomas did it lightly enough to awaken the President, who would cough slightly to show that he was awake, but still softly enough not to disturb the sleep of Mrs. Kennedy, who arose around nine.

Mrs. Johnson heard the invitation for breakfast, and she is up, her nightgown covered by a robe. She pushes the stray locks of dark hair back and lifts the phone. The accent is Texas abridged, which is to say flat and sharp with precise diction. She calls her maid, Helen Williams, a Negro who has been with Mrs. Johnson seventeen years. "Helen," she says, "please ask the butler to bring me a tray. I'd like to have some coffee, fruit juice, and a little toast and jelly." Mrs. Williams is bright and cheerful, and there is an understanding between her and the First Lady.

Mrs. Williams gives the order in the kitchen, and hurries into the bedroom. Mrs. Johnson is already in the bathroom. She will not join Lyndon without looking her best. She is not only his love, she is his assistant, his guide in the wilderness of Washington society; she knows how to select his good ear for whispering, tolerates his bristling attitude but now and then issues an ultimatum of her own: "Lyndon, I have phoned you three times to come to dinner. If you're not here in five minutes, I am going to bed." In five minutes she retires.

She moves about the bathroom, brushing, washing, putting a dab of make-up on, walking around the official *White House Guide* which lies on the tile floor, knowing that any moment her husband will be at his door, roaring, "Bird, this breakfast is getting cold." When the last stray strand of hair is in place, she adjusts the robe, comes out of the bath nodding good morning at Mrs. Williams, and hurries to the door of the President's room.

Mr. Johnson is a big man for family affection. From each of his girls he expects "a kiss, a hug and a grunt," and as Mrs. Johnson slides into bed beside him he gets his husbandly due and turns on the rarest smile the White House has seen since Calvin Coolidge occupied the mansion. Mrs. Johnson, petite and efficient, smooths the bedclothes so that the tray will fit around her little body.

The President eats while answering his wife's questions, and he eats swiftly, sometimes lifting the dish of melon balls to a point under his chin as he spoons them to his face. His spec-tacled eyes are on the television set across the room. He is watching the Today Show. Hugh Downs is talking to an au-thor whose book has just been published, and Mr. Johnson shows a momentary interest. Sergeant Glynn moves silently about the room, crossing to pick up some laundry from a hamper, returning to adjust the presidential trousers so that the creases are straight, walking across to the bathroom and back. On the last trip between Mr. Johnson's eyes and the TV set, the President roars, "Paul, you can make more moves than any man I ever saw. Can't you pick that stuff up at one time?" Glynn says, "Yes, sir." He masks a knowing smile, because he always thinks of the President as an impatient drill sergeant. But whenever Mr. Johnson "chews" him out, he knows that within a minute or two the President will leaven it with a compliment. He waits, putting the room to rights, and Mr. Johnson turns the television off and picks up the phone.

Over the top of his glasses, the President glances at the sergeant, smiles and says, "By God, Paul. That's a nice tie you're wearing." Mrs. Johnson addresses herself to her breakfast, but is always aware of what her husband is doing. She is silent when he is on the phone, but there is no intonation of his voice which she cannot interpret, and nothing that she cannot recall to his mind later if he asks about it.

The President phones Marvin Watson. He is in a teasing mood. Watson, at his desk in his office, receives the words as a penitent listens to gospel. "We're going to need a little help on this bill, Marvin." Mr. Johnson thinks of Jake Jacobsen, who has a brother-in-law who cares nothing about politics. "Don't ask Jake about it," he says seriously. "He'll call his brother-in-law for advice."

He phones McPherson. "The speech I read last night will do. It's all right, but I think we ought to support it with a few more statistics." The next call is to Courtenay Valenti, tiny daughter of his one-time assistant Jack Valenti. "Hello," he says seriously. The child, who is two and a half years of age, likes to pick up a ringing phone. "I know," she says. "This is the Prez." Johnson dons self-pity. "Nobody loves the Prez," he says sadly. "I do," she says. He plays the flirtation a moment longer. "Nobody really truly loves the Prez." "I do!" the child screeches. Mr. Johnson seems to be placated. "All right, then, Courtenay, I want a hug, a kiss and a grunt." She thinks a minute, and says, "I can't, right now." "All right, then," he says, "I'll wait, but you'd better be ready."

He hangs up and phones Joseph Califano, Jr. Joe is a legislative assistant, thirty-five, a New Yorker who once worked with Thomas Dewey. Califano represents tomorrow and next week to the President, because he works on a State of the Union

Message in the summer, five or six months before it will be delivered by the President to Congress; he also works on next year's Congressional bills.

Behind the high brown leather chair are two French windows looking out on the old State Department Building. Califano has no interest in his surroundings, only in his work. Once the President said to him, "You just get me some good programs. I will take care of getting the legislation through." It was the *omnia dicta* of the Califano post. The young lawyer never forgot it, and often drew up progressive legislation which pleased the President and sometimes, as in the case of proposing four-year terms for members of the House of Representatives, won the approval of Mr. Johnson but lost the fight in Congress.

The President discusses anti-inflation measures with Califano, and wants to know what is being done. As they talk, Joe remembers the time, a few years ago, when he received an urgent phone call from his wife that one of his two little boys had swallowed all of the aspirin in a bottle. It was a frightening crisis, and Califano had raced to a hospital just in time to hear a doctor tell Mrs. Califano that the stomach had been pumped; the child would live. Joe remained to comfort his wife. When he returned to the West Wing in the morning, he kept the subject out of his conversation. And yet, when the first summons came from the President's bedroom, the question was: "How is the little fella doing, Joe?"

A year later a Congressional bill on drugs came to the President, and without studying it, Johnson said to McPherson, "Anything in this about putting safety caps on medicine bottles so that children can't get at them?" McPherson was confused. Nothing had been said about the incident, and nothing regarding it was in the bill. "I won't sign it," Mr. Johnson said. "Get

8:00 A.M.

something in there about safety caps."

Califano wanted to know what the President's wish was this morning. Johnson asked details on seven separate problems, only two of which were in Califano's field. Besides worrying about the future of the Johnson administration, and working far in advance of the others, Joe also commands such unenticing subjects as water shortage, transportation, the New York blackout, inflation, and strikes which create a national emergency.

He did not say, "Mr. President, those other five matters properly belong to Bill Moyers, Walt Rostow, and McPherson." The words were: "I'll get on it at once, sir."

The work in Mrs. Johnson's suite goes swiftly. Helen Williams knows that the First Lady, more than any other occupant except Mrs. Eisenhower, spends most of her day here. For Mamie, it was a refuge from a noisy and critical world. For Lady Bird Johnson, it's a den, an office, a beehive. For Mrs. Kennedy, it was a cocoon; for Bess Truman, it was the waiting room for the homeward trip to Independence, Missouri.

The bedroom is high-ceilinged, as all the rooms are, and has an off-white aura. Over the fireplace is a painting by Mary Cassatt depicting a mother, a young girl, and a nude infant. It is called "Carisse Enfantine." There is a double bed with five pillows and a quilted coverlet folded across the bottom. There are also two plain night tables with phones flanking the bed, an off-white rug, chests of drawers, a dresser on which stands a photo of Johnson when he was a United States senator, and another painting, this one of the Johnson's beloved hill country of Texas.

: 31

A Day in the Life of President Johnson

The sitting room is smaller and was probably once used for sewing; it overlooks the old Rose Garden and the President's office. On Mrs. Johnson's desk, which faces the window, are two dictionaries, a Uher tape recorder, a rack of books, and a gold clock with a harp and the figure of Columbia. The wallpaper is patterned in gay flowers and butterflies. An old settee is used not for guests, but for papers, letters, and memoranda, each marked with a tab depicting the day, the week, the year. In the bathroom is a lithograph of a monster, pasted on the wall by Lynda. On it is scrawled: "This is what will happen if you don't brush your teeth."

Although the Lincoln Room, with his big rosewood bed, is at the other end of the corridor, an inscription on the mantel in Mrs. Johnson's bedroom proclaims: "In this room Abraham Lincoln slept during his occupancy of the White House as President of the U. S. March 4th, 1861–April 13th, 1865." Mrs. John F. Kennedy also placed an inscription here: "In this room lived John Fitzgerald Kennedy with his wife, Jacqueline, during the two years, ten months and two days as President of the United States."

Most First Families know when they will leave the White House and plans for moving are made far ahead of time. Mrs. Kennedy's leave-taking was tragic and unexpected. The Johnsons begged her to take plenty of time, but she fled the premises precipitately. Her orders were swift and firm. The inscriptions on the marble mantels were quickly chiseled. She ordered her husband's ship models, high-backed chairs, rockers, Acapulco-caught sailfish, such personal papers as could be found in the files crated and sent away to appear some day in the Kennedy Library in Massachusetts.

Most First Ladies have seen the White House as a glittering social platform. A rare one, Abigail Adams, despised it and hung her wash in the formal East Room. Mrs. Lincoln, a hysteric, purchased two hundred pairs of gloves at a time for White House functions, and asked her friends to address her as "Madame President." Lou Henry Hoover moved in and used the house as a place of seclusion. Edith Bolling Wilson tried to rule while her husband was incapacitated; Mrs. Kennedy, who had the noblest purpose of them all, used her time to restore the old house as a historical monument, refurbishing the public rooms in the proper period of time, restoring armchairs and sofas which had, through one hundred and sixty years, been sold or stolen.

Lady Bird Johnson looks at the big house and sees triumph and grief hand-in-hand. In the privacy of the family, she talks of the White House as a "temporary abode." She is one of the few First Ladies who refused to adjust to the pomp and circumstance of the White House, and when she first moved in, walked out front one morning to hail a taxi to take her to a beauty salon. Mrs. Johnson had to be reminded by the staff that she has limousines and chauffeurs at her disposal. Nor was it easy for her to appreciate that an offhand jest or an offhand opinion might thunder on the front pages of the morning newspapers as presidential gospel.

While the President is on the phone, Mrs. Johnson pauses at breakfast to scan the *Washington Post* and the *New York Times*. She also picks up the phone on her side of the bed to check the day's scheduled events with her personal secretary, Ashton Gonella, a young red-haired woman of energy and a sense of humor. Mrs. Gonella reviews and arranges the letters selected for Mrs. Johnson's personal attention from the approximately 1,500 addressed to her each week.

They talk about today, and Mrs. Gonella, in her third-floor office, thinks it is wonderful that this may develop into a dull one. Mrs. Johnson says that she may use the morning—"if the girls don't get to me first"—to answer mail. Much of it is from women who ask personal questions, or want recipes or descriptions of furnishings. Some refer to her husband as the worst man ever to grace the White House, and Mrs. Johnson reads these and tries to think of something kindly to say.

The beautification of the United States is her gigantic project, and she works at it like a diminutive Johnny Appleseed, suggesting parks and playgrounds, flying to national shrines to ride the rapids in a rubber boat, planting trees in her "A" skirts with gleaming shovels.

She is also a manufacturer of spare time. She hasn't any, but she literally holds the hands of the clock to listen to her husband read a draft of a speech, to bend an ear to Lynda's grandiose recitation of poetry, to respond with motherly asperity to Luci's striving toward adult freedom, to study the Spanish language weekly with a group of women friends, and to phone old friends.

The position of spouse of the President of the United States has become a semi-official post since Mrs. Franklin D. Roosevelt began to act and think as a national figure. A First Lady is expected to have opinions—not always in concurrence with her husband—on a wide range of subjects, with the exception of politics, when she is usually silent.

Besides Ashton Gonella, as personal secretary, Mrs. Johnson utilizes the services of Liz Carpenter as a press secretary, and Bess Abell as her social secretary. Mrs. Gonella, of course, takes care of all personal mail; Mrs. Carpenter sees her boss twice a week for possible public statements; Mrs. Abell works out the guest list for state dinners, receptions, and family invitations to dinners.

The President finishes his breakfast and asks his wife what

her plans are. They discuss their respective work freely, and neither is reluctant to make a corrective suggestion to the other. If Mrs. Johnson is about to launch a ship, cut a ribbon, dedicate a park, or entertain orphans, her husband displays interest and says, "What are you going to say, Bird?" Whatever her remarks may be, they are sensible.

It is not a glamorous phrase to apply to a lady, but Claudia Alta Taylor Johnson was born with strong horse sense. In Karnack, Texas, where she grew up, the only playmates she had were the children of Negro sharecroppers. Her mother died when she was five years of age, and at a time when most girls were reading Louisa May Alcott's *Little Women*, Claudia was listening to Uncle Claude Patillo expiate on the joys of reading books on finance and stock market trends.

In spite of her intelligent and practical approach, Claudia was a shy child who needed something or someone to make her more gregarious. The someone turned out to be Miss Gene Boehringer of Austin. They visited often, and Gene is as close a friend today as she was when she and Claudia were twelve. What Gene had to offer was a natural, outgoing personality. She could tell a story, laugh uproariously at something girlishly ridiculous, be introduced to a stranger, inaugurate a good conversation. Sometimes, when Mrs. Johnson is working in her room, Gene will come to mind, and she will say, "I'm a friend-lier and more confident person because of her."

Claudia also became a shrewd assessor of people. She never tarried around girls who listened to off-color stories, or ne-glected college work for a dance date. One vacation, Claudia and her roommate, Cecile Harrison, planned a trip to Wash-ington. They had an interest in boys, but not to the point of chasing any, so when Gene suggested that Claudia stop in the House of Representatives and see young Lyndon Johnson,

Miss Taylor said yes, but thought no.

"He knows every bit of Washington," Gene said, but nothing could be further from the truth. He knew every inch of Congress, and very little more except the hill country of Texas. Later in that summer of 1934, with the country still deep in the despair of depression, Claudia was at Gene's house when Lyndon Johnson walked in. Miss Boehringer introduced them. No one knows what the young politician thought of the alert, birdlike girl, but asked her to visit Johnson City and meet his folks.

On her part, Claudia looked him over. She felt that she had met someone "quite remarkable, but I don't know what. He's thin, good-looking, black wavy hair and he has the most outspoken, straightforward determined manner I have ever seen." The assessment was made at once. He said he was staying overnight in Austin—Johnson was then secretary to Congressman Kleberg—and he asked if Claudia would join him for breakfast at a local hotel.

Young ladies usually encourage men to talk about themselves, but Lyndon didn't need the prod. He ate his breakfast as though starved, and he talked about his father's work in the Texas legislature, how his father went broke, his own jobs as ditch digger and road builder, how he disliked school and dropped out to go to California with other boys, where he flipped hamburgers at a roadside stand, and of an assortment of menial jobs, back-breaking and poor-paying. Most of all, he discussed his mother, Rebekah Johnson, who tried to kindle a fire in her son to go back to school.

He related the hardships of trying to pay $30 tuition, of how he gave up a visit home at Christmas in order to save money to stay in school, of a pal who emptied his bank account of $80 to help Lyndon keep alive, and of how he, in time, became a teacher at Cotulla High School. He said he enjoyed his work in Washington, and felt a strong inclination to remain in politics. Everything monumentally good or bad, he said, originated in Washington. It was the seat of government, the source of power, the wellspring for making a great nation greater.

After the breakfast Lyndon Johnson went home and told his mother he had met the most interesting woman of his life. This did not please Mrs. Johnson. She was alarmed. In the first place, her boy Lyndon was not a girl-chaser. He was more of a tease in mixed company and was never serious about any girl. Now he had met "the most interesting woman."

He was twenty-six, eligible for marriage, but his mother had no desire to share him with another woman. On the other hand, she was intelligent and shrewd and she knew that the worst thing to do was to deride, decry, and discourage. She asked her son to bring this remarkable girl to the house. The young man was caught in a situation common to many, and, as always, he was the last to know it.

When the women met, they became cordial contenders at once. Rebekah wanted Lyndon—her favorite—to carve a career and remain at her side, as she aspired to remain at his. Claudia saw the storm flags, but saw no cause for alarm. And yet she was irritated because she felt that Mrs. Johnson might think that she was one of those cheap girls who trap a boy into marriage.

When Lyndon was in the kitchen making lemonade, Claudia stared straight at her rival and said, "Don't you worry about me, Mrs. Johnson, I have more sense than that." She didn't say more sense than what. The boy's mother smiled. If there was to be a battle, she was happy to know that it was going to be clean all the way.

One of the few things that Miss Taylor got across that evening was that her family never called her Claudia. A Negro maid who cradled her as an infant had said, "She looks like a little lady bird." No friend ever called her Claudia after that. Lyndon liked the nickname. Within a week Lady Bird invited her new friend to visit her home. Her father, Thomas Jefferson Taylor, the staid owner of a general store, had little to say until Lyndon said goodnight. Then he said, "You've been bringing home boys. This time you brought home a man."

Within a few months Mrs. Johnson lost the battle. Her strong-willed, straightforward son had made up his mind that Lady Bird was the only girl for him. There was no other, there would be no other, and there was no point in anyone's telling him to think it over.

The marriage was quickly set, and when the Episcopalian girl and the Christian Church boy met for the ceremony, he had no wedding ring. He sent a friend down the street to the Sears, Roebuck store and told him to bring several, and hurry. The one which fit Lady Bird's finger cost $2.98. She has never removed it. When the newlyweds left for Washington, the joy was in Lady Bird, the sadness was in the heart of Rebekah Johnson. But at least she was now convinced that the little birdlike creature could do something Mother couldn't—tame that boy.

So in late November, 1934, Rebekah sat down and wrote a letter which, for its expression of conciliation and good will, comes close to being a masterpiece:

> My Precious Children: Thinking of you, loving you, dreaming of a radiant future for you, I someway find it difficult to express the depth and tenderness of my feelings. Often I have felt the utter futility of words, never more than now when I would wish my boy and his bride the highest and truest happiness together. That I love you and that my fondest hopes are centered in you, I do not need to assure you, my own dear children.

8:00 A.M.

My dear Bird, I earnestly hope that you will love me as I do you. Lyndon has always held a very special place in my heart. Will you not share that place with him, dear child? It would make me very happy to have you for my very own, to have you turn to me with love and confidence, to let me mother you as I do my precious boy. My heart is full of earnest wishes for your happiness. From a mother's standpoint, however, I can scarcely say more than this. I hope, and hope you know is composed of desire and expectation, that Lyndon will prove to be as tender, as true, as loyal, as loving, and as faithful a husband as he has been a son. May life's richest blessings be yours, dear little girl.

My darling boy, I rejoice in your happiness, the happiness you so richly deserve, the fruition of the hopes of early manhood, the foundation of a completely rounded life. I have always desired the best in life for you. Now that you have the love and companionship of the one and only girl, I am sure that you will go far. You are fortunate in finding and winning the girl you love, and I am sure your love for each other will be an incentive to you to do all the great things of which you are capable. Sweet son, I am loving you and counting on you as never before.

Now, my beloved children, I shall be longing to see you soon. Wire me. Enjoy your honeymoon in that ideal setting, then hurry home to see us.

My dearest love to you both,

Mamma

The "ideal setting" was a small one-bedroom apartment in Washington. Lady Bird, who had been accustomed to moneyed living, had to adjust to an almost impoverished life. Her husband earned $267 a month. Out of this he had to keep $100 to cover lunch, tuition at George Washington University night school, where he was studying law, installments on a small car, and gasoline.

This, for a girl who never had to count pennies, was difficult. But there were other trials. He thought she dressed too plainly. He constantly admonished her: Cut your hair. Be more fashionable. Get rid of those tailored suits and get a form-fitting yellow dress. I love yellow. You'll look great in it. Why do you

: 39

wear low-heeled shoes? Throw them out. Get those big spikes . . .

No enduring marriage is one-sided. Lady Bird waited her turn. When some money had been saved and Lyndon was doing well as a member of the House of Representatives, she told him she had found a small house she liked, and wanted to buy it. At the moment Lyndon was talking to John Connally. He looked at her and resumed his conversation. Lady Bird stepped back a pace, drew in a long breath, and roared, "I . . . want . . . that . . . house!" and left the room.

Lyndon bought the house. The marriage, over the years, was ideal inasmuch as both parties became more firm in their love. The husband never openly asked for a son, although he has a singular understanding of young boys and could "live" a sand-lot baseball game by watching one. In ten years four babies were expected, but did not arrive. Then Lynda was born, and later, Luci.

Mrs. Williams draws a bath for the First Lady. She adds an oily bubble concoction to the water. She knows that as 9 A.M. approaches, Mrs. Johnson will be back. The maid is relaxed in her work because the Johnsons are predictable in their personal lives, with the exception of meals. Their individual likes are as firm as their dislikes. Helen and Zephyr sometimes feel that they know the Johnsons better than they know themselves.

Lynda awakens in stages. Luci reaches consciousness like a fireman halfway down a brass pole. The President has a built-in clock for sleeping, awakening, bathing, dressing, appointments, television newscasts, reading reports—he ignores it only

8:00 A.M.

when it approaches time to eat, or when he wants to phone assistants at a late hour. None of his team, for example, ever goes to a motion picture without leaving the phone number with the White House operators. Once, late at night when the President wanted immediate counsel, he could not reach his man. In the morning the greeting was: "That must have been a hell of a good picture you saw last night."

There is no set time for breakfast, lunch, or dinner at the White House for any member of the family. Mrs. Johnson joins the President for breakfast in bed because her presence elevates his spirit. It makes him feel that somewhere outside of all the pontification and crisis and international tension, there is a serene world of man and wife, a place where nothing matters except to pass the jelly without getting it on the bedspread.

Helen and Zephyr know that, commonly, the members of the family will eat at separate times, and there is little agreement between them on what to eat. The President doesn't like ham. He is fond of soft, fattening foods—chipped beef, creamed chicken, beef stroganoff, lamb hash, stuffed peppers, ground meat. He loves tapioca pudding so much that Zephyr often makes it every day until the President asks her to switch to rice custard.

A homemade pie makes Mr. Johnson swallow with anticipation, but Zephyr stopped baking them because they create a weight problem. He doesn't like vegetables, but will eat them if Zephyr will make them taste "different." When she serves something he refuses to eat, his eyes grow cold and he points to the food and growls, "Zephyr. I . . . don't . . . like. Don't make it any more."

He said this once too often, and Mrs. Zephyr Wright stared at the President of the United States through her glasses and snapped, "Anybody who works for you for a long time has to

: 41

love you, because you kill yourself and everybody else too." A moment later the President and the cook broke into laughter, because both realized that Lyndon Johnson's loyalty to Zephyr is as unyielding as hers is to him.

Mrs. Johnson enjoys breakfast foods. She likes scrambled eggs, bacon, ham and red-eye gravy, pancakes, waffles, omelettes, and fried chicken. She doesn't share her husband's appreciation of chicken livers or stuffed peppers. She also likes a juicy steak, baked grits, hamburger, and broiled tomato. On one food both husband and wife agree—thick-sliced bacon.

Lynda's favorites are tuna fish, steak, spinach, and peppermint ice cream, and she is the only member of the family who will eat just about whatever Zephyr puts on the table, whether she likes it or not. She rebels when it comes to onions and garlic, but otherwise, the young lady is tractable. Given a choice, Luci will ask for breaded veal cutlet, green beans and corn, breaded shrimp, green peas, and hamburger. If she can beat her father to the tapioca pudding, Luci will do it.

9:00 A.M.

A fresh relay of operators mans the eight switchboards in the Executive Office Building. They work in the dusty, desolate basement, a place which inspires uneasiness. For a time they insisted on having a White House policeman outside the door. He was finally replaced by a heavy lock and a buzzer. The solemn gray pile of stone is Victorian and once housed the State Department. It sits like a grouchy old lady across the street from the pristine White House and is used for presidential functionaries who cannot fit in the Chief Executive's house.

The ceilings are high; the lights are dim. Old parquet floors creak with age. In the vast spaces, air conditioners hiss venomously and a clerk with a lively imagination might hear Admiral Nomura and Ambassador Kurusu telling the old Tennessee judge Cordell Hull that they have been instructed by the Japanese government to see him precisely at 1 P.M. on December 7, 1941; or an earlier Secretary of State, Robert Lansing, murmur the litany of World War I: "We made the world safe for democracy."

The telephone operators feel better in spirit in their rest-

: 43

room. The rug is warm gold and new. The switchboards are the most modern. Their chief operator—Beverly Cole—who has been saying "Yes, Mr. President?" for almost a quarter-century, arranged for them to have a restroom where they can sit and sip coffee, or puff a cigarette, or flip through a fashion magazine. There are twenty operators, including two men who work the midnight-to-dawn shift.

Unlike previous Presidents, Mr. Johnson can identify the individual voices of the operators. At the ranch in Texas, for example, if he punches the wrong button, he may be answered by one of the operators who accompany the Johnsons to the hill country. "No," he will say, "I don't want you. I want the White House." The eight switchboards, or positions, are duplicates of each other. Each has five hundred extensions and trunk lines. Some are marked: "Pres. Johnson," "Pres. Johnson," "Pres. Johnson." Others are marked with Mrs. Johnson's name, and the names of men of importance in the federal government. There are direct lines to faraway places.

Behind the switchboard room, there is a much larger one, empty of humans. It contains large metal frames encasing color-code telephone lines and automatic switches and relays. The telephone company recently installed what it feels is a foolproof system of communications—of which this room is the heart—for more than $2,000,000. If all power should fail, the system has its own Diesel engines which cut in automatically.

The operators sit in silence, watching the winking lights. Behind them, Beverly Cole walks up and down, studying the communications traffic and the responses. The voices of the operators are more neutral than musical. They simply say, "White House," but to many on the other end of the line, there is a special thrill in the words.

At one time when President Johnson was busy cutting expenses by turning lights off, he decided that some phones were not being used; that a few executives had more extensions than needed. So he asked that a record be kept of all traffic—with phone numbers of the callers—on each extension. The newspapers of the country referred to it as a Gestapo ploy, and made it appear that the President examined the thousands of slips of paper every morning. The operators say that he never showed any interest in the records, and expected them to tell him which extensions were seldom in use and which had heavy traffic.

The Secret Service became interested, because part of its work is to trace crank calls threatening the life of the President. Chief James Rowley wanted a record of every threatening call, and the number of the caller. This is still done by the operators, but they no longer keep track of other calls, except incoming ones directly to the President or to Marvin Watson, his appointments secretary. Both men requested this extra service.

The quiet man studies reports. Lem Johns, in charge of the White House Secret Service detail, has an office in the feminine side of the building, the East Wing. He sits in a room containing three desks, and his job is to anticipate the unanticipated. In almost every way Mr. Johns is medium: size, skin tone, hair. If he differs from millions of men, it is in his voice, which is an octave lower than usual.

Room 200 holds neither excitement nor hurry. The three men at the desks, in addition to Miss Kennedy, a receptionist in an outer office, could represent the trust department in a branch bank. The movements of all of them are careful and precise. Johns sits at the rear desk, near the window, and studies a sheaf of plans for the new Secret Service training academy at Beltsville, Maryland. Bob Taylor, deputy agent in charge, picks up a phone and whispers, "Hello." Clint Hill, the assistant agent in charge, gets up from the front desk and carries a signed letter to Miss Kennedy.

The memory of John F. Kennedy's assassination may dim slightly in the rest of the world, but it remains sharp here. When procedure is discussed, one hears "before Dallas" and "after Dallas." And yet no Secret Service agent wants to discuss the event, because the loss was theirs. It is a highly personal thing. Chief James Rowley, gray and competent and quiet, says, "I live with Dallas every day. All of us do."

Lem Johns and his men must know everyone who is in the White House. The building is a sort of fortress protecting the President of the United States and, to keep it so, these men must know every servant, every clerk and executive, every guest, every reporter, every delivery boy who gets beyond the front gate. The President, for example, may not walk through the ground floor of his own mansion while tourists are in it from 10 A.M. to noon.

The coffee pot behind Lem Johns shoots a small geyser of steam and Clint Hill pours a cup black. Hill too was in Dallas; it was he who jumped off a running board and grabbed the trunk of the Kennedy limousine as Mrs. Kennedy climbed back over it. The duty of the Secret Service man is not only to anticipate trouble, but to place his body between the President and an assassin, if possible. If someone must die, the Secret Service man knows that, under the rules, it's him.

Before Dallas, the White House unit functioned well. But a young man crouching in a sixth-floor window with a cheap rifle taught these men that no amount of care is enough. Even though the dinner tonight for President Marcos of the Philippines has a guest list of government officials and their wives, Lem Johns and his men have been working on it for three weeks. If the President goes to the Shoreham Hotel tomorrow, for a Filipino reception in his honor, every street, every rooftop en route, every car passing, will be scrutinized by men armed with the latest and most powerful weapons.

Every waiter, every service entrance, the guest list of foreign ambassadors and ministers, is studied. The Shoreham will be "sanitized" by this evening, and Secret Service men will be stationed at precise posts to see that it is not contaminated. The presidential automobile, a seven-passenger Lincoln, is bulletproof top and sides. Some windows in the White House which face Pennsylvania Avenue are now as thick as a woman's hand.

The organization has recently been revised. At one time the Secret Service was a small elite organization, concerned with narcotics, the protection of currency in the United States Treasury, and the lives of the President and Vice-President and their families. Since Dallas, the unit has been augmented both in manpower and sources of information. The force had 600 men; it is now more than 900. There are 225 uniformed men in the White House police force, and they too are part of the Secret Service.

The office itself is plain. There is a wall map of the world, a few phones with sixteen buttons apiece, a television set on a file cabinet, and an inaugural photo of Lyndon B. Johnson. Lem Johns is dealing with a President who doesn't like to reveal his plans until he is ready to move. The Secret Service would like to have three weeks' notice so that preliminary work can be done—an automatic computer now spews information on subversives and obsessively sick persons in every city Mr. Johnson may visit. Research is important to the Service. So too is something called optional alternate. When the situation becomes dangerous for the President anywhere, Mr. Johns has a safe alternate procedure ready.

He runs down the check list with a pencil. "You got Mr. and Mrs. Roy Butler of Austin, Texas," he says softly. Taylor nods. "Personal friends of the Johnson family," he says. "He runs a radio station in competition with the Johnson station, and he also has a Lincoln car agency. The President buys his car there."

In a secret office the military signal board is tested by a soldier. Communications between the President and his Secretary of Defense, the generals, the admirals, the bases across the seas, the strategic bombers in the sky, the Polaris submarines around the world, must be instantaneous. If, as the military phrase it, "the balloon goes up," the President of the United States must—whether in his office, bedroom, bathroom, on the ranch, in a car waving to friendly people, or in his Texas speedboat—be able to give the coded phrase for counterattack within a few seconds.

There will be no time for consultation in the event of nuclear attack because the "birds" require only a half hour to reach their targets, and the best a President can hope for is twenty or twenty-five minutes between the time of radar sighting of clutches of invisible arrows heading toward the United States and the moment of impact. In that short span he must make up his mind, give the order, and mount a massive counterattack in time for the birds to pass each other in flight.

This is the gravest burden any President faces. His personal death at the hands of an assassin does not match it in weight. Each President begins his term of office fearful of either or both. As the days turn into months and then years, he becomes more confident. It will not happen, he thinks, because there is no gain for anyone in either event. Sometimes the fear returns, as when Harry Truman heard the shots of assassins and police outside his window at Blair House. It came back to John F. Kennedy when he sat in the Situation Room one night and made up his mind to tell the Soviet Union that the United States would hold Russia responsible for any missile activity in Cuba. It hits Lyndon Johnson just as hard when he holds out an olive branch in one hand and a mailed fist in the other, and watches Ho Chi Minh select the fist.

The soldier completes his relay check of the military board and reports to his superiors that all is in order. Now all he has to do is remain awake through the long, dull hours, watching for a signal.

Outside the east gate, citizens three abreast wait in line for a tour of the White House. The line stretches along the fence, around the corner, and down between the White House and the Department of the Treasury, around the bend of the President's Park on the south side, where it ends with a group of teen-agers in tight slacks and short skirts singing songs and clapping rhythmically. They will wait until 10 A.M., when the line will start to feed through the public rooms of the ground floor and first floor. They will listen to a taped voice tell the story of the Executive Mansion, and some of the notable events which occurred in each of the rooms.

In the West Wing, White House correspondents sit in the

big reception hall reading morning newspapers in the recessed lighting which diffuses on the ceiling. Outside, in the bright sunlight, a few television cameras are already set up, ready to record image and voice of presidential visitors as they leave. Some reporters are in the press room, and the sporadic sound of typewriters clacking arches over the wood screen at the entrance.

The reporters stand watch all day. They wait for handouts, press conferences, distinguished visitors who have just left the President. They evaluate the substance of a copy of a report on farm prices, an opinion of Senator Everett Dirksen, an appointment of an under secretary, a statement delivered by the President within the hour, and they ask questions about Mr. Johnson's reaction to current world news. A few have "pipelines" to someone inside the White House who can recite Johnson's opinions. These are called "leaks," and some leaks are intentional and some are not.

All of the 290 employees of the West Wing are now present, except for the few who are scheduled to work late tonight. In the office across the street are 1,365 more White House workers. The White House police department has uniformed men standing in every hallway, at every gate. Softly, politely, they stop every stranger to ask for "your White House pass." Even after a visitor is admitted, if he leaves an office alone to go to another one, he will be stopped.

Upstairs in the west bedroom, Mrs. Williams lays out Mrs. Johnson's wardrobe for the day. Like her husband, the First Lady has little feeling for the feathers of adornment. In the early Congressional years she triumphed over Lyndon's desire to see her wear clinging silk dresses and spike-heeled shoes. She returned to the "sensible" clothes she preferred, and now she resents the necessity, as First Lady of the Land, to buy more and more gowns and dresses for more and more state occasions.

She has her hair shampooed and set twice a week. Until recently, Mrs. Johnson did it herself. Once a week she will visit a beautician to have the hair ends trimmed, or to luxuriate in having someone else work her hair into a modified coiffure. Mrs. Williams hangs the clothing in the bathroom and, in a few minutes, Mrs. Johnson is ready for work.

When Lady Bird strides into the sitting room, Ashton Gonella is waiting. Mrs. Johnson is wearing a brown pleated skirt, brown shoes, a white frilly blouse, and a silk scarf with the knot on the right side of her neck. "Morning, Ashton." Then she turns to Mrs. Williams and says, "Go down the hall and ask the girls to come and chat with me." An hour ago she thought she might not be able to see them because of work. Mrs. Gonella displays the calendar of events for the day, and Mrs. Johnson sits, facing her desk, and reads it. She is relieved because there is little of consequence.

It is going to be a family day. Lynda and Luci are home, and the President said at breakfast that he expected this to be one of those rare days. Mrs. Johnson picks up the folder of mail and begins the task of responding to strangers. Between letters, she picks up the phone to ask the operator to call an old friend, or the wife of a member of the Cabinet, and she goes over the White House grocery list item by item, as though she were paying the bills.

Bess Abell stops in for a moment to consult about a formal dinner which is three weeks away. The women chat, and as is customary among relaxed females, the subjects skip to many matters as they come to mind. Mrs. Johnson says that last night she sat alone in the small White House theatre on the ground floor and saw a color film about the Texas hill country, and

: 51

another film of her travels with Secretary of the Interior Udall through the Big Bend.

The women discuss pending appointments. Mrs. Johnson dreads affronting people; at times she is overly considerate. Often, as Bess Abell knows, when Lady Bird Johnson is unsure that she can accept an invitation, she will decline. However, the date of the event is always noted in a book, and when it arrives, if the First Lady is not committed elsewhere, she will phone the hostess and say, "This is Lady Bird Johnson. May I still come over?" She will not visit a city or a country without personally researching the place, so that, on arrival, she knows something about the people and their problems.

She doesn't like to make speeches, but if it must be done, Mrs. Johnson will dictate one, and when it sounds right, she will stand alone in her room and deliver it aloud. It must "make sense" before delivery. She knows when it is right because she took a course in public speaking and knows the value of simple declarative sentences and sharp, clear diction.

Many Americans hear the flat wooden clack of Texas in everything that Mrs. Johnson or her husband says. The President, who was a champion in school debates, is proud of his hill-country speech and wouldn't alter it if he could. It is as sectional as Kennedy's down-East twang, or Harry Truman's Midwestern monotone. Some advisers have tried to modify the President's inflection, but they have hardly heaved the mountain an inch. He is at his most effective when he speaks naturally and departs from the script. When he is angry or irritated, his mouth forms a huge "O" and he sounds like a hog caller.

Lincoln often squeaked when he started a public address. Andrew Johnson faltered in his phrasing and committed the unpardonable oratorical crime of repeating the words. Coolidge didn't like the sound of his voice and made as few speeches as possible. Wilson pontificated, and made the speech at the planting of a tree sound like a classroom drill in statecraft. Franklin D. Roosevelt invented the personal touch with his fireside chats, and charmed the nation with his "You and I know . . ."

Kennedy, who suffered from stammering until after his first term as a Congressman, made greater strides in public speaking than any President. He practiced modulation of voice and gesture and surrounded himself with writers who could take hackneyed phrases and polish them until they gleamed with freshness. He could not correct a sectional weakness for dropping "r's" in words like butter, which came out "buttah," and putting them into words which did not have "r's," so that Cuba became "Cuber."

Almost all of America's Presidents—with a few exceptions such as Thomas Jefferson, F. D. Roosevelt, Wilson, and Washington—spoke two English languages; one was formally correct, the other was a native patois. In home surroundings, they lapse into the vernacular of boyhood, using sectional pronunciations and local expressions. At other times, the manner becomes presidential and the sentence structure is welded into precise words. Truman and Kennedy, among cronies, spoke in the vernacular and often laced their spoken thoughts with short ugly words.

Lyndon Johnson is the best example of all because his two languages are further apart. The one he speaks in public is correct and almost professorial. When he stands among his neighbors in Texas, he wouldn't dare to say, "Aren't those birds pretty!" It would be considered snobbish, so he falls easily into saying, "Ain't them birds purty!"

Like most Presidents, he can switch from one kind of speech

to the other without strain, just as all of them learn to switch from topic to topic without confusing one with the other. Eisenhower once said that he redesigned his mind in the White House so that at one minute when General Persons came into the office to discuss, let us say, Matsu and Quemoy islands, he could do it and concentrate completely, while, in the next moment, Mr. Feldman was in the office talking of the slow spiral of inflation and he would concentrate on that— even though, a few minutes before Persons arrived, Jim Hagerty had been in to brief the President on a forthcoming press conference and the questions most likely to be asked.

In the President's bedroom, Sergeant Glynn picks up the clothing from the wooden valet and hands them to his chief. Johnson's frame is big and broad, a legacy of the teen-age days when he helped to build roads in Texas. It is stolid rather than graceful, and as he dresses, the President walks back and forth across his bedroom like a heavy-footed bear.

Ideas come to him, even with one leg thrust into the trousers. He returns to the telephone again and again. He calls Jake and asks him to check on the bill regarding federal rights to shore land along Great Salt Lake. He listens for a moment and says, "I know. But this bill must be signed by midnight or it becomes a pocket veto. Now if Utah wants to give us some assurance that the federal government isn't going to be stuck with their lessees, then okay. Otherwise, I won't sign it. Now you get in touch with those people, Jake. I mean now. Tell them they can't have it both ways."

He hangs up and the other leg goes into the trousers. The sergeant wonders if there will be another call before the shirt and tie are donned. It is possible. Johnson turns his mind to the nation's affairs when he awakens and turns it off when he snaps the night light out. There is no time—even when he is

9:00 A.M.

relaxing with his family—that he isn't receptive to a fresh notion on how to resolve American problems. Sometimes they
occur to him; sometimes they are suggested in conversation.
He never knows where or when the lightning of solution will
strike, and he will listen to Zephyr Wright with only slightly
less attention than he accords Dean Rusk.

The knot is almost in his tie when he thinks of something
and walks to Mrs. Johnson's door and calls, "Bird!" She is
dictating letters to Ashton Gonella but stops at once. "How
about a boat ride tomorrow night?" the President says. Mrs.
Johnson is accustomed to unscheduled events. "Might be a
good idea," she says, raising her voice, "if the weather stays
warm." He straightens the tie. "Well," he says, "think about
it."

There is a small office sandwiched between Marvin Watson's
and the President's. Called the "Little Lounge," it has a couch,
a chair, a table, and miniature television sets mounted high on
the wall. Here, Dwight D. Eisenhower composed himself for
naps. So did Mr. Truman. It is so small, so well insulated on
all sides from receptive ears, that President Johnson sometimes
uses it for personal chats or secret conferences between appointments. The man who has just walked into it is Jack
Valenti. Like the room, he too is a well-decorated miniature.

For the first two years of the Johnson administration, this
man was as close to the President as Sherman Adams was to
Eisenhower, as Harry Hopkins was to Roosevelt. The press
referred to him as a whipping boy because Johnson articulated
all his early frustrations to Valenti. If there were "bastards"
and "sons of bitches" in Washington who were pouring sand

: 55

into the Executive Department machinery, Jack Valenti stood and listened to the raging because he knew that it had nothing to do with the President's deep affection for him.

If the President, in times of stress, worked all day and all night, Valenti was at his side, whispering, finding proper documents, making phone calls. The early photos of this duo depict the President frowning and bending his big ear down toward the slight man at his side. When the time came for Valenti to leave and earn a far bigger salary as a "czar" of motion pictures, Mr. Johnson permitted him to go, but only because it would penalize the Valentis economically to ask him to stay.

Valenti sits in the limbo of the little room waiting to sneak in between appointments. Watson stops in for a moment, and they chat about their families and the President. Both are possessed of the feeling that Lyndon Johnson has already proved himself to be the greatest President of all, and so, when they speak of him, one expresses superlatives and the other underscores it with ditto marks.

"The lesson I learned best," Valenti says, "is that he will not tolerate temporary solutions. We took turns offering a way out of many problems, but he rejected them on the ground that they'll be no good in the next generation. He told me that all the stakes are in tomorrow—not today." Jack Valenti never discusses the strain of being close to President Johnson. Most of this strain is caused by the President's impatience, but Valenti isn't ready to concede any Johnsonian weakness. The President may not require a word from a man for a whole week, but when he wants him, this instant is almost too late.

Every one of the assistants has, at one time or another, raced down a White House hall to hear the President say, "Where the hell have you been?" He holds himself at such tension that a squeaky door can unnerve him, because having heard it twice, he will wait for the next squeak. Once, when Valenti was on the phone as President Johnson strode into his office, the Chief Executive hollered, "For Christ sake, do you spend all day on the phone?"

Postmaster General Lawrence O'Brien walked in one morning to tell the President the results of a nighttime legislative battle. The President didn't want to hear it in the morning. "Wake me up," he said, "I want to bleed with you." He has rebuked stenographers to a point where they have burst into tears. And yet when Princess Margaret visited the White House, he invited all of them to the White House dinner because he heard that they would be thrilled to meet a real live princess.

A few offices down the hall from where Jack Valenti waits, Bill D. Moyers, the President's press secretary, makes the final turn into his outer office, walks through it, and makes a left into his private office. He walks fast, thinks fast, is young and slender—an ordained Baptist minister engaged as a buffer between Johnson and the press. And he is more than that: Moyers is the President's confidant and counselor.

He has intelligence, judgment, and discretion. He has a deep voice with a tonal crack in it, and with his dark clothes, owlish glasses, tight-lipped mouth, and speed, looks like a runaway mortician. Like most of the assistants, his title fails to describe his work. Some reporters estimate that Bill Moyers spends twenty-five percent of his time doing presidential press work and seventy-five percent as adviser and speech writer. One of his functions, a news magazine said, is saying "No" to President Johnson. This leaves the implication that no one else has the nerve to stand up to the President and refuse to go along with his notions. This is untrue. Almost all of the men in executive positions in the White House have said "No" more than once, and survived it.

Johnson would be a one-man Executive Branch of government if no one was permitted to disagree. All he asks is that the word "No" be supported by an argument with substantial statistics. The President is uneasy in the presence of the chronically agreeable. He is just as ill at ease in the company of those who wait until all the opinions are in and then say "No" merely to attract attention.

He taps the intelligence of all the men around him for their best thinking, and then makes up his mind what course to pursue. In a manner of speaking, Bill Moyers is the "good boy" young Lyndon aspired to be. Besides being a reverend divine and a good student (University of Texas and University of Edinburgh), he is a political neophyte who started at the top, and so far as anyone recalls, hasn't lost a major engagement. Moyers is only thirty-two years of age, is married, and has three children. He has been working full time for seventeen years.

Moyers replaced Valenti as the man who sits in the President's ear. Mr. Johnson gave Moyers the authority to attend National Security Council meetings, where top-secret defense moves are discussed, Congressional breakfast debates, and Cabinet meetings. The young man is an attentive listener, and sometimes can bring the President to a skidding stop by cutting in with "That wouldn't work because . . ." And yet the President insists that no one can replace Valenti. "He's the man who knows me best. I trust him completely." Mr. Johnson said this after Valenti resigned his post to sign a seven-year contract as president of the Motion Picture Association of

9:00 A.M.

America. In fact, Valenti was executing confidential missions for Johnson long after he "left" the administration.

The barber shop is open. The men and women who make the tidy sandwiches and salads at the White House commissary are already chopping and mixing. The tables are empty, but in a couple of hours they will be surrounded by some of the most active mentalities in the nation. Others will be around tables at the Senate restaurant. Few eat alone. Conversation and food go well together, and most lunches are composed not of steak and statecraft, but hamburger and gossip.

On the lower floor the imposing face of Bob Kintner is screened by a speech. It is neither great nor important and will be read to schoolchildren late this afternoon, but the secretary to the President's Cabinet goes over it carefully. Kintner is the newest member of the inner circle. He is chubby, has thick lips, a round face, tinted glasses, a striped bow tie, a crew haircut, and puts his feet on the desk.

His voice is a whiskey growl. Mr. Kintner has held high posts. At one time he was president of the American Broadcasting Company; at another, he was head of the National Broadcasting Company. Earlier this morning he marshaled all the information required for the Cabinet meeting. He will sit a foot behind and to the left of the President of the United States, whispering, suggesting, making notes, keeping the discussion to the agenda.

Of course, he has other duties, such as the school speech. The President has also paired Kintner off with John Macy, chairman of the Civil Service Commission, as talent scouts.

: 59

A Day in the Life of President Johnson

When vacancies occur in the Executive Branch, Johnson expects his assistants to make suggestions for filling them, and they have learned not to suggest friends or political hacks. The President looks for top talent and top efficiency; the only political aspect which might enter into consideration of a candidate is if he is viewed as anathema by the senators and representatives of his state. Then, considering talent as a constant commodity, another man will be selected.

In a few minutes John Macy will stop by to discuss some names suggested by Moyers, McPherson, and Califano. Kintner finishes the speech, makes a single minor correction, and walks to Marvin Watson's office. They discuss it, and it goes to the President's desk. Lyndon Johnson, being human and a man of moods, does not always react favorably to a good suggestion, nor negatively to a poor one. Normally, he is shrewd and swift and can respond with a yes or no to a proposition as it is being expounded. When his judgment is in error, the President scourges himself as he does other malefactors.

Probably the most stirring speech Johnson made was a night address to the joint houses of Congress, where he literally tossed the script aside to point a strong straight finger at the lounging, listening membership and told them that he would not wait eight or ten months for action on a civil rights bill—he proposed to keep prodding them until they passed it.

That night Lyndon Johnson was boss. The representatives and senators—even the distinguished gallery—listened attentively, and they applauded the toughest phrases. In substance, it said: "If the Negro wants to vote, we're going to see that he gets the right. If he desires to achieve full citizenship and enjoy the privileges which are rightfully his, you are going to consider this bill and pass it quickly, and I will implement it. We are going to stop wasting time."

9:00 A.M.

Kintner is something of a West Wing anachronism because he thinks deliberately and walks deliberately. He sounds more like a Franklin D. Roosevelt man who has been locked in an office for twenty years. In a way, this is so. Bob Kintner is now fifty-five. His first big political opportunity, as a young writer, was to be with Roosevelt on a campaign train. On the same train, a young Texas Congressman named Johnson followed the gleaming teeth, tilted chin, and polished spectacles with adulation. Kintner met Johnson. Neither forgot it.

The last of the special assistants has been working for two hours. This is a stout, graying man from Alabama—Douglass Cater, a man who doesn't permit his Harvard master's degree to show. He has four children, smokes cigars, and speaks with an unusual accent—Alabama with a thin spread of Boston on top. Mr. Cater has plants in his windows. They look more orderly than his desk, and his desk looks the way it does because, like the others, he works in so many disparate fields.

The phone rings. He picks it up, first removing the cigar to avoid collision. The caller is Congressman John Brademas, a Democrat of South Bend, Indiana. He wants Cater to know that the bill called the International Education Act is coming up before the House in four days on a consent motion. This is a Johnson favorite because it blends education and work. It will give money (grants) to universities to build up departments for the study of foreign affairs, and will allow graduate students and faculty to contract for a developmental project. The choice could be in the fields of health, agriculture, assistance in education.

It sounds dull and nebulous, but it isn't. In its provisions, the

Peace Corps is empowered to enable American colleges to literally "adopt" neglected schools in other nations. It will cost less than $20,000,000 a year to administer, and there is little opposition to it, but Cater, taking no chances, phoned the executive editor of the *Washington Post* and suggested that a lunch with Congressman Brademas might produce a favorable editorial on the bill. This, as Douglass Cater knows, helps Congressmen to make up their minds.

Cater's primary liaison is with the Department of Health, Education and Welfare, but he also draws bills into legalistic lingo, writes a draft or two of presidential messages, has a special concern for elementary and secondary education, and, of course, studies speeches. He averages eleven and a half hours a day at his desk, but wouldn't trade this opportunity to stand close to the source of power even for a more exalted position.

In her sitting room, Mrs. Johnson works alone with a tape recorder. She has sent Ashton Gonella off to find a carbon of a letter, and now the words pour into the silent spinner. When the First Lady desires to send a letter but not dictate the whole thing, she says, "I'm speaking to you"—meaning Ashton—and gives the sense of what she wants said.

The machine is switched off, and Mrs. Johnson says to no one in particular, "Now where are those girls?"

10:00 A.M.

Everything in the White House is inherited. Lynda Johnson's room once belonged to Caroline Kennedy. Luci's Coke bar-room was Harry Truman's poker den; it was also a Kennedy schoolroom. Prior to that, it was what it was intended to be: a solarium. The mansion can never really be home to anyone. Only the ghosts last more than two terms.

Lynda Johnson sits on the bed on her crossed ankles, thinking. The bedspread is white; a brown satin quilt is folded at the bottom of the bed. A yellow dust ruffle with flowers adds additional femininity to the bed. The drapes are pinned back, and there is a view of the front lawn, the big elms, a cascading fountain, and Pennsylvania Avenue.

The young lady is reciting a poem from memory. No one listens. A small tape recorder plays music. There is a matching bed a few feet from the one on which she sits. This is for books and records and studies and girl friends. Around the room are stuffed animals, staring glassy-eyed at nothing and looking pathetic or idiotic. The music is an admixture of Mantovani and Nat King Cole. On the shelves, the knowledge this girl

: 63

seeks is on display: history and poetry. She is a pretty person who thinks pretty.

Lynda Johnson always presents her cultured side. The sentimental side is there, but she hides it. In the room is a photo of her father, signed: "To the sweetest, best girl I know, with all my love, always . . ." Another from her mother says: "To my dearest Lynda, my best companion, with a heartful of love . . ."

Like the rest of the family, Lynda is accustomed to speaking her mind: "I'd rather play bridge than have a date. Fellows get scared off by the press. I don't know what the future will bring. I must always be careful that a bad press doesn't upset my parents.

"This is a bright room. Mrs. Truman's mother died in it. So did Willie Lincoln. You know what? They even performed the autopsy on President Lincoln right here. Some people don't believe in ghosts—but he does walk at night. It's great fun. Sometimes the phone rings and the operators tell me, 'I didn't ring you.' Well!"

If there is a dark side to Lynda's thoughts, it doesn't show in the room. There are flowered pens on the desk, a red pillow at the headboard of the bed, a crucifix, a lion bank, two traveling hatboxes, an old bride doll, a pink radio alarm clock. At college she was a good student, a girl with a dimpled smile and bright teeth. Like many graduates, she is introspective and intent on self-analysis.

The phone between the beds rings, and she talks for a moment to a girl friend. "Oh," she says, "I'm not too arty. I mean not too much on opera. I like museums and ruins." She has learned the phrase "guilt complex" and thinks her parents may have one. Texas is the place of preference, but the LBJ Ranch, Lynda feels, is inhibiting. Still, it is wonderful if you invite people you like. Then the natural beauty of the ranch comes alive for her. "I don't like to walk, ride, or swim by myself."

She is a tall, slender girl with thoughtful cocoa-brown eyes. Her hair is brown, full, and flipped. "I'm the more studious, the more refined of the two. I'm cast as the old maid." Her sympathy and understanding apply to everyone except herself. When she tries to bubble, Lynda just talks too fast. "I don't care for phones; people talk and talk because it's the thing to do.

"I like books. Maybe I inherit this from my mother." Lynda giggles. "Somebody said that at their wedding they exchanged books and their tastes were so dissimilar that each one took back his own to read. Mother says she'd like to get sick so that she can really read. On television, she likes *Gunsmoke*. Never misses it. She thinks divorce is dreadful, and once I reminded her that Jim Arness is divorced and Mother said, 'That's all right, as long as he's kind to Miss Kitty.'"

Nat King Cole concludes his final song. Lynda untangles her legs, and pouting, walks to the machine and shuts it off. She is wearing a beige-yellow A-line dress with a zipper all the way down the front, and a crushable floppy white hat. In a minute she is out in the ghostly corridor to visit Mother.

The competition between sisters usually dies when one marries or one becomes mature. The competitive instinct is usually stronger in the younger sibling. The more spread of time between their births, the more combative the younger one becomes. "In this family," Luci says, "I rank just before the dogs."

This is self-assertion. The statement isn't intended to be ac-

: 65

curate; it asks denial. Pat Nugent, bridegroom-to-be, is off on a business call, so Luci sits at the Coke bar, trying to think of new ways of defying the world and at the same time play the mature conformist. She is eighteen, short, a fast walker and fast talker, a clutch of Texas arrows held together by the string of parental authority.

In a minute she wants to see her mother. On the Coke bar is a song sent by friends. It is called "Luci A Go Go." She reads the lyrics, nodding assent:

> Luci is legal
> That should be regal
> But it ain't—why?
> Well, her father is Prez
> And as everyone knows
> The Press and Secret Service are with her
> Where e'er she goes.
> So, although she's legal
> There'll be no Chivas Regal
> She'll have to be hep
> With diet Dr. Pep.

She thinks about it. The premise, she feels, is about right. Now and then, sitting on the end barstool of five, she flicks her head to toss the thick dark brown hair from her eyes. Heavy matchstick drapes screen the beautiful south view of the President's Park, the Washington Monument, and the veiled haze of the Potomac. On the other side of the room is a coral couch with a fraternity pillow, a desk with an electric typewriter, nursing-school books, and a television set.

On a shelf is a broken champagne bottle that was used to christen this room. This is her den, her refuge, her joy. When her mother tried to help by buying chintz for curtains and couches, the independant Luci asked to choose her own. Also, she didn't want any books in the room which she had not read.

"You see," she says, "I love my mother and father. And now that I am grown up, I understand them more and more. I don't even drink or smoke, out of respect for them. And what about Pat? I am Lyndon Johnson's daughter and whatever we do will reflect on them."

This too is mere monologue, because Luci is sensible, quick-witted, and sure-footed. If her father was a garbage man in Austin, she would still behave as she does today—extend both love and hostility as well as understanding and laughter, because this is the character of Luci. "I look at it this way," Luci says, "when they get out of here, Lynda and I will have some forty years or so to do as we wish."

Lynda. Now there is another thought. Dear, darling sister Lynda. "I do lots of things Lynda wouldn't think of doing. She wouldn't think of having her ears pierced. Mine are. I started innocent little dates at the age of eleven. I've had lots of boy friends. She hasn't." She lapses into silence and studies the lyrics again. They do not seem as profound as before. "Nothing is possible in this fishbowl," she says. "And yet we have much more family unity here." The little shoulders come up tight in a shrug. "This is the most family life we have ever known.

"When I was fourteen," Luci says, "I dated this boy. He was anti-Johnson. When he heard that I felt a distance between me and my father, he tried to widen it. Almost automatically, I started to defend Daddy. The more I explained why my father was forced to do the things he did, and live the life he lived, the more I began to understand him. My mother understood that she had to go with him wherever he went, to hold a good marriage together. I didn't. She did it out of love, not out of

: 67

love of politics. The more I talked, the more I understood.

"Now, of course, I love him more than I can say. He teases me more than Lynda. It hurts when it's near the truth. Now, Lynda—she's logical and she will argue that point. I never debate with Lyndon Johnson. I listen. I smile. I kiss. I run.

"I love Lynda too. She isn't a snob. She has an innate decency about things. The competition between us may have been started by my father. He said that Lynda had a business head and was smart enough to grow up and make a living for herself. Luci Baines, however, is so appealing and feminine that there will always be some man around willing to make a living for her."

The President used to tease Luci about being the only member of the family with blue eyes. She was thirteen when she was asked to say a few words to a mixed racial group, and Lyndon Johnson listened respectfully, with the audience. "I don't know what to say to you folks," the child started. "I often think of my mother, who has dark hair and brown eyes. My daddy and sister do too, while I have light skin and blue eyes." She studied her shoe. "But we all get along fine together. If we do, why can't everybody, without thinking of the color of people's skin or hair or eyes, or even how they worship God?" Lyndon Johnson never teased Luci about blue eyes again.

Luci pushes the little song aside and starts down the corridor to her mother's room. She enjoys the warmth of a family talk. She will not only participate, but will dominate it if she can. Luci tries hard to be the "old head." Her deepest admiration is reserved for her mother. "She pulls us all together. The rest of us have tempers, but Mother is the calm soul who smoothes us down and makes us feel closer than ever."

Still, there is a remnant of the little girl in Luci. She has a childish lisp, and she crayons round baby faces on the windows of her den. She draws on her personal loyalty to friends as though the account were inexhaustible. Her conversion to Catholicism is, in a way, a personal indication of adulthood and independence. It proves that she can take giant steps by herself. Her marriage is of utmost importance, not only because of the beauty of love-in-sacrament, but because it is the final step in a campaign by the youngest in the family to assert herself.

"Just think," she says, tossing the dark hair as she bounces down the second-floor corridor, "I can phone them once a week from my own home."

Sergeant Glynn is behind his desk. He gets up to say good morning as Luci goes by. Two minutes later he is on his feet again. The President has emerged from his bedroom. He carries a fresh folder of papers. The stride, as always, is fast. He covers the distance to Glynn's desk before the sergeant can pick up his walkie-talkie and intone: "The President is on the elevator coming down." A buzzer is pressed, and on the first floor in the center hall, three beeps come from a ceiling fixture.

At once the Secret Service agents and the uniformed White House police scramble. The men at the ends of the corridor look for strangers in both directions. The men at the station opposite the elevator are beside Dr. Burkley's door. One goes to the elevator to accompany the President; the other looks for an all-clear wave from the ends of the corridor. It comes, but nobody relaxes.

The elevator door makes a small click as it opens. The President comes out, head slightly stooped, hair slicked back. He nods as one mans falls into step at his side, and they walk west.

: 69

A Day in the Life of President Johnson

A White House policeman holds one of the double doors open, and the President makes a left turn past the old greenhouse and then continues along the walkway with the gardens on his left and the swimming pool and bowling alley on his right. At each turn, a White House policeman at the next post studies the area ahead and waves the Secret Service man an all-clear.

Before he reaches the French doors of his office, the word has been flashed on scores of phones in the White House that the President is en route to his office. The time is logged. Secretaries in many offices hang up the phones and say to their bosses, "The President is now in his office." To some, the news is only incidental intelligence. In the Situation Room, the Pentagon, the press room, Secret Service headquarters, the State Department, the appointments secretary's office, the news has substance.

The President steps into the office of Juanita Roberts. "What's new?" Mrs. Roberts smiles and hands over a few let-ters which have just arrived. He glances at the young and dark and pretty face of Victoria McCammon. "That's a good hair-do," he says. Miss McCammon glances up briefly from her rapid typing and says, "Good morning, Mr. President." Two years ago he heard her say that her mother was lonely for her native Budapest. It was a casual thing. The following year, when he named a commission of august personages to attend an international trade conference in Hungary, Vicki almost fainted when with no warning she copied off a list of presi-dential commissioners and found her mother's name. She was so astounded that she didn't know how to break the news at home. Her mother wept. As an emigrant from Hungary, Mrs. McCammon returned home in style.

Pretty Vicki is to be married, and the President knows it. If he can find a way to tease, he will do it. The institution of marriage, in truth, slows President Johnson's work. He acquires the services of those who he feels are best qualified for White House positions and, in time, they either get married and leave, or they are married and want to get home for dinner. "What I need most of all," he said one day, "are more bachelors."

The President moves on through the small white door leading to his office, which is a large oval space, perhaps fifty feet by forty. The morning sun brightens the big pale green rug, which is rimmed with fifty embossed stars with the seal of the President in the center, and the sound of soft music fills the room with neutral melodies, as it does so many of the offices. There are vases of fresh flowers judicially set around the room. A painting of Henry Clay and one of Andrew Jackson stare solemnly at whatever happens in this place.

The office isn't really oval. The outside wall, pieced together by deep French doors and gossamer curtains, forms part of an ellipse. The inner side of the office is composed of two right-angle walls—one leading to Mrs. Roberts' office, the other to the West Wing corridor. There is a tone of natural majesty and simplicity. The mahogany desk, made in the Senate workshop around the turn of the twentieth century, has a green leather top and doors flanking a screened center. On it are a cup of pencils, a yellow pad of foolscap, two telephones, a date pad, a wooden tray for mail, a pen, a framed schedule of appointments for today, and a small thermometer. Senator Lyndon Johnson used this desk a long time.

There is a big green leather chair, wrinkled from long use, a signing table against the windows, which are flanked by the American flag and the President's banner. The table holds a thermos of water and a brace of glasses on a tray. There is also a white telephone plus half a dozen reference books dealing with government and legislation. Hidden under the President's desk is a small footstool. Two cane-backed chairs stand on either side.

Across the room, facing the President's desk, is a marble fireplace. On it are framed photos of Mrs. Johnson and their daughters. Two comfortable settees flank the fireplace, with a coffee table between. The President—like his predecessor—has a rocker facing the settees. To the left of his desk, there is a console of three television sets with off-white doors which open and close automatically. Although news is presented to the President at once, almost simultaneously with its occurrence around the world, he has an Associated Press as well as a United Press International news ticker. The latest dispatches from these are now on his desk.

Anything of importance is placed on the foolscap. When the President cannot find something, he speaks to Juanita Roberts through a green microphone standing on his desk, and she usually answers, "On your yellow tablet, Mr. President." Marvin Watson opens the door on the President's left—the door through which most visitors approach the Chief Executive—and he says, "Jack Valenti is waiting in the 'Little Lounge.'" Johnson nods. "I'll be right in." He is studying the most recent news-ticker reports.

"Nobody here to see me?" he says. Watson, half out the door, shakes his head no. Because of the forthcoming Cabinet meeting, Watson has had to alter a few appointments, but he doesn't concern the President with this. It is possible that Mr. Johnson is the only President ever to be happy when someone arrives early for an appointment. Often he will interrupt his work and say, "Show him in."

Once the early arrival encountered trouble. James Saxon, Controller of the Currency, had an 11:30 A.M. appointment.

10:00 A.M.

He arrived at eleven. Many of the faces in the reception office were new, and Mr. Saxon was not recognized. Mr. Johnson was about to sign an important bill, and the ushers assumed that this man was a part of the signing ceremony, so he was ushered in quickly and placed in a Congressional group behind the Chief Executive. The moment the President had concluded with the dispensing of signing pens, the party moved out into the old Rose Garden for pictures.

Mr. Saxon was elbowed away from the President. He tried to say something, but was hushed into a silent smile for the photographers. When the pictures were finished, the President waved farewell to one and all and hurried back into his office. Ushers and White House police assisted the signing party out through the west gate. Mr. Saxon was carried by the political tide. When he got outside, he had a difficult time convincing the sergeant in the sentry box that if he was not readmitted at once, he would be late for his 11:30 appointment.

The President leaves his desk and walks through a door near the television sets. In the tiny office, he exchanges greetings with his old friend, and relaxes on the couch with his big hands cupped over his head. Jack says that he has just returned from a series of conferences in New York with motion picture executives, and has stopped by to say hello. They talk about Valenti's new job. Mr. Johnson says he's thinking of taking a short trip on the *Honey Fitz* tomorrow night, and how about coming along with his wife, Mary-Margaret, and little Courtenay. Mr. Valenti thinks for a moment, and says, "I think we can make it. I'll call later to see if you're firmed up on it."

Marvin Watson sticks his head into the room and says the Under Secretary and Assistant Secretary of Defense are in the Fish Room. The President says goodbye and returns to his office to scan the desk. There is nothing on it but a sample of unsolicited mail. This is important to some Presidents (Johnson and Kennedy, for example) and unimportant to others (Wilson, Harding, Coolidge, and Hoover). Mr. Kennedy requested that every fiftieth letter sent by citizens be placed on his desk for a random sample.

Bill Hopkins, who is in charge of such matters in the Executive Office Building, is expected to scan all letters—favorable and unfavorable—and to select a sampling every day for Johnson's perusal. The mail may range from 6,000 letters a week to more than 25,000, and in addition to the letters from officials of the government and personal friends, he wants to read enough unsolicited material to apprise himself of what the people think of his work.

Sometimes Hopkins, in collusion with Mrs. Roberts, will slip into the pile a letter or two which they know will lift the President's spirit. He stands thumbing through the pile and stops at one which appears to be all heart and no grammar:

> Dear Mr. President: Here I am sending you this picture of Raul. He is my son. We are verey prout of him for we are a big family of ten children. Daddy and me we are very prout of him. Until three years ago we come to Colifornia Where we had some halp from the children in summer in the crops and keep them in school. We had to stay in a laber camp for we don't have a House to live in.
>
> With a big family it is not easy. We don't have much place for them to study. And Raul come up with a schoolerchip 3000 dollars a year where only millionaires go. seems like a dream to us and still its true. He is going to Harvard University in Sep. with God's halp. Mr. President we as parents want to thank you for the big oportunidodes that weall have in America. We are Mexicans from Texas. And that no matter who we are. rich or poor. we all have the same right if we work for it.
>
> Resive the love of our children my husband and me. I pray that when my boy gets to Harvard his teachers and friends will make him feel at home for it is not easy for him feeling different from the others. Anyway, in his heart he is rich . . .

10:00 A.M.

He calls Mrs. Roberts on his squawk box. "I want somebody to check on this boy mentioned in the letter. If there is any information, clippings in local newspapers for instance, I want to see them. Also remind me to write a reply to his mother." He drops the letter and leaves.

In the Fish Room, applause breaks out as the President crosses the hall and steps to a lectern. Twenty men, all ranking immediately under Secretary of Defense Robert McNamara, come to their feet. These are executives and each heads a bureau or department. They are McNamara's team and they are present for an informal chat. The President feels that in the pyramid of bureaucracy, it is easy for the second-echelon men to feel unappreciated, because they seldom see the President.

He waves them to their chairs and, with no prepared notes, begins to speak in a soft tone. "I'm in a sentimental mood and want you to know that I have never seen a more selfless, competent group working in this Congress. I recognize it and am thankful for it and want to say so on behalf of all Americans. You are the biggest part of the government. With the security you give us, we are able to move ahead in many other fields . . ."

The more flamboyant the superlatives used by the President, the more his sophisticated audience is prone to tighten the seat belts. Mr. Johnson continues in the soft tiger-stalking tone, and the secretaries began to light up in glassy smiles. The first fork of lightning comes with no thunder: He talks about the sale of United States bonds, and tells the Defense Department that the Chrysler Corporation, a private organization, has a better record of employes who subscribe part of their salaries to it than the Department of Defense. "Some of your admirals need inspiration." He criticizes the bond subscription record of the Department of the Air Force. The speech becomes more of an extemporaneous monologue, and as thoughts come to mind, Lyndon Johnson enunciates them with considerable impact.

He has no desire to charm. "Bear in mind that you support the whole government, not just part." He studies the individual faces of the men, skipping, pausing, locking eyes. If the President must choose between admiration and obedience, he will take obedience. He doesn't castigate *per se.* It is a technique his mother once used on him: it begins with praise and reward, hits a peak with shortcomings which can be eliminated, and closes on a folksy friendly note.

His words also nail down policy for their departments: Korea and Viet Nam prove that the Soviet Union and China have always misjudged American intentions. To speak of peace and of reasoning together is translated as fear and an unwillingness to take a firm stand. To speak of men of good will appears to be the offering of a cowardly olive branch. "You men are my managers in a department which spends over fifty percent of the budget," he says, pointing a finger at them. "I want you to think, to be ready, to make certain that the American fighting man is the best-equipped soldier, the best-supported soldier in history. Do anything and everything you can to help your country and Secretary Robert McNamara.

"Ask yourself after a day's work, as I do: 'Have I done anything to help my country today?' I don't mean to just run off wildly on new tangents. Be alert and think and always count ten before you do whatever it is that your department can do to help." His hands grip the sides of the lectern. A new thought is on the way to his tongue. "I like the way you spend. Next to the Secret Service, you can spend more money on nebulous projects than any bureau I know." The faces before him try to maintain the bold smiles.

"My desire is not to make you feel defensive about what you

spend, but to make you look at those dollars and to see that the American people get a dollar's worth of products and service for their money." The executives have heard this before. Mr. Johnson re-emphasizes the point because he is certain that the United States can maintain the best defense establishment in the world while, at the same time, cutting the purchase of, for example, ten thousand wastebaskets and the unnecessary items which the wastebaskets symbolize.

"Bob McNamara would be the happiest man in the world to be able to cut his spending by ten billions of dollars. Not so much to cut taxes but to be able to take that money and put it to work helping, let us say, poor children. I want you men to think of other departments besides your own. McNamara and your President would feel proud if you would get out once in a while and tell how you feel about Medicare, or civil rights, or the Poverty Program. I want you to keep it in mind."

This follows the Johnsonian thesis of a single team with a single purpose, rather than many departments in competition. Part of the work load he dumped on Harry McPherson this morning did not properly belong to the man; but it is a governmental philosophy of the President's that he wants everyone to be acquainted with what everybody else is doing, and, above all, to be interested and helpful.

"I want you also to think of the fact that I have never heard Rusk say one word of criticism of anything Bob did. In fact, I have never heard of any member of this Cabinet who placed blame, even indirectly, on other departments. Bear this in mind too. I'm proud of this Cabinet because they now work— not each one for his department, but for the United States of America. It should have been like this all along."

One more thing. Just one more. "If De Gaulle wants us to get out of his country, I am going to do as I would do if I was a guest in your house. I'm going to take my hat and leave, as a guest should. But we plan to be doing business with France long after De Gaulle is dead and gone."

The monologue is over. "I must get back to work . . . Remember, what affects you affects me. What is a good day for you is a good day for me. The best we can do, gentlemen, is to serve intelligently and loyally." The hands release the lectern. Applause echoes against the rounded walls where once John F. Kennedy hung a sailfish caught on his honeymoon. President Johnson snaps on his briefcase smile and is gone.

At his desk, the President has six minutes of open time. He scans a summary of damage done by bombers over North Viet Nam. The reconnaissance photos are good. A report by General Westmoreland is digested. Mr. Johnson asks Mr. Watson to step in. A memo from McPherson describes a civil rights conference composed of over two thousand doves and about twenty-five hawks. McPherson observes that the hawks always make the most noise and achieve more complete coverage in the press.

The President phones Bob Kintner and asks him to be in the office in five minutes. The Associated Press and United Press International wires are searched for fresh news. A button is pressed, and the off-white lids of the triple television peel away from three glass eyes. Watson comes in, and the President says he doesn't know how long the Cabinet meeting will last, but to modify the presidential appointments so that people aren't kept waiting.

Mail is delivered every fifteen minutes, and Mrs. Roberts brings more letters to the desk. They are read, and there is no comment. Kintner peeks in, and is waved to a chair beside the desk. Luci looks in from Mrs. Roberts' office and Mr. Johnson beams, gets up, and walks across the room for the morning kiss, hug and grunt. His daughter says that she has lots of shopping to do and waves and says, "Toodles."

There is a list of persons who have phoned the President while he was in the Fish Room. He asks Mrs. Roberts to call two of them. In all cases, he says "Hello" and gets to the point. Sometimes, as he listens, he dons his glasses and scribbles notes on the foolscap pad. He brooks no social conversation, such as a mutual exchange about families, unless there is illness in one. A phone call to Jake Jacobsen gives him a rundown of the Congressional agenda for today, and the President tells him whom to call if there is a problem.

As he sips a glass of water from the carafe on the signing table behind him, Mrs. Johnson phones to say that the idea of a boat ride tomorrow is a good one. She wants to know who should be invited. "Oh," the President says, "invite anyone you please," and then proceeds to recite a list of names. "I don't know," he adds. "I'll try to get out of here sometime around seven-thirty or so. Just get a group of people together."

Marvin Watson returns to the President. "The secretaries are in the Cabinet Room." The President looks up from the television sets. "All in?" "Yes. As you know, Ball is sitting in for Rusk." Johnson nods. "All right. I want to talk to Bob for a minute."

11:00 A.M.

"Now, Bob," the President says, "let's have one more look at that agenda." He glances at the white sheet vertically, and folds and slips it into his pocket. Kintner says it's a tight schedule for a Cabinet meeting and he summarizes the items to be discussed. Mr. Johnson is pleased. When he first presided over these solemn conclaves in November, 1963, the President was appalled at the meandering pointless speeches, the jollity between secretaries, and, above all, the lack of preparedness.

When he asked a question of the Department of Commerce, or State, or Interior, the secretaries would scribble it on a pad and say, "Mr. President, I'll check on that and phone you." This is not the Johnsonian system; he handcuffed his patience for a while and then one day burst into the roaring protest he reserves for time-wasters. He expected his secretaries to have answers prepared, and didn't want them "looked up" later. If the secretaries could not remember the problems and proposed solutions to departmental matters, then bring assistants to the meetings who could furnish the material to the whole Cabinet.

The protest was not an indictment of the men who help him

to run the country. If it had been, Johnson would have permitted some of them to resign. To the contrary, he believes that he has the best possible Cabinet. What he wanted was to make the meetings more efficient, more productive. In all departments and bureaus, Johnson's desire is to gear everyone up to his standard of driving oneself all day and part of the night at high speed. A few years ago, when he quit work at 10 P.M., he toured the offices, turning lights off. When he came to one where a man was still working, the President smiled.

An unwritten rule in Johnson's administration is that everyone should be on duty twenty-four hours a day. At home, on a visit, in bed, a man may be contacted by the President in the late night hours, and Johnson has no qualms about making the call.

The President looks at his watch. The time is 11:07 A.M. "Let's go," he says, and moves out before Kintner. The Cabinet secretary has arranged this meeting according to the rules laid down by the President. Several days ago he contacted the members of the Cabinet and told them that the President was planning a meeting. What topics would they like to discuss? Would they please think it over and let him know quickly? Each one did. The gravel-voiced man brought the sheets of paper to the President and, item by item, they were discussed three days in advance. Some were dropped for reasons ranging from untimeliness to unimportance or something the President wanted to talk about privately. Others were kept on the active list.

The day before the Cabinet meeting, Johnson sent a memo to Marvin Watson. It said: "Kintner. See me." Watson studied the appointment pad and found time. Then he advised Bob Kintner. In the late afternoon the President and his secretary made the final cuts and reduced the topics and problems to a manageable number. In all cases, the President makes the ultimate decision.

His authority to administer the welfare of the country, and the limits beyond which he has no authority, are spelled out in 223 words of the Constitution:

> The President shall be Commander in Chief of the Army and Navy of the United States, and of the militia of the several states, when called into the actual service of the United States;
>
> He may inquire the opinion, in writing, of the principal officer of each of the Executive Departments, upon any subject relating to the duties of their respective offices, and he shall have power to grant reprieves and pardons for offenses against the United States, except in cases of impeachment.
>
> He shall have power, by and with the advice and consent of the Senate, to make treaties, provided two-thirds of the senators present concur;
>
> And he shall nominate, and by and with the advice and consent of the Senate, shall appoint ambassadors, other public ministers and consuls, Judges of the Supreme Court, and all other officers of the United States, whose appointments are not herein provided for, and which shall be established by law;
>
> But the Congress may by law vest the appointment of such inferior officers, as they think proper, in the President alone, in the courts of law, or in the heads of departments.
>
> The President shall have power to fill up all vacancies that may happen during the recess of the Senate, by granting commissions which shall expire at the end of their next session.

Thus, in an instrument simply conceived, broad power was given to one leg of the governmental triad, even granting additional power over another leg—the Supreme Court—by permitting the President to name the members rather than have them face general election, as the Congress and the President must. Intentionally or not, this gives each President additional power on the Court inasmuch as he may be expected to name such interpreters of law as agree with his philosophy of government. A President and two sympathetic judges out of nine can swing the balance of power. If the opposition to the President's philosophy loses three of the remaining seven members, it has lost the decision five to four.

The table in the Cabinet Room is a single slab of boat-shaped dark oak. The President never sits at the head of it. His high-backed chair is in the middle, with his back to the windows. The members of the Cabinet stand chatting easily, their aides in chairs against both walls. Three doors are closed, and guards stand outside. The President bursts into the room from Mrs. Roberts' office, with Kintner a step behind him. The conversation dies in mid-phrase and the faces turn toward the big man in the blue suit. He starts toward the middle of the table, and stops when he sees that the fair skin of Lawrence O'Brien, Postmaster General, is sunburned.

"Must be nice at the beach, Larry," he says. O'Brien, balding and blue-eyed, chuckles and says, "I knew you'd say that, Mr. President. There isn't a chance of convincing you that I got this in the backyard." The President shakes his head and grins. He is wearing his glasses, and as he glances around, the rare mellow smile appears. Practically every face is pleasing to him, and by pleading, cajoling, pounding his fist and shouting, he has welded these men into a unit. His policy is to have the most efficient government in peace. And where some pundits think they see policy falling off the rails, Lyndon Johnson maintains that anything which will contribute to peace and efficiency is welcome at the table.

The President sits. At once the gentlemen pull their chairs out from the table, sit, then draw them in. There are immaculate pads and pencils before each man at the table. The room, for a few seconds, is in silence before an array of wax replicas. He shuffles papers, and begins to speak softly, as though the meeting—this particular Cabinet meeting—deserves a preface. The theme is Medicare, which, after much travail, is law.

Two flags on standards are against the wall behind him. A bronze bust of John F. Kennedy stares across the table at Lawrence O'Brien. A chart at the end of the table stands tall and says: "89th Congress, Second Session." On the walls are portraits of Thomas Jefferson, Andrew Jackson, and Franklin D. Roosevelt.

Johnson talks of the millions of elderly people and of their many concerns. "They worry about cancer and arthritis and lack of income and the cost of medical care." He sighs. "Now we have taken some of the worry off those nineteen million people." There is a pause. "They get sad, just like we do. They laugh, like we do. They even cry, like we do."

No one who knows the President can imagine him weeping, but there is no doubt that there are moments of frustration. He will not hang his head in public; his attitude is: "We win 'em all, but what we can't win today, we'll fight again tomorrow."

His administrative record is good; better than good. But any defeat, however light in historical significance, is borne by the President like a cross. He reacts to the heavier defeats as Eisenhower did: flushed silence. Viet Nam, for example, has been a chronic sore spot in the last three administrations. It waited until Lyndon Johnson's tenure to escalate in blood and cost. In his eagerness to settle it and pull out, the President's biggest mistake was to appeal to reason. The sound of logic is often lost on oriental ears. There is no Vietnamese word for "candor." Reason is interpreted as a diversionary subtlety.

One might say that the very existence of socialist Cuba

: 84

proves the true democracy of the United States, but no government in the world sees it that way. The nations view each other as strong or weak, not good or bad. Many of them cannot understand a partial commitment, such as the shabby U.S. role at the Bay of Pigs. Conversely, they appreciate Russia's action in crushing the Hungarian revolt. Total action or no action is comprehensible. Johnson has done nothing in Cuba, and, by doing nothing, he has caused Cuba's life insurance policy to lapse. This treatment is expected to make the Communist government poor and impotent.

In the United Nations, the American ambassador fights seating Red China, but intellectual Americans seem to feel that there can be no true United Nations if the most heavily populated of all countries has no seat. Contrariwise, few appreciate that China, trying to unify 700,000,000 people who must learn to equate communism with patriotism, needs the United States as an enemy. In this, which is a battle of propaganda, the Americans have lost world opinion. American tourists, who see the United States as altruistic, are shocked to find that a large part of the world looks upon this country as rich, fat, and fearful.

It is not the kind of image to which Lyndon Johnson aspires. He would like to teach the poor countries to be self-sustaining as, once upon a time, he helped a man refurbish a ranch home and taught him to be self-sufficient. He would like to deal with the few rich and powerful nations in a field of mutual respect and businesslike efficiency. These are idealistic improbabilities. He will try, again and again, because he knows that this is the right path, but, in time, his faith may be shattered.

Domestically, there have been defeats which have made him wince. The civil rights movement, blueprinted carefully by the Kennedy administration, scrapped the chart in favor of guer-

: 85

rilla civil war in city streets. Some of the new Negro leaders in their extremism force the Negro to paint himself black inside as well as out. The riots make the Negro appear to be what the narrow-minded white man suspected all along: ignorant, rapacious, shiftless, and thieving. The majority of moderate leaders are unheard in the cauldron of communications because the newspapers and radio and television find more drama in fire and riots than in reasonable actions.

Labor and management have never been in exact balance, and until the Franklin D. Roosevelt administration, it can be fairly stated that management sat in the narrow driver's seat of the nation's economy. FDR's social legislation, designed to equalize the two, had the effect of tossing management out and putting labor in. The nation loses hundreds of millions of man hours in crippling strikes, billions in profits and wages, and Congress cannot devise legislation which will put both in the driver's seat. Nor can President Johnson.

Crime progresses almost to the point of squaring itself. Police morale is down; criminal morale is up. The Supreme Court, in a series of notable decisions, has taken the handcuffs off the prisoner and put them on the police. The decisions were objectively equitable for a free society, but the effect has been to put law enforcement on the defensive.

Inflation is a world-wide problem, but so is typhus, and the United States found out it could correct that in continental isolation. Economics, however, is a multiplex and experimental subject in which schools of thought wax and wane in popularity, and the only provable dictum is that if one earns more than one spends, one saves. Privately, Mr. Johnson worries about inflation and will listen to anyone with a panacea. There is none. Now and then the President orders the government to stick its finger in the dike by selling off surplus ore or grains, but the watered-down dollar squirts around the finger.

As he sits talking to his Cabinet, Johnson himself is undergoing a postgraduate course in government. He learned much in Congress; he learned more as Vice-President; now, as President, he absorbs some bitter defeats as he totals the broad spectrum of victories. If he receives another mandate from the people for an additional full term, Lyndon Johnson may put in more time as President than any other except Franklin Roosevelt. And like all other Chief Executives, he will be studying and learning all the way.

None of this will alter the high personal goals he has set for himself. He was at the LBJ Ranch one Sunday morning, lying in bed watching two astronauts on television. They had landed a few miles from the carrier *Wasp*. Someone sitting by the bed had asked the President what his personal feelings are about the world and his work.

"I'm going to watch these astronauts for a few minutes before I shave. When they get aboard the *Wasp*, I want to phone and congratulate them. Also, I want to promote one of them. Normally, they phone the President from the carrier, but I think I should call *them* the minute they get on the flight deck."

He kept watching from a semisupine position. It was obvious that it would be another half hour before the spacemen reached the *Wasp*. Mr. Johnson watched, but began to speak. He made no attempt to marshal his thoughts into gleaming phrases; he spoke like a man enunciating an old prayer:

"We must try to learn to live together. No people want to learn to die together, so we have only one option. The trouble with this philosophy is that it sounds so simple. We must understand our fellow man to a point where no one will want to destroy him—a world in which all men are not only free to speak and act and write and print, but can be free of prejudices and bigotry and the hates engendered by his differences in religion and skin."

As the President talked, he kept watching the television screen, not seeing it really, and the voice reached the low, almost indecipherable growl of a man talking to himself: "I would like to banish ignorance and poverty, if I had my way. I would like to see science prolong man's life and minimize his sufferings. The ancient enemies are disease and ignorance and war. Just because no one ever beat them before doesn't mean that they are unbeatable."

He began to think in terms of what has been done, not what might be done. "We have the greatest conservation and education administration in history. We dare to do, and we have done, and will do more. I think that in our time the people who are opposed to us on the other side of the world will become more tractable."

He sees a real God in heaven moving man toward a more compatible existence. Lyndon Johnson doesn't always go to services on Sunday, but he goes often enough to participate in the psalm-singing and the prayers. Whereas Kennedy the Catholic said that he prayed once a day—at bedtime—Johnson says a quick thank-you to the Supreme Being every time he hears good news. It does not even formulate itself into words: he hears something good from Walt Rostow or Jake, and an image of Jesus Christ comes to mind and the gratitude Johnson feels is expressed in a spontaneous prayer.

"I would estimate that I say a prayer about a dozen times a day. I say it every time I am confronted with a difficult situation or if something good happens." The thoughts move on to

11:00 A.M.

his workday. "Some say I work too hard. I don't see it that way and I don't feel that I am pushing myself. I don't play golf at Burning Tree and I'm not a social butterfly, so that leaves work. In my case, this can take the place of golf or cocktail parties. From five or five-thirty P.M. until seven I try to see the people who are going to be gone in the evening. Men like Rostow, Watson or Jacobsen, and Ferris Bryant.

"The schedule is never the same, but from seven until seven-thirty I might watch the news on television. I also study the next day's schedule. I revise. I also study proclamations and bills written up during the day. I try to gather up my night reading. I also glance at the late ticker news and call such assistants as might help me at the moment with new problems.

"I am sure in my heart that my mother had a strong bearing on my morals and habits. My father was a hard-working man who applied himself at all times to whatever the problems at hand might be. He took them in order of priority, one at a time, and worked them over. I like to sing and dance. But I do these things rarely; I do it to forget my troubles. I used to take a ride with my father in the late afternoons in the hills. He looked at cows and sheep and he philosophized on land and cattle-raising and grazing land.

"Now, when you see me dancing with many ladies at a White House party, it is not because I am a good dancer, or even because I like to dance. I feel that when a lady goes to a White House party, she knows that when she gets home the children are going to ask, 'Mommy, did you see the President?' I want her to be able to say, 'I danced with him.'"

He switched the television set off and called Jake. "Let me know the minute those fellows get on the *Wasp*. Tell the Secret Service that as soon as the call is finished Mrs. Johnson

: 89

and I are going to church." His pajamas were rumpled, like his face. "If I had a hobby—I don't think I'm going to have one— but if I did, I think it might be horseback riding and swimming. They can keep a man in pretty good condition."

Starting from the foot of the table, nearest the President's office, and moving clockwise, the titles on the backs of the Cabinet chairs read: Secretary Weaver, Housing and Urban Development (Robert Wood uses the chair today); Secretary O'Brien, Post Office; Arthur Goldberg, United Nations; Vice-President Humphrey; Secretary McNamara of Defense; Secretary Freeman of Agriculture; Secretary Wirtz of Labor; at the head of the table is Secretary Gardner of Health, Education and Welfare; then, coming down the sunny window side, Secretary Connor of Commerce; Attorney General Katzenbach of the Department of Justice; George Ball (sitting in for Secretary Rusk) of the Department of State; President Johnson, with Kintner sitting slightly behind him; Secretary Fowler of the Treasury Department; and Secretary Udall of the Department of the Interior.

In all, fifteen men sit against the walls listening. One of the men against the right-hand wall is Gardner Ackley, of the Council of Economic Advisers; against the other wall, behind the Vice-President, is Charles Schultze, director of the Bureau of the Budget; against the far wall, behind Wirtz, is David Bell, director of the Agency for International Development.

Johnson opens the agenda by praising the work of Secretary Gardner of H.E.W. in getting Medicare in operation so quickly. Among the professionals, Gardner is regarded as an amateur in politics and there was some fear that the problem of getting Medicare in motion by July 1, 1966, would be too much for Health, Education and Welfare because it involved not only an understanding of the complexities of the bill and its proper administration, but also the job of convincing millions of fearful oldsters that they should relinquish their relatively expensive private health policies for a cheap government one. There was, moreover, the task of lining up a large number of hospitals to qualify as agents of Medicare.

The President says he thinks that Health, Education and Welfare did an amazing job in such a short time, and he feels that his personal gratitude, and that of the government, should be extended to Mr. Gardner. The others nod approval. But then the President's superlatives go beyond what the effort merits. Those who know Mr. Johnson begin to frown. A storm is coming. He leans with one elbow on the arm of his chair, the fingers of the other hand indenting his cheek.

"One more thing," he says. "It has come to my attention that you fellows are busy sending out publicity releases. Some of the members of Congress are complaining that they don't know what is going on in your department until they read it in the paper. Now"—the voice rises, and the finger against the cheek begins to point—"I've told you fellows before to stop this practice. You need friends in Congress and I don't like to see publicity about matters which haven't been reported out of committee. I told you before, and if you don't stop it, I'm going to put a couple of professional politicians in your office to show you fellows how to do it."

The table is silent. Some men scribble. Others study a blank wall. The President nods. "We're ready for the briefing." Mr. Gardner stands with an assistant beside a big Medicare chart and points out how many old people are enrolled, how many hospitals, how much the bill is expected to cost the first year, and so forth. All faces are turned toward the chart because the President wants all departments to understand the problems of the others.

"A remarkable achievement," Humphrey says. The President half stands to get a better look at the figures on the chart through his bifocals. "This plan is going to be popular," he says, "but you fellows should be ready to be blamed for all problems which arise." He studies the next item on the agenda and growls, almost to himself: "We have wrecked the farmer, we have wrecked labor and business—people assume that all we have to do is push a button to put everything in working order. I want you fellows to expect major criticism. Any questions?"

Silently he points his yellow pencil at each face around the table. Ball says that being opposed to Medicare is going to be as unpopular as being opposed to Social Security. The pencil completes its rounds. "Thank you, gentlemen." The subject is closed.

Kintner whispers to the President. "Dave Bell has done a wonderful job," Johnson says, "and he finds himself in deep trouble and I think we may be able to help him." Mr. Bell, who is in charge of foreign aid, has been sitting behind the Medicare exhibit. He gets to his feet with a chart which explains, in color combinations, the types of aid he offers to other nations. The blue lines indicate a "supporting" assistance, while the yellow indicates "development" aid.

The program has become increasingly unpopular among the people, especially the "supportive" money, which critics claim is a means of buying friends abroad. To the contrary, "development" money is spent to help people in other countries learn how to support themselves with better farming, better tools, better merchandising. Mr. Bell knows this, and he shows that in the next fiscal year the United States can expect a rise in the yellow lines of developmental aid and a decline in supportive money.

"We have been making progress," he says, "in moving each nation from straight support money to development. Of course, support money does little more than feed and medicate people. Development money"—the pointer moves from the blue lines to the yellow—"helps nations to buy and use the tools to help themselves." The story is hackneyed. Everyone around the table knows it, but all, including the President, listen attentively. He rubs his big nose and is aware that Congress enjoys cutting this appropriation each year.

A door is opened and Bill Moyers comes in, tiptoes around the table and crouches beside the President to whisper. Mr. Johnson listens and nods. Bell continues by relating the proposed Congressional cuts in foreign aid. He says that the Congressional committee "is operating under a misapprehension." Moyers leaves the room noiselessly as the President interrupts the speaker. "Have you told the committee about their misunderstanding, Dave?" Mr. Bell nods. "Right." But he didn't convert anybody.

As always, Mr. Johnson is aware of the number of votes he has "in his pocket" and the number needed. In this, he never requires a chart and his memory is prodigious. He stops the talk to corral a few more votes. He points the pencil at the Postmaster General. "Let Larry O'Brien take a few members." The pencil moves. "Goldberg will take a few. And Hubert will contact some, and if all of us know which ones—and who has the ball—we are pretty sure to get the ten votes we need for committee action, and maybe a few more." As Johnson speaks, Humphrey keeps nodding, like a doll with a spring in its neck. The President is aware of any interruption, such as a rattle of

: 93

paper, a cough, or even the noisy dropping of a pencil, and his head swings to the source of the sound.

The attitude of the President at a Cabinet meeting is neither bossy nor dictatorial, but rather that of a teacher reviewing the work of a group of gifted freshmen. Speeches are forbidden; facts take precedence over opinions. The President refers to Congress in the manner of a Moslem talking about Mecca. "Go to them," he says. "Tell them it's their country and we must do it.

"If each of you got out of your offices and took two or three people apiece, we'd have them all. . . . Don't phone them to explain anything. Go over there. You, George, Larry, Arthur, Hubert—get the names and addresses of the Senate Appropriations Committee—make a major effort." He has an intensity as he speaks. Vice-President Humphrey strokes his eyebrows. Wirtz chews on his glasses. O'Brien is fascinated with the locking and unlocking of his fingers.

An assistant comes in and, impatiently, the President listens. "Tell him I'm in conference, and if it is urgent, I'll go to the phone." Ambassador Goldberg asks a question and the President doesn't answer. He points to the next chart. Mr. Johnson discusses the need for new people working in government. Once upon a time such a discussion would be superfluous: all a President had to do was send such a list to senators and representatives, and he would be inundated with nominations overnight. In the process, he would pick up some votes of gratitude. But that time is past.

Johnson tells them he wants his Cabinet to spend a little time thinking about people who should be working for the government. "Bring them in," he says bluntly. "We'll put them under the microscope when they get here." There is a hint of sharpness in the tone, as though he is irritated that they have done so little about this matter. He stares at John Gardner and says, "John, will you explain something about how these gentlemen can help us to get desirable and talented people to work with us?" The nonpolitician, the Secretary of Health, Education and Welfare, begins by admitting that it is a continuing problem. It cannot be solved by any number of presidential appointments, because people are always leaving government service and "we need constant renewals."

The assistant returns and whispers and the President stands, glances at his Vice-President, and leaves the room. The meeting continues. In a moment Mr. Johnson is back, crashing into the room and sitting, with a fresh assortment of papers in his hand. The meeting gathers momentum. Mr. Johnson has the agenda and he also has his say. Then he invites discussion by asking, "Any questions?" Sometimes yes, sometimes no. Like Kennedy and Truman, the President is unafraid to descend to the use of common language among his confreres.

"Your mistake was you brought in your one-eyed girl and hid your Miss America." . . . Pointing to a chart on a rent supplement bill: "Never mind the details. Tell them to get practical. We want to stop the rats from eating kids' ears . . . we don't want to start handing out the cigars until we're sure about the wedding . . ."

Johnson likes to think idealistically, and promise a better life, but he knows that there is a long finger of retribution in the November vote if promises are unkept. "We promised health care to our elderly," he says, ticking off items on his fingers, "we promised decent housing and opportunity to our poor, we promised education to our youth, new benefits to our military people, clean water, pure air, parks and open country to all citizens, new skills to our workers, security to our farmers. We have promised to extend the longest and greatest period of prosperity—to give our people a greater share in it."

He looks around the table with a sigh of resignation, as though he cannot understand their inertia and they cannot comprehend his speed. He expects more than time from each of these men. He expects them to execute his will, and also to take the accomplishments to the American people.

"Go tell them. Tell them the record of the Democratic Congress. Get on the air. Remember, they don't pay you to come in second. We don't want to fail in November. Go out and sell them."

Johnson nods to Nicholas Katzenbach, the Attorney General, who sits two removed on his right. Katzenbach is tall enough, seated, to look over the red hair of Under Secretary George Ball at the President. A report is given on a civil rights congress, which, Mr. Katzenbach feels, is not exactly a civil rights congress but perhaps a meeting of disparate groups under one roof. There was the usual ornithological separation of doves and hawks, and Mr. Katzenbach names them.

The President points out that violence is not progress and, in self-defense, asks if any administration has moved as fast as this one, or as far, in the matter of implementing Negro rights. The Cabinet knows the answer to that one as well as he, but the President cannot understand why any sensible leadership would advocate violence as a tool of progress. He singles out Floyd McKissick of CORE as a disruptive influence, and wonders aloud why the newspapers give so much coverage to the apostles of riot and fire.

Katzenbach suffers the interruptions, and continues his report. He is a bald man with a professorial lisp who analyzes the situation as dispassionately as a cook skimming fat from soup as it comes to the boiling surface. His attitude reflects a philosophy that no matter what they say or do at the civil rights congress, and no matter what we do or say here, this country is going to endure long beyond our time.

Mrs. Johnson is on the second-floor porch with Luci. There are two cartons of crystal goblets on the floor. The girl holds them up one at a time and asks her mother which pattern she likes better for the Nugent home. Mother has learned that her approval, rather than her opinion, is being solicited. She has something nice to say about each of the samples.

Mrs. Johnson wears a blue wool dress. Her morning chores are done. She sips a cup of coffee from a White House silver service set. This porch is the favorite place of both Lyndon Johnson and his wife. It is called the Truman Balcony, and it commands a noble view of the green of the President's Park, the Washington Monument, the glaze of the Potomac, and the young hills of Virginia. The sun makes the hummocks of trees wear a deeper green than the grass and lazy birds fly downhill from sturdy branches to insects on the lawn.

Luci puts the goblets back in their respective holders and does not notice that her mother is half-dreaming in the sunlight. Luci mentions something she read in the newspaper this morning, and asks if Mother read it.

"No," she says softly, almost far away. "No, Luci. I don't read the newspapers. Your father laughs at this, but there is too much in them that hurts. I don't want to be masochistic about what I read." Luci listens with her mouth half open. Then she grins, and picks up the cartons and walks inside.

12:00 NOON

To Americans, the White House is beauty, dignity, power, a temple, a valentine, pomp and circumstance, heritage, tradition and glory. It is the fulcrum, as well as the aspiration, of the nation. It is a symbol of might and majesty, a banner for which many have died, a place of historic moments of decision —and tragedy too, because of the last twenty Presidents, four have been assassinated.

It is everything but a home. The occupant feels akin to the curator of a museum. He has 131 rooms ranging from the magnificent golden splendor of the East Room to the small neat servants' bedrooms on the third—or attic—floor. The Presidents and their families are squeezed into eight rooms on the second floor. The living room is part of a corridor.

One President did not live in it: George Washington. He lived in the temporary capitals of New York and Philadelphia. When the states of Maryland and Virginia agreed to cede property for a capital city, the place was called the Territory of Columbia and Pierre L'Enfant designed the national capital within it. He drew huge spokes on a chart and said that it would be a city of magnificent distances.

The Congress offered $500 or a gold medal to anyone who could design a palace for the President of the United States. James Hoban, an Irishman, submitted the design which won, and he accepted the medal for his service. The Congress and the first President rode through the leafy woods and could "see" the stately capitol and the palace. Everyone was pleased until Congress asked for estimates to build the house. The lowest was $400,000.

The members acted as though they had been betrayed. The sum was enormous. The year was 1793, and President Washington knew that the place could not be built in time for his occupancy, but he felt that an executive mansion was as important as a capitol. "It was always my idea," he wrote, "and if I am not mistaken, Mr. Hoban coincided in the propriety and practicality of it, that the building should be so arranged that only a part of it should be erected for the present; and that upon such a plan as to make the part so erected an entire building and to admit of an addition in the future as circumstances might render proper, without hurting but rather adding to the beauty and magnificence of the whole as an original."

This was conciliatory, and Congress responded by appropriating modest amounts of money every few years. German laborers were employed, and they lived in Foggy Bottom, south of the White House, where a tributary canal wandered southwest into the Potomac River. They worked when money was available; they took other jobs when funds ran out.

The first President retired to his home in Mount Vernon, Virginia, in 1797. By this time everyone but George Washington was calling the capital city "Washington." Another Virginian, Thomas Jefferson, left his beloved Monticello to serve in Philadelphia as Vice-President to John Adams. This was still the capital city until such time as quarters were completed on the Potomac.

In June of 1800, President Adams moved the capital permanently to Washington, but he and the Congress were disappointed because they had exchanged the effete refinement of Philadelphia for the crudity of a frontier town; the gray and blue and lavender flagstones for tawny mud; the beautifully gowned women and crystal chandeliers for harridans and candlelight. The new capital contained less than fifty houses.

The White House was not completed, and Congress grudgingly gave $25,000 to furnish it. Abigail Adams despaired when she found that there were not enough candles to light the building at night. There were servants, but no means of summoning them. The main building, without wings, was completed in 1803 and measured 170 feet by 85 feet. It was big and damp and discouraging. Thomas Jefferson was the first President to look upon the building happily. He could see it, in his mind's eye, as a white edifice with long breezeway walks flanking it, and fluted columns across the entrance. He called the architecture "Greek Revival." Across the front lawn he planted saplings with his own hands, and he could see those too as stately elms guarding the entrance.

When he left office, the White House became the abused toy of succeeding Presidents. One wanted the tables and chairs to give a crowded appearance; another wanted mother-of-pearl screens; some demanded more fireplaces; others removed the furniture of predecessors, sold it at public auction, and asked for a Congressional appropriation for new. Some saw the mansion as bright and gay; others demanded that it be formally funereal. For many of its years the President's office was on the second floor, and office-seekers slept in the corridors.

Tad Lincoln kept goats on the lawn. Little by little the First

Family was inched toward the west side of the second floor, a refuge from gapers. Theodore Roosevelt decided that the retreat had gone far enough. He badgered Congress into building a west wing in 1902 for $500,000. But the Legislature expected more than that for its money. It wrote into the bill that the architects were expected to repair and refurnish the White House, build covered ways and walks, and wire the house and grounds for electricity.

The firm of McKim, Mead and White shouldered the burden. The fee was small but the prestige was great. Besides, Sanford White had an idea that he could consult Hoban's old records and maintain the White House as it was originally intended to look, inside and out. In the autumn of 1902, when the work was finished, Theodore Roosevelt had a mansion, with a walkway to the President's office, offices for secretaries, a room for the press, a large reception room, and files and closets in a basement.

The divorce between living and working quarters was an intelligent dream, but public demand to see the public rooms of the mansion made it impossible to expand the living quarters of the First Family. A companion east wing was built to match the other one. This too had room for offices. The result was a continuous and stately structure running all the way from East Executive Avenue to West Executive, with spacious grounds and a curving driveway and fountain in front, and a fenced-in park behind. In all, it occupied eighteen acres, but the august prisoners had to live on one part of one floor.

More Presidents made more changes. Franklin Roosevelt put a swimming pool in the west walkway. Harry Truman put in three bowling alleys. He also had to move across the street to Blair House while the entire interior was gutted so that steel beams could replace termite-infested wooden ones. Everything removed, even bits of flooring, was numbered and replaced; in fact, the whole house was reassembled, and a new and deeper basement was dug. To add a solitary touch of his own, Truman built a family balcony on the south side.

The exterior was now attractive and impressive. When John F. Kennedy became the thirty-fifth President, his wife decided to restore the interior to its original grace and elegance. She inaugurated the White House Historical Association, which, with the co-operation of the National Geographic Society, undertook this major work. It is said that she drew the idea of refurnishing the mansion after a tour of the White House warehouse, where she found historic items raging from James Madison dinnerware to velvet-upholstered chairs designed for the Blue Room.

A call went out for patriots to donate or sell original White House furniture, rugs, and paintings, which for a hundred years or more had been lost in a maze of auctions and presidential gifts. The result was encouraging. A presidential library was furnished on the ground floor. The diplomatic reception room was done over with scenic wallpaper and wall settees. The East Room, used for massive receptions, attained its old golden glitter.

The Blue Room was refurnished with some of the pieces bought by James Monroe in France in 1817. The Green Room was walled with jade damask and Daniel Webster's sofa was placed near the white marble fireplace. A painting of Benjamin Franklin, done in lively colors in 1767, dominates the room.

The Red Room—or third formal parlor—has a Dolly Madison sofa and a gallery of presidential portraits. The walls are in cerise silk with golden borders. The State Dining Room, large enough to seat 120 persons, was not refurnished, but the walls were restored to their original clear oak paneling, which is offset by white Corinthian pilasters. The main table, which stands before a fireplace, is decorated by an elaborate bronze-doré plateau.

The smaller dining room was ignored, except to add a Healy portrait of President Tyler. It is now used for presidential breakfasts and luncheons. Little was done to change the assortment of bedrooms on the second floor. Joseph P. Kennedy, in the early days of his son's administration, liked to sleep in the Lincoln bedroom. Lincoln did not sleep in the big ornate four-poster. It comes from a guest room. However, the room in which the bed stands was Lincoln's Cabinet Room and here he signed the Emancipation Proclamation in 1863.

On the same floor is the Treaty Room. The war with Spain was ended in this room in 1899. The family dining room, down at the west end, is simple and small and decorated with scenic blue wallpaper. The windows facing Pennsylvania Avenue are bulletproof. The Rose Guest Room, a frilly and feminine room, is now called the Queen's Room because Britain's two recent Elizabeths slept there. So have Queens Wilhelmina and Juliana of The Netherlands, and Frederika of Greece. The lavatory is the only one in the White House with a wicker hamper to disguise it.

The chore of restoring the interior of the White House was practically finished when John F. Kennedy was shot in Dallas, Texas. Mrs. Kennedy never regretted the time spent doing the work, but she never returned to appreciate it.

A group of men, a few fairly young, most of them in middle years, stand in a square room, holding pencils and paper. Two White House stenographers sit with pads on crossed knees.

The men stare—some frowning, some tense—at a tall young man with Lincolnesque lips. This is the daily White House press conference. It is more formal than friendly; more a game of wits than the dispensing of information; more getting than giving on both sides. What the press and Bill Moyers have in common is suspicion.

And yet the exchange is "Yes, John?" "Well, Bill . . ." "No word on that appointment yet, Joe." The White House feels that the press twists, bends, and breaks the news. The press corps—which now totals over a thousand accredited correspondents—is just as certain that Lyndon Baines Johnson is a sly fox who uses the press to enhance the image of his administration. The handful of regular reporters who pound the daily beat face two men they like—Bill Moyers and Assistant Press Secretary Robert Fleming. No matter which face they see, the words they hear belong to the President. They seldom like the words, but they always ask for more than are given.

They dig hard, but Moyers and Fleming rarely go beyond terse announcements. This makes the work difficult for both sides, but it has always been this way. James Garfield once permitted reporters to walk into his office to ask questions. Lincoln seldom tried to correct a personal abuse in the press, but he would sit with a coterie of newspapermen and sometimes a man with a jew's-harp would oblige when the President asked him to play "a sad song."

Coolidge had a crony in the press corps and would walk with him on the south grounds while Mrs. Coolidge exercised her two collies. Herbert Hoover didn't trust reporters, and kept away from them. Franklin D. Roosevelt was the first to hold the mass press conferences which have become so popular. In his honeymoon with the press—almost all Presidents have one

: 104

which dies in divorce shortly after the first kiss—Roosevelt permitted them to congregate outside his office, and four sang barbershop harmony, knowing that he could hear it inside. His favorite song was "Home on the Range." One night he phoned them in the press room and, disguising his voice, said that he was Ernest Flugelheimer of the Flugelheimer Pickle Works, and he was looking for a quartet for his national radio program. Would they be interested? A short conference, and the men said they would. The President could not contain himself. He collapsed in laughter.

The pundits have syndicated columns and they feel that good news is no news, so they specialize in public worrying and pontificating. They know what the President should do about Viet Nam, Cuba, inflation, the Soviet Union, and the next election. Sometimes they are right. Sometimes they are not. In either case, the President—whoever he may be—is ruffled.

Usually he cultivates publishers and editors by inviting them to his office for an off-the-record visit, or a lunch. Sometimes he sells himself well, and the attitude of the newspaper in question becomes friendly or less truculent. Sometimes he fails, and the publisher leaves the meeting with ammunition for a personal blast on page one.

The men and women who have desks in the White House press room have to live with Lyndon Johnson every day without seeing him. Theirs is the difficult task of taking the sparse announcements uttered by Moyers and Fleming and trying to turn them into stories worthy of a headline. Sometimes the material they get isn't worth two paragraphs. In either case, editors badger the "regulars" to find out what the President thinks of this or that embarrassing development, and the reporters are often left with a vacuous "No comment." This hurts them with their bosses, especially if there is a later "leak" of the story to another reporter.

Mr. Johnson, for a time, tried to treat the press like old buddies. He called them into his office and took walks with them on the service road outside his office, briefing them on certain matters, giving valuable background material on others, requesting that certain quotes remain unquotable by citing "a high White House source."

Fencing with pens is an old White House pastime, and it will continue regardless of the feelings of the President. Mr. Johnson now and then tries the public press conference, complete with auditorium, lights, television cameras, and radio tapes. Like Kennedy and Eisenhower, he looks for raised hands and he tries to select those he can trust. And like former Presidents, he must first undergo a briefing on what questions are most likely to be asked, and what are the answers.

FDR fought the press successfully by resorting to the "fireside chat." In this, he went over the heads of the journalists and appealed directly to the people by giving his version of events in an intimate, and sometimes jocular, manner. Since the advent of television, the Presidents have used the medium freely to get to scores of millions of Americans personally. It worked especially well for Kennedy, who had presence; and in his pre-election debates with Richard Nixon, television brought John Kennedy enough extra votes to tip the election in his favor.

Mr. Moyers asks, "Are there any questions?" and a reporter, scribbling, says, "Bill, with the conduct of the war in Viet Nam figuring as an issue in the Congressional primaries involving Mr. Cohelan and Mr. Brown, since they both won, I wonder if the White House has any comment." This is a reference to contests for open Congressional seats, and the reporter wants to know if the escalation of the Viet Nam war is helping or hurting the Democrats.

Moyers is prepared with names and facts. "I think you can say," he says dryly, "that the President is very satisfied with the day the Democrats had yesterday. There are a number of reasons for that. First of all, not one Democrat incumbent lost his seat. Second, the number of Negroes who voted in Mississippi was larger than at any point in history, and that is a healthy sign and an encouraging one, in the President's judgment. I think another factor is that as of right now a Democrat is leading in the special election to fill the seat of a Republican who died in office, Mr. Baldwin in California. Mr. Waldes is leading out there with fifty-two percent of the vote."

"What seat is that, Bill?" Moyers is well armed: "The fourteenth district of California. In 1964 the Democratic candidate polled thirty-five percent of the vote. In 1962 the Democratic challenger polled only thirty-seven point one percent of the vote. So, as of right now, this morning, the Democrat is running ahead with fifty-two percent of the vote . . . I think those are the reasons the President would think that it was a good day yesterday."

It is a hurrah-for-us point, but it doesn't excite the press. A reporter says, "The question dealt with the factor of Viet Nam in the election. Would you care to comment on whether you thought there was any approval *or lack of it in* the vote yesterday?" Moyers feels the point of the barb and decides to take the President off it at once. "The fact is," he says, "that we didn't discuss that at all this morning. We didn't get into that. I think the President generally tends to believe that in conditions like this, local issues are important."

The match is a draw. The journalists fidget with their pencils. Some have arrived prepared with questions; others wait for a subject, then think of a question designed to exploit it.

"On a related subject," another reporter says, "what is the President's reaction to the Gallup Poll last week, indicating his popularity at the lowest ebb since he took office, and attributing the drop in some substantial measure to Viet Nam?" This is a wide-breaking curve, a hot question which requires a cold reply. "I don't have a specific reaction to pass on, John," Moyers says.

The subject of polls is raw skin at the White House. The President was once a scoffer. When Louis Harris called a few elections correctly within tenths of a percent, Mr. Johnson was not only converted, he became an avid follower of polls of all kinds. But like Trendex ratings in television, polls are believable when they are palatable to the subject, and anathema when they cut him down. Johnson is an avid poll watcher and has an assistant whose function it is to paste up all the polls and trends, local and national, in the fifty states. When the ratings were warm and friendly, the President carried clippings in his jacket pocket. At such times as the press seemed to taunt and hurt him, he would whip these out and recite them down to the last decimal point. When the polls showed that endorsement of the American public had declined, Mr. Johnson stopped carrying the clippings. Last summer, when the President had an informal meeting with the press, the gentlemen tried to ram the adverse polls down his throat. As always, he rose to the challenge, and in his harsh tone, snapped, "We have had a dozen polls, I guess, in the past week. You don't read about the favorable ones though, I observe." He recited one which favored him with fifty-five-percent approval. "That," he said, "is what you reported as a landslide in General Eisenhower's administration."

12:00 NOON

Caustic reproval of the press may make the President feel better, but it wins no friends. The reporters and columnists emphasize his pique. The schism between the two widens. Often he quarrels with their so-called slanting of the news. "There were 2,500 men and women in the civil rights congress. And there were a few antis, about twenty-five, who were there to disrupt the work of 2,475 people. It is no tribute to our press to notice that more attention was paid to the twenty-five than to the 2,475. Any jackass can kick a barn down, but it takes a pretty good carpenter to build one."

The press is not above pursuing inconsequential subjects when it is in the mood. The following is the exchange reported when Robert Fleming was holding a briefing about Mexican-Americans being invited to the White House. "Bob, what is the project out back?" "Purely to save your time, as anybody who has had a lawn in this part of the country knows, the hard summers are hard on the lawns. The experts have advised that a different combination of seeds be planted to provide a lawn that would last through the summer. The other grass is being removed. I have been advised that for six years they have been fighting a fungus strain."

"As a man whose lawn is in a mess, may I ask what the combination is?" "I lack the proportions. It is fescue and Kentucky blue grass." "Bob, are they going to build, back there, a heliport for the President, a more permanent heliport?" "I know of no plans to change anything back there at all. I was told they are going to get new grass." "Are they seeding or sodding?" "I haven't looked . . ."

The President holds informal press conferences on an average of every few weeks, and he approaches them brusquely. On these occasions the Cabinet Room is filled with sitting and standing reporters and Mr. Johnson tries to discourage hot questions with cold replies. Sometimes he refuses to answer a question; at other times he asserts that it has been answered time and again and he refers his audience to an earlier briefing; once in a while, he decides to ad-lib his hopes, his goals for his country, and to recount America's few slight ills in relation to its many healthful aspects.

Nowhere has Johnson done better in a monologue on domestic and international matters than in press conference number 63, held in the early summer of 1966. His attitude was icy, but he permitted himself to be drawn toward terse explanations of his accomplishments and goals.

Viet Nam: "We are watching the situation very closely. We believe everything possible should be done to bring the various factions to an understanding of the need for unity while the constitutional process is moving forward. That is what our people are trying to do . . . The South Vietnamese are trying to build a nation. They have to do this in the teeth of Communist efforts to take the country over by force. It is a hard and frustrating job, and there is no easy answer, no instant solution to any of the problems they face.

"We are not in Viet Nam to dictate what form of government they should have. We have made it abundantly clear that it is our wish to see them increasingly able to manage their own affairs with the participation of an ever broader share of the population . . .

"The longer we are there, the more sacrifices we make. The more we spend, the more discontent there will be. The more dissatisfaction there will be, the more wish and desire there will be to get out. Leading that parade is the President. If you want to feel that it troubles you one hundred percent, just double that and make it two hundred percent for the President. Say his concern doubles yours. I am glad to say that a substantial majority of those that you refer to do approve of the course of action that we have taken. They do support their government.

"There are others who have different plans. Some would pull out, run out. Some would run in further. Some would just stand still and do nothing. You are aware of our plan. We think that under the circumstances we are doing the best that we can. We would like to have peace. We have had two bombing pauses. We have had economic proposals. We have had diplomatic invitations extended to all 115 or 120 countries. We had two hundred conferences privately. We had visits to forty countries publicly. We have been unable to get the other people to sit down and talk instead of fight. We are trying to provide the maximum deterrents that we can to Communist aggression with a minimum of cost. That is our policy . . ."

Inflation: "I think that the public generally feels that we should get a better price for the things we sell and have a lower price for the things we buy . . . I think there is somewhat more concern now than you would have in a normal period because we are coming close to reaching our objective of full employment. As we do, as labor gets scarce, as commodities get scarce, there are increases in prices . . .

"Here is a chart I had made last night that I asked for in connection with price statistics. You will see the consumer price here as 100 for 1960, and here it is for 1966. In Japan it is now 140; in Italy it is now 130; in France it is 120-plus. In the United Kingdom it is 120-plus. In Germany it is 115, in that neighborhood. In the United States it is 110. It looks like about 108 . . .

"We are reaching a point that we have worked for for so long, trying to get employment for most of our people. When you reach that situation, you run into other problems. I would rather face the problems I face now for this reason: increases in wages have come faster than the prices. The fact that the people have work, and the fact that we have income coming into our Treasury to permit us to increase our educational efforts, our health efforts, our beautification efforts, our conservation efforts—I would rather have these problems than problems that come when unemployment is high and income low."

Spending: "The deficit this year is going to be less than was estimated. We are appropriating almost ten billion more for education and health since I became President than we were the day before. We are spending about two billion more on poverty each year, not to mention what the states, counties and cities are doing . . ."

The press complains that the President lacks modesty. He often wants to "point with pride," and the more he senses the desire of the press to exploit his weaknesses and failures, the harder he tries to prove by statistics that other countries are worse off. The school of politics in which he grew to maturity was one which arrogated to itself all the right, and isolated all the wrong to the other side of the aisle. Earlier in life, in and around Johnson City, Texas, Lyndon Johnson found that it was easier to take credit than to wait for someone to grant it to him. The struggle for recognition was so long and so frustrating that the only way he could achieve it was by pointing to a rural electrification station or dam or road and yelling, "I got it for you."

One difference between Johnson and other ranking politicians is that he is more direct in stating his aims. Teddy Kennedy ran for the United States Senate, not on a platform of helping the nation, but by shouting, "If you elect me, I can do more for Massachusetts." Robert Kennedy, who lives a good part of his life in McLean, Virginia, and some of it at Hyannisport, Massachusetts, convinced the citizens of New York State that he could do a great deal for them in the Senate. And yet his friends make it clear that his personal ambition is the White House. Johnson's personal ambition is to be the best President in the history of the United States, and he is not going to be shy or subtle, nor is he prepared to concede errors of judgment.

This is true also of the men around him. The intelligent and knowledgeable men of the West Wing can get better-paying jobs in private industry, but they not only work long hours and sustain insufferable tasks, but fight to remain at the side of the man they say is "America's greatest President." They support him to a degree above and beyond the call of duty, and they bristle when they read criticism of Johnson in the newspapers.

A reporter says that Republican leaders charge that Johnson is withholding the facts on Viet Nam, and Moyers blandly replies, "All I saw was a statement by Senator Dirksen." The reporter says, "Dirksen and Ford." And the press secretary says:

"I think that the President has had more briefings for more members of Congress than has generally been true under past administrations. At his own personal instruction, the key officials of this administration have been spending hours on the Hill, testifying before various committees, briefing members privately and collectively . . . The President recently visited the majority leader and the minority leader in the hospital to keep in touch with them. He informed both of them, at that time, that he would be happy to provide whatever information they thought they needed, or he had . . .

"He has invited every member of Congress, House and Senate, to the White House this year for briefings and meetings. He has long ago instructed every member of the administration to keep the Congress informed in depth. There is no information in this government which is not available, on a bipartisan basis, to the Congress."

Information vital to the public welfare and public confidence is lost in word-quibbling. The reporter says, "The dispute seems to be over invitation, then?" and Moyers shakes his head negatively: "I don't recognize a dispute." A few other reporters decide to hone their semantics: "I have the impression that the thrust of his [Dirksen] remarks was not so much that Congress was not gettting the facts—but the people."

"I don't know what more the President can do," Moyers says, dropping a briefing paper on a desk, "more than he has done over the course of his administration, Ray, to keep the people informed." Another reporter says, "You said you thought the people would decide whether they have been informed sufficiently. What do you mean by that?" "I just think the people will have to make the judgment." "How?" "However the people go about making judgments on public issues." "Would you include polls . . . ?" "However they go about making their judgment." "Do you interpret any of the recent primaries as an indication that they are expressing their—" "I try to stay away from the business of interpreting primaries. I leave that to you."

"Bill, there is a published report this morning that charges, in effect, the President and the White House have been selling invitations to dinner at $10,000 a year." "That charge is so absurd that it does not warrant comment." "Is there such a thing as an Elite President's Club?" "I don't know of one." "Is

there a $10,000 donation club?" Moyers is now irritated. "I told
you the charge is so absurd as not to warrant comment. Period,
end of quote."

The President has his arm on the table and he takes a glance
at his watch without drawing attention. He does not want the
others to see him because he does not want the meeting short-
ened. Still, he wants to maintain his schedule. Gardner Ackley,
of the Council of Economic Advisers, has the floor. He is short
and emphatic. In thirty days the fiscal year will close and the
men around the table want to know whether the United States
is going deeper into debt, holding its own, or doing a little
better than expected.

Mr. Ackley and Charles Schultze, the director of the Budget,
have been conferring about the 1967-1968 budget, and as
goods and services cost more for the housewife, they do also
for the United States government. Schultze sits against the left
wall, opposite the President, listening to Ackley. He is talking
about a "cash budget 1966 estimate."

It is clear, from the figures, that some departmental spending is $200,000,000 more than was estimated last year, when
the budget was drawn. Still, Mr. Ackley says, using his pointer,
"corporate and personal income were up, and a surplus of
$1,500,000,000 can be expected." The most prosperous nation
in the world spends more than anyone in the world, but the
returns in taxes are higher and ever higher. The National
Growth rate is up four percent, or about $16,000,000,000 a
year. Employment is at an all-time high. This brings a faint
nod of pleasure from the President, but Ackley warns the administration against "any further tightening of the labor mar-

ket." The unemployment rate should level off next year, Ackley says, at about three or three and a quarter percent of the labor market.

Everyone agrees that the country is healthy. Mr. Johnson passes the compliments in silence and asks Secretary Orville Freeman about food prices. The President knows that the Congressional campaign for election will begin in sixty days, and he doesn't want the Republican party to be armed with misleading figures. "You want to show the survey on price rises and food costs," he says, "so that we won't be selling a dead horse two months from now."

Freeman, behind glasses, looks confused. "Prices are coming down some," he says defensively, "but we don't have the figures for the current month." Johnson stares steadily. "I do," he says softly. "I have them for mid-month. Instead of being up seven-tenths of one percent, which we caught hell for, they are up four-tenths of one percent over two months ago." The Secretary of Agriculture is in a slightly embarrassing position. "I don't have that," he says. He sits across the big table between Wirtz and McNamara. Mr. Freeman jerks a hand at a chart which shows price rises in many countries. By comparison, the United States looks good. "I'd rather dance with the girl that brung me," he says.

President Johnson looks at Lawrence O'Brien and points a pencil at him. The Postmaster General, who has many duties besides seeing that the mail is delivered, begins to speak about government-employee subscriptions to government bonds. Mr. Johnson has already been through this subject, so while O'Brien talks about the percentage of employees in each department who have signed for bond payroll deductions, the President tiptoes from the room. As O'Brien calls off the figures, some secretaries cut in to add their knowledge to the total. They have been doing this for over an hour and a half. The interruptions are not for the purpose of disagreement; it is part of the Johnsonian policy of ordering each man to be interested, and be a participant, in the problems of all the others.

Defense Secretary McNamara chews on the end of a black pen. Ball, sitting in for Rusk, who is in Brussels, makes notes for his chief. Udall, of the Department of the Interior, is a squirmer. He is the athlete of the group, and protracted sitting forces him to keep changing position on the chair. Wirtz, of the Department of Labor, puffs on a dark pipe. Bob Kintner shuffles his papers to make certain that every approved item has been discussed.

The President returns, as softly as he left. Kintner turns the chair for him, and Mr. Johnson listens to O'Brien and agrees that the bond figures are good but can be improved. Kintner whispers that the agenda is now complete.

The President clasps his hands before him on the table. He looks from face to face to see if there is anything else to discuss. Nothing. "I hope," he says, "that every Cabinet member will sit with the appropriate Congressional committee chairman and talk things out *now*. Congress talks about adjournment, and if you don't get your program on the agenda now, you may find yourselves out of the ball park. If you don't get on the Congressional agenda now, you might as well junk the programs and wait until after elections.

"Have we done our homework on this subject?" Good. He advises the Department of Housing and Urban Development to stop giving out press and television stories on the day their bills come before Congress. To the Cabinet in general, he repeats an old warning: "You may have good academic men, but if you don't learn to work with the men on Capitol Hill, I'm going to put a couple of politicians in your departments."

He shakes his head dolefully. "One more one-vote victory and I'm going to have to do something." Then, enunciating each word separately, he says, "If . . . you . . . don't . . . get . . . your . . . legislation . . . passed, all . . . the . . . announcements . . . will . . . do . . . you . . . no . . . good . . . at . . . all."

The President is ready to close the meeting. Joe Califano, one of those against the wall, gets up and walks slowly around the table, asking each secretary for names of senators who are not sold on certain legislation, "but are willing to listen." He makes notes rapidly. He also asks for legislation which is in committee but can be moved to the floor for a vote. "I want cases where we need two votes before we can move," he says.

Mr. Johnson is still thinking of public relations. While Califano is making the rounds, he asks the Cabinet to route "material of national interest through Moyers and Kintner. We'd like to get aboard some of these projects, and yet, on the other hand, I expect all of you to get on television and get out proper releases from time to time. We have to have some sort of procedure so that you people are not announcing things that we know nothing about." His hands are on the arms of the chair, ready to lift his body.

"If you have speeches you're particularly proud of, we want you to make them and we want to know something about them before you make them." He looks around. "If no one has any further business to bring up, I'll declare this meeting of the President's Cabinet adjourned." As he strides toward Mrs. Roberts' office, Johnson again glances at his watch. The time is five minutes to one.

12:00 NOON

Within three minutes the President is back in the Cabinet Room. He looks over the familiar faces of the newsmen who have come in. He wastes no time. "Bill thought that an efficient and effective way for handling your problem of coverage would be for me to review what transpired in our Cabinet meeting and to ask those who made the presentations to stay here"—he nods at some of the Cabinet members, lounging in groups around the room—"and make a brief report to you, or at least to be available for any questions that you might have." Quickly, as though there is never enough time, the President recalls, by looking at the agenda, each speaker, and, in recalling the speaker, the President seems to be able to remember the multitude of figures and percentages of the reports. He also tells the press which ones please him, and why.

When he concludes, the press directs its questions not at the Cabinet member involved, but at the President. This is understandable, because in the eyes of readers, it is more authoritative. However, as hands are raised and new voices crowd the table, the newsmen depart from the President's report and begin to take dead aim on Viet Nam.

"We didn't really go into Viet Nam here today in the Cabinet," Johnson says patiently. "But if you want to spend a little time on Viet Nam, if you have a particular interest in it, I will answer your questions." He knows he is running overtime on appointments, but if he concludes the interview now, it will appear as though he is afraid to discuss the problems of a little country which for many years has been disemboweling itself.

The solitary question turns out to be a query about elections in Viet Nam. Will they be held in September or not? The President doesn't know. He is hopeful. Another question concerns a White House "priority" for certain legislation pending

A Day in the Life of President Johnson

before Congress. Mr. Johnson says he doesn't believe in such priorities; they irritate the department heads whose bills are not on the list.

Another writer asks about optimistic reports on legislation. "I don't believe in those 'optimistic' or 'pessimistic' terms," the President snaps. "Probably thirty-five or forty percent of our bills are already signed, and that many or more are already out of committee and passed in one house. If you had that kind of a batting average when the session was over, you wouldn't consider it a disaster. We want to make as much progress as we can, and we are doing that." Mr. Johnson is trying to convince anew the skeptics who see trouble where there is none and dissension where he knows there is harmony.

"I picked up the ticker the other day and read, I believe, over a period of an hour, where there had been several real denunciations [of a certain bill]. When it was added up, it didn't amount to much. At the end of the day they passed the bill they were denouncing by a substantial vote." The President decides to fire a broadside. "There is nothing as dead as yesterday's newspaper and criticism. What we want is to get that legislation passed . . .

"The answers are good. The economy is good. The employment is good. The wages are good. The profits are good. The farm income is good. So, as a people, we are doing well. We all have ambitions. We have higher goals and we want to do better . . ."

The high sun is hot, and from office elevators and stairwells the working people of Washington drift into the street to talk of eating in a new place, or to give the old one another chance.

12:00 NOON

Pretty girls walk in pairs and pass old ladies who clump along slowly, squinting at the "Don't Walk" signs. Hundreds of thousands of government officials, great and small, join the sidewalk crowd. In the Pentagon, uniformed officers carry trays in cafeterias, with an eye over the cup of coffee toward empty tables. The White House barbershop is full; the little restaurant in the basement has two empty tables. The House and Senate are in session, and citizens present passes permitting them to sit in the galleries and listen.

In the United States Printing Office, the first stenographic material from the House of Representatives is being copied, and will soon be set in type as more and more of the speeches are brought in. The reporters who were in the Cabinet Room a moment ago are back in the press room. Those who represent afternoon newspapers are on phones, reading their notes to rewrite men. Those who work for morning newspapers are, for the most part, at typewriters, trying to think of a newsworthy lead, anything except the President's feeling that everything is uniformly good.

The word is flashed around the White House that the President is now in his office. Labor Leader George Meany hobbles to the desk on crutches, one leg in a cast, and sits on the chair indicated by Mr. Johnson. Marvin Watson knows that the President is slightly behind schedule, and he will have to speed other appointments or cancel one. In the private dining room on the second floor, Lynda Johnson sits alone, eating lunch, speaking sporadically to Zephyr as the cook comes into the room, then goes back to the kitchen. On the south lawn, a man is walking the President's beagles. They sniff at grass, wag their tails, and look sad. A shimmer of haze lies over Washington.

1:00 P.M.

In his office, the President listens as George Meany recites the problems of labor. Guidelines have been set up for increases in wages and these average about 03.4 percent per year, roughly commensurate with the rise in prices. Mr. Meany, president of the American Federation of Labor, feels that labor will ask more, and get it. The President is sure that this will impel industry to jack prices beyond the guidelines.

Labor legislation is watched closely in the White House, and there is no doubt that A.F. of L. and C.I.O. lawyers study the bills before they reach the assessing eyes of Congressional committees. In the postwar years labor has become stronger politically, even though many doubt that there is a unified labor vote. In 1952 the so-called labor vote helped elect a Republican, Dwight D. Eisenhower, who was opposed by the Democratic liberal Adlai Stevenson. In 1960 John F. Kennedy romanced labor to the point where at 6 A.M. he stood in zero cold in Wisconsin shaking hands with laborers reporting for duty in factories. In spite of labor's promise of bloc support, he barely squeaked through to victory over Republican Richard Nixon. Thus, a President of the United States who fears the

loss of support of labor must walk a legislative tightwire between granting economic liberties to unions, and fighting that
old glacial and inexorable enemy, inflation. The forces oppose
each other, and no one can support both.

The President strides slowly beside the labor leader as
Meany limps toward the door. The chat has been pleasant, but
of no great consequence in the affairs of the state. The men
wave in the corridor, and President Johnson walks into the
Cabinet Room. This is his third meeting there and a lectern
has been set up with the President's seal on it.

The governors of forty-one of the fifty states are present.
The matter of highway safety is under consideration. Americans kill each other in motor vehicles at an annual rate of
about 50,000. The governors and the President are agreed that
the number can be cut—but how? Ferris Bryant, head of the
Office of Emergency Planning, is in charge of the federal program for highway safety and he speaks a few words, introduc-
ing Mr. Johnson.

The doors are closed. Some of the governors are political
allies of the President. Some are his enemies. All sit in rapt
attention as he makes a short speech. In this case, he has little
actual power and no means of imposing his will on these men,
because motor-vehicle laws are state rather than federal matters.

Mr. Johnson stands at the lectern, smiling down on familiar
faces as the governors applaud his presence. ". . . No doubt the
key to solving this problem," he says, "is in your hands. Responsibility rests back home. You have a responsibility. People
are getting killed on roads everywhere. For this, we have a
moral responsibility although the governors issue the license."

The President stresses the importance of state car inspection
on a regular basis. State police, as well as local police depart-

ments, must assist in the enforcement of traffic laws. Our people are aroused and concerned. Three times as many people have been killed in automobiles as in all the wars the United States has fought. Today more servicemen are killed in autos than in military action. Over the Memorial Day weekend 540 Americans died in accidents. This is the highest toll in our history.

"Something must be done. Anything which affects the lives of so many citizens asks for action. We are going to get it. Gentlemen, view this problem squarely. There is a need for a safety program. Legislation will give us the resources to find out what causes accidents. This involves your roads, your drivers, construction of safer automobiles, safer highways, and so forth.

"Action is needed now. We can't postpone it. Governor Bryant must have help to move this badly needed program forward. We can stop senseless slaughter on the highways. Credit will then belong to you leaders of the fifty states . . ."

On his way back to his office, the President pauses to shake hands with some of the governors. Their applause is still ringing as he shuts the door behind him. He entered the Cabinet Room at 1:22 P.M. and he is out in time for a social call from Richard Strout and Seville Davis of the *Christian Science Monitor.*

Watson comes in to tell the President that the appointment with Ted Heath, Leader of the British Conservative party, has been changed and will follow this one. These are the midday short appointments, personal in character. Some involve but a moment or two; others extend and threaten the tight schedule: even distinguished visitors are sometimes eager to establish a special friendship in ten minutes and show photos of their children and grandchildren. The clock watcher, Marvin Watson, interrupts these by standing in the doorway and telling the President the time.

In the trips back and forth to the Cabinet Room, the President has advised Juanita Roberts of several matters which have come to mind. Two involve dictation of letters; two are phone calls to other departments; one is to ask Califano to see him later. The President always works through the lunch hour, and the responsible people of the West Wing are not away from their desks when the President calls.

Rostow is at lunch. Instead of eating it at his desk, he sits with an assistant in a more uncomfortable place, a settee and a low coffee table, which permits little leg room. Walt Whitman Rostow is as articulate as the man for whom he was named, and almost as intriguing. Mr. Rostow spears a salad and fruits, and sips hot black coffee. The salad is to keep him slender, but the leaves of lettuce are laced with a tasty fattening dressing.

He is talking about the change in reaction times. In the era of World War I, he points out, the United States was interested solely in the Atlantic community, and when cables or advices told of trouble, the White House attitude was to do nothing, or, at best, express a pious hope that all would turn out well.

This now is the time of the poised rattlesnakes, all in a common pit and all believing that none will strike. The attitude of remaining coiled with head erect is a chronic strain, and Rostow knows that this is the true danger. "The world," he says as he refills the coffee cup, "is a small community of dissidents. If something in a small nation like Ghana imperils

: 125

peace, it is of immediate interest to Moscow, Washington, Peking, London, Warsaw, and Tokyo. Everyone reacts."

The presidential phone buzzes. Mr. Rostow is on his feet quickly; he threads the narrow aisle between sofa and coffee table, grabs the phone, and listens. The grave expression relaxes. "I hear you loud and clear," he says. "Right in my lap." The phone is reset on its cradle. It is not only nations but people in government who have instantaneous reactions. It required six seconds for Walt Rostow to get from the sofa to the scrambler phone, and even though it was only an operative test, a nuclear missile covers five miles in the time he needed to traverse fifteen feet.

He picks at the salad, finished with it but nibbling because there is some left on the platter. The President's personal aide in foreign affairs is still a teacher at heart, and he enjoys briefing his assistants on his political philosophy. He is talking of the Soviet Union and China, and like President Johnson, Rostow enjoys weighing now against tomorrow.

"They have unrealistic doctrines," he says, and his assistant nods absent-mindedly. "In time they will realize this and come around to a softer attitude with less tension. These doctrines may very well fail first in Moscow and Peking. At this moment we happen to be the balancing power. If we weren't, Moscow and Peking might, for a time in history, enforce their harsh doctrines on the world and make them stick."

He gives up on the salad and sets the fork down. "Political inefficiency is an important phrase." His eyes are on the soundproof ceiling. "It is inefficient, and therefore costly in treasure and progress, to bring a group of nations together under a Communist dictatorship. The price of satellite nations is high. Protecting them from the non-Communist world requires vigilance. Protecting the mother country from a coalition of satellites entails neutralizing their military power, but must be achieved without rendering them helpless.

"And yet, there is nothing on the Asian mainland, except United States forces, to stop the Chinese from overwhelming all of it. In Europe, there is nothing to stop the Russians from blackmailing countries into subjugation, except NATO. Above all, I think we must realize that we're just a bunch of guys working on problems too big for any one of us. But then, you must think of your adversaries as just another bunch of guys in a similar situation. The difference between us and them, I think, is that we never confuse ourselves with God."

The President is at his desk, alone. He has found a few minutes for the signing of mail. Eisenhower and Kennedy had signature stamps made, and these were so cleverly executed that it was difficult to tell a real signature from one stamped by a secretary.

President Johnson doesn't like to use a stamp. He wants to read the note, then sign it by hand. Each day he averages fifty personal letters and he reads each one carefully, then squiggles his signature, which looks like a series of mountain peaks pressed together from the sides. His appreciation of neat secretarial work is sincere. Sometimes, before reading an incoming note, he will hold it aloft and say, "Isn't that a pretty letter!" In sending epistles, he wants the recipient to know that it comes from the President's hand, so he often pens a personal postscript.

He has told Watson to show Ted Heath in, and when the Briton appears, the President arises from his desk and walks around it to shake his hand. Mr. Heath's Conservative party has been out of power since the political retirement of Winston Churchill. Thus the meeting is politically perfunctory—a social call, so to speak.

The President escorts Heath to the settee and then sit in the rocker. Each is careful not to say anything which might be considered news, and each agrees that the United States and the United Kingdom are now, and in the foreseeable future, walking arm in arm through history. The clipped understated British accent contrasts sharply with the broad Texas twang, and when the Englishman rises to take his leave, the President is obliged to ask him not to rush off. This is good manners, but potentially dangerous to his tight schedule. Mr. Heath insists, and Mr. Johnson shows reluctance in permitting him to depart. The door closes and the President again begins to read and sign letters.

He has made the job of Chief Executive one of dynamic industry, but slowly, steadily, he has come to accept the truth that everything cannot be accomplished today. At first he felt that all he had to do with each problem was to implement a reasonable solution, then stand back and watch it work. To his dismay, he found that few of his duties could be executed that easily.

It was almost as if everyone around him were afflicted with what Lincoln called "the slows." Presidential temper and tension broke through the emotional dams and he began to holler for even more action. When Marvin Watson showed him, one day, that the Johnson administration had passed more Congressional legislation in one year than any other in the history of the United States, the President shook his head and said, "We can do a lot better if we can get everybody on the ball."

Little by little, the President is learning to live with time. In the third year of his tenure he was more tractable, more forgiving of mistakes, than in the first two. The flashes of speed and the insatiable demands for it are still present, but he has learned to settle for something less. The further he draws away from the press, the more he courts the people in personal confrontation. He reaches through fences to shake hands, exchanges pleasantries, flies over the land and pauses to make speeches, becomes folksy with farmers and factory workers, and like his predecessors, brooks no interference from the Secret Service.

Personal habits too have been altered. Once he gorged himself on catfish and Texas barbecue, and he didn't care whether he put on weight or not. Since his heart attack in 1955, Lyndon Johnson has learned to eat sparingly, and has given up smoking. In the locker rooms of Congress, he used to join the others in emptying bottles of Cutty Sark. Today he asks for a diet cola. His only indulgence, outside of an occasional drink, is tapioca pudding.

He understands the august character of a presidential whim, and he enjoys exercising it. The President still does not know the city of Washington, but if he is in the mood for a walk, he will take it. He is prone to decline invitations to parties, and then pop in late. Those who protect his life prefer to have plenty of notice before planning a trip, but President Johnson often makes up his mind late, and is off to the helicopter pad on the back lawn of the White House, trailing a comet-tail of Secret Service agents.

He chafes under rules of presidential decorum. When he wanted to walk with Mrs. Gandhi, Prime Minister of India, to her abode at Blair House, the alarm bells rang in all the security offices. Johnson took the lady by the arm and walked across the street. If he desires to sit on the office floor and play games with tiny Courtenay Valenti, the worried expression on the handsome face of Marvin Watson in the doorway will not stop him. And if he desires to leave his desk and hurry upstairs to embrace his wife and daughters, an appointment of state may have to wait.

Sometimes, when the mood is on him, President Johnson will drop his work for ten minutes and walk outside to the Rose Garden to lie supine on a couch and soak in the sun. He enjoys strong hot rays, and will close his eyes behind sunglasses to feel the pleasant warmth on his leathery skin. By instinct he is an outdoor man, and this has conflicted with his career, which calls for indoor work. The opportunity to go home to Texas is, to Johnson, akin to a Christmas present. His spirit is renewed before he leaves Washington; his attitude becomes jovial, boyish with anticipation. At the ranch, he spends as many hours as possible outdoors, and sometimes when he returns to Washington he will stroke his face and say, "I got a lot of sun over the weekend. Does it show?"

Sometimes in the early evening Mrs. Johnson coaxes the President to stop working and "come up on the balcony for a cup of coffee." The flow of energy which keeps him burning bright all day seems, in this, his favorite place, to ebb. He sits relaxed with his wife, speaking in a voice low enough to be a mumble. He sips his coffee and he listens to her recital of her day, or the plans of their daughters. He will promise to try to get upstairs early this evening, and both know that he will be unable to keep the promise. The direct brown eyes gaze off across the deep green lawn, the trees, and pick up a jet climbing behind the Washington Monument toward the White House. He will continue to talk in that low confidential tone, and keep his eyes on a gray squirrel, darting, stopping, racing halfway up a thick elm to stand immobile, then moving across a branch, balancing with the sway of a furry tail. For a mo-

1:00 P.M.

ment a squirrel becomes an important thing, as it must to any
ranch boy.

Then he will slap his knees with big palms and say, "Gotta
go, Bird," and he will kiss her as though the office were miles
away, as though he might not see her for days.

An usher brings lunch to Mrs. Johnson in her room. It isn't
much: a bowl of soup and a sandwich. She eats alone, and uses
this opportunity to make up an informal list of people to invite
aboard the *Honey Fitz* tomorrow evening. As additional names
come to mind, she makes a small sound and writes them on a
pad.

It reads: "The Rostows, Riordans, Valentis, Juanita, Vicki,
Marie Fehmer, Dr. Young . . ." It includes senators, writers,
and Cabinet members. She will not phone any of these until
she is certain that Lyndon will have the time for a cruise down
the Potomac.

Mrs. Johnson thinks of the White House as a temporary trust
granted to her husband by the American people. The ranch is
their true and only home. While she is in the Executive Mansion, Mrs. Johnson appears to stand a pace behind her husband; in truth, however, she exercises more influence over him
than anyone else. His faith in her inherent intelligence is so
complete that a whisper from her can often change his course
and his mood. She knows a lot about government and government policies, but she confines her attention to the niceties she
wants him to display. If he lacks consideration for the feelings
of his co-workers, Mrs. Johnson is overly considerate. If he is
brusque, she is solicitous. Where he fears to show his natural
sympathy for people who are hurt, and will exercise it surrepti-

tiously, Lady Bird can radiate sympathy and warmth without being "gushy."

She taps her mouth with a napkin, rings a bell for the tray to be taken to the kitchen, and gets back to work.

Others remember, with some chagrin, that when Mrs. John F. Kennedy occupied this house, the young First Lady could not understand why the wife of the Vice-President had to appear to be subservient to her husband's wishes. Mrs. Kennedy saw the role of wife as that of a co-equal. When the mood was on her not to accompany her husband, she didn't. White House photographers had to learn not to incur the wrath of Mrs. Kennedy by taking photos unexpectedly. She saw herself as one who led a life with her husband, and a life separate from her husband.

When time stopped for the Kennedys in Dallas, the skimpy string of friendship between the Kennedys and the Johnsons broke. As Vice-President, Lyndon Johnson deferred to the young man who only a short time before had been the junior senator from Massachusetts, subject to the majority leadership of the senior senator from Texas. He was willing to be John F. Kennedy's assistant, his buffer, his errand boy to foreign countries, his adviser, anything serviceable but not his court jester.

There were some taut moments between the two, but in any dispute, Johnson could not afford to be a winner against his President. The Kennedys, representing the East, were not charmed by a practical politician given to hill-country homilies, a man who studied reports assiduously and quoted statistics at random at Kennedy meetings. Johnson, who was certain that he would never be President of the United States, wanted to conclude his political career as the most accomplished Vice-President. His desire to help led to trips abroad. President Kennedy, at his evening "bang-board" hour, could always draw a smile from his assistants by asking, "Whatever became of Lyndon?"

On the plane back from Dallas, there were two camps: the Johnsons in front and the bereaved Kennedy group around the casket in the rear. From that day on, no overtures of sympathy or friendship were acceptable to the Kennedy family. The new First Lady had a floral plot designed on the southeast lawn and decided to name it the Jacqueline Kennedy Garden. Mrs. Johnson was advised by White House historians that it could be called the First Lady Garden, but that it was against tradition to name it for an individual. Lady Bird Johnson, however, did name it for Mrs. Kennedy, and invited her to come to the White House to dedicate it.

The invitation was declined. President Johnson sent an invitation to all the Kennedys to dine with him. This too was spurned. Mrs. Johnson nevertheless dedicated the garden to Mrs. Kennedy and asked that it be maintained in perpetuity in the name of her predecessor. She sent a large color photo of it to Mrs. Kennedy.

2:00 P.M.

The air conditioners, like the personnel, work quietly. Marvin Watson leans back in his high-backed blue chair and checks the appointment calendar. It is on schedule again. Bill Moyers, Willard Wirtz, and J. E. Wolfe have just been admitted to the President's office for an off-the-record talk. Mr. Johnson, watching the hourly news on television, waves them to sit down for a moment. He wants to listen.

All over the West Wing, steel file cabinets carry temporary red tags marked "Open." Bill Hopkins stops in at Juanita Roberts' office with a fresh batch of mail. In the basement, a messenger drops an envelope on Rostow's desk. Across it is printed: "For Mr. Rostow: Extremely Sensitive." The President snaps the television off and tries to open a French door leading to the gardens. The door sticks a moment. He returns to his desk, ready to talk to his three visitors, but first addresses the intercom to Mrs. Roberts' office: "Get somebody to fix those doors so you can open them without a college education."

Mrs. Johnson phones Lem Jones of the Secret Service that the President expects to take a cruise tomorrow. The word is passed at once on walkie-talkies to those agents who will be

2:00 P.M.

on duty on the *Honey Fitz*, also to those who will be on the thirty-foot cabin cruiser which follows the presidential yacht. The event is not yet "firmed," but two Secret Service agents go to the dock to examine the boat and its personnel and quarters at once. Watson hears about it and murmurs, "Well. Short day." It isn't, really. At this moment the President has completed seven hours of work, and expects to put in three more before quitting.

The chat with Moyers, Wirtz, and Wolfe is concluded secretly and succinctly. The President meets with a group not listed on his calendar: the assistants who serve Secretary of State Dean Rusk as experts for various parts of the world. This time there is no lecture. Mr. Johnson looks them over, one by one, eye to eye, and asks them to state their problems. The men are mostly career men, and they know that their troubles are small compared to his. They speak up because he asked for it. When they finish, the President nods approvingly and enunciates a few refinements of American policy as it relates to the Middle East and Eastern Europe. The changes are not monumental, but if the assistant secretaries do not remember the nuances, Mr. Johnson will.

He learns from experience rather than books, and his memory for governmental detail is phenomenal. He likes baseball, but he will fall silent if asked if the Washington Senators won or lost a game yesterday. However, if anyone mentions an old and forgotten Congressional bill, a minor appointment of an earlier administration, or something that Carl Vinson once said about naval construction, Lyndon Johnson will quote the date, the year, the political moves which prompted the event, and, quite often, is able to recite the essence of the speeches made on the subject.

He is the first President of the United States who is never

: 135

away from his desk. From the helicopter or from Jet 26000, he can pick up a phone and dictate a letter to Mrs. Roberts, query Harry McPherson about a first draft of a speech, or ask Lawrence O'Brien what is going on in Congress at this moment. He can call from his little speedboat on Lake Lyndon Johnson ("This is Volunteer; get me Bill Moyers") and it doesn't matter if Moyers is at home or driving in his car—the President speaks to him. Mr. Johnson can be driving his Lincoln over granite in the Texas hills and pick up a phone and talk to Moscow or the Joint Chiefs, or even Dale Malachek, his ranch foreman.

Eisenhower had good communications; Kennedy improved them; Johnson perfected them. Nothing he says can be plucked out of the air by eavesdroppers, because of the scrambler system. Even when he is walking alone with his wife, a Secret Service man is within a few seconds of the President, armed with a system of communications light enough to carry. The military men who walk behind also carry secret codes in case war must be declared. When the President sleeps, these men rest within a few yards of his bedroom door. The system works two ways, so that classified information is outbound as well as inbound. Aboard *Air Force One,* for example, it may be unimportant that the President has just said that he will retire for a nap, still, the news is flashed; and back in Washington, the press information officer of the State Department may be completing the draft of a public response to the newest Chinese threat. It is important that the President read it before it is publicized.

If the system of constant world-wide communication had not been devised when President Johnson assumed office, he would have ordered it to be invented because he is, above all, a "nosy" man. He wants no surprises, good or bad. His insatiable desire to know everything about everything was not acquired; Lyndon Johnson was born with it.

Part of the system—especially on trips—is manned by the Secret Service. They make excellent use of walkie-talkie sets hooked into switchboards with direct lines to the White House, Secret Service headquarters, the Departments of State, Defense, and so forth. As a group, the White House detail is young, tall, muscular, crew-cut, and dedicated. They wear small colored pins in their jacket lapels and neutral smiles.

The relationship between President Johnson and the Secret Service is, at best, tender. But most Presidents of the United States learn, in time, to accept the onerous aspects of the job. History shows, however, that none ever learned to accept the Secret Service with grace. The man who attains the most exalted position in the country is shadowed at all times. The unremitting presence of men who are neither personal friends nor strangers aggravates the man in the center. The longer he remains in office, the worse it gets. He starts by trying to understand that they will protect his life, and the lives of his family and Vice-President, but the longer he lives without threat, the more certain he becomes that the presence of the Secret Service isn't always necessary.

John F. Kennedy chafed at the whole system. Leaving Sunday mass, with two agents in front and two in the rear, he used to bend his knees as he walked up the aisle, flexing them until he became smaller and smaller. Then he would whisper to the men in front in a sinister tone, "If there is anybody up in that choir loft trying to get me, he's going to have to get you first." On the morning of his visit to Dallas, President Kennedy sent an order to the Secret Service not to trot beside his car, and not to stand on the rear bumpers. His credo was: "The people come to see me, not the Secret Service."

Lyndon Johnson is the only President who was a witness to

an assassination. The horror of it will never leave him, but the scar is not visible. (The President agreed to co-operate with William Manchester, Mrs. John F. Kennedy's choice to tell the story of the tragedy, but he refused to grant him a personal interview. Manchester had to submit his questions in writing because Mr. Johnson felt that the author and those associated with him were "on the make.")

If Johnson is fearful of his life, he hides it well. He walks freely among strangers at cattle auctions in Texas, shakes hands through the fence of the White House with strangers, sometimes speaks before crowds in as many as six cities in a day, poses with Lady Bird for camera groups outside the church, and admits two or three hundred strangers to the Rose Garden outside his office for informal chats on whatever legislation interests them. Johnson knows that fresh millions of dollars have gone into the Secret Service since that day in Dallas, and he isn't sure it is worth it.

The Secret Service must always combat the homicidal psychopath on the one hand, and the President on the other. The men with Chief James Rowley work under an inflexible rule: "Protect the President with your life." By instinct, Rufus Youngblood, in the Vice-President's car, threw Johnson to the floor when the shots first snapped around Dealey Plaza in Dallas, and dropped on top of the Vice-President. This is the way it is supposed to be.

The Secret Service has three functions: to detect and stifle traffic in narcotics; to protect the currency and bonds in the United States Treasury, and to preserve the life of the President from those who would take it. It is not a detective agency, nor in the case of the President, a police agency. When Kennedy was shot, it was not the function of the Secret Service to hop from the cars and find the assassin. Their sole duty was to stay with him and do anything possible to maintain his life.

Under Rowley, the Secret Service had a good working agreement with the Federal Bureau of Investigation to exchange information, but there was a day when the system didn't work. Today the Service has written agreements with the F.B.I., the Central Intelligence Agency, the State Department, the Department of Defense, the National Security Agency, and the Immigration and Naturalization Service to funnel information about extremists, rabid Communists, neurotics, dangerous aliens and those who have uttered or written threats against the government and the person of the President.

About seven thousand items of interest come in each month, and these are processed for future use. When the President plans a trip to New York, the data for that city and its environs are automatically printed in the computer. The information is good, but the burden is great because the machine now demands fifteen thousand separate investigations each year.

The President, alone in his office, lifts a stack of departmental reports from the "In" box, places them on the desk blotter, and props his chin on his fist as he reads. They cover a range of subjects, from the size and cost of missile engines to a fishery dispute with Japan. Understandably, this would be a tax on any human mind. A man who is president of General Motors finds his work sufficiently difficult in maintaining an up-to-date knowledge of motors, subcontracts of parts, and the market for automobiles. In effect, the President of the United States is the chief officer of several hundred corporations of the size of General Motors, and each requires a separate knowledge of interrelated and independent subjects. Some Presidents learn to delegate authority over the various bureaus and agencies, or run the risk of trying to do all and accomplishing very little. Roosevelt had Harry Hopkins and Ickes; Eisenhower had Sherman Adams and General Persons; Kennedy had his McBundys and O'Briens; President Johnson has himself. He could, if he chose, share the complex power of the Presidency, but he holds all the reins himself.

This is not to say that the members of the Cabinet are powerless in the face of a willful and industrious President. It means the President expects them to tell him of major decisions before anyone else knows about them, and he expects to be able to veto those decisions without rancor if he disagrees with them. He does not alienate his deputies; the President shepherds them, protects them, and counsels with them on matters great and small. The fact that Johnson, at any given moment, can recall exact dates, statistics, and arguments about departmental matters does not excite the admiration of his Cabinet and department heads as much as it kindles dismay. It hurts them to start a discussion and, in mid-flight, learn that the President has superior and sometimes contrary knowledge.

The wound is seldom deep enough for bleeding, but the President makes it plain that he is the President, and is therefore reponsible for all decisions made in the Executive Branch of government—the bad ones as well as the good. Kennedy desired all his old cronies to stop calling him "Jack" and to address him as "Mr. President," not so much for the respect such a title engenders, as to remind them constantly that his was the ultimate power, his was the ultimate responsibility. Johnson will permit old friends to call him "Lyndon," but he is so obviously the enforcer of power that he doesn't require a proper form of address to impose his will on the men around him. They know.

The task of the President is almost impossible, even with seventeen special and administrative assistants, in addition to Cabinet secretaries, assistant secretaries, and under secretaries who supervise. President Johnson is a combination of father-and-boss, stern and shouting, sentimental and appreciative. He is at the tiny end of an intercontinental-sized funnel, and he drowns in statistics and detailed report. He collects, absorbs, remembers, uses. He sometimes knows how much a subordinate owes on a car.

To give an idea of the scope of the Presidency: The President is Commander in Chief of the Army, Navy and Air Force; the Bureau of the Budget is responsible to him; so is the White House office and personnel; add to these the Council of Economic Advisers; the National Security Council; the Central Intelligence Agency; National Aeronautics and Space Council; Office of Economic Opportunity; Office of Emergency Planning; Office of Science and Technology; Office of the Special Representative for Trade Negotiations; Department of State; Agency for International Development; Peace Corps; United States Mission to the United Nations; the delegation to UNESCO; Treasury Department and the Internal Revenue Service; Bureau of Customs; Bureau of Engraving and Printing; Bureau of the Mint; U. S. Coast Guard: Department of Defense; Department of Justice, Federal Bureau of Investigation, and other sections; the Post Office; Department of the Interior; Department of Agriculture; Department of Commerce; Bureau of the Census; Maritime Administration; Bureau of Public Roads; Weather Bureau; Department of Labor; Department of Health, Education and Welfare; Office of Education; Social Security; Food and Drug Administration; American

Battle Monuments Commission; Atomic Energy Commission; Civil Aeronautics Board; District of Columbia; Farm Credit Administration; Export-Import Bank; Federal Aviation Agency; Federal Communications Commission; Federal Reserve System; Federal Trade Commission; General Services Administration; Defense Materials Service; Department of Housing and Urban Development; National Archives; Urban Renewal Administration; Federal Housing Administration; Indian Claims Commission; Interstate Commercce Commission; National Aeronautics and Space Administration; National Labor Relations Board; Securities and Exchange Commission; Selective Service; Small Business Administration; Smithsonian Institution; Civil Service; U. S. Information Agency; Veterans Administration; Commission on Civil Rights; there is even a Citizens Advisory Council on the Status of Women.

And more. Under the law, there is some question whether it is proper to use the word power in connection with the President. It is possible that the word should be responsibility, because each agency is limited in its functions, and power implies personal political latitude. Under the American form of government, the President has enormous prestige, tremendous scope to appoint and dismiss, and the constitutional authority to set policies foreign and domestic.

There is no likelihood of a Chief Executive's becoming a dictator. To the contrary, a weak President could become a pawn of Congress.

Lyndon Johnson makes a note on the last report and speaks to the desk intercom. "Tell Zephyr to fix a little lunch. I'll be right up." He depresses a button on his phone. Down the hall,

2:00 P.M.

Bill Moyers picks his phone up. "Yes, Mr. President?" "Come right in. We'll go up and have something to eat." He rings the Watson button. "What's next?" Watson studies the appointment sheet. "Children from Cotulla at five, Congressman Tom Curtis at five-thirty; senior citizens at . . ." "Okay."

The President hangs up. Juanita Roberts bustles into his office with some mail. "Leave it on the desk," he says, and walks past. In the hall, a Secret Service man falls into step beside the President. The phones ring all over the White House, informing interested parties that the President "has left his office for lunch in the mansion, and will be back at five P.M." Behind Mr. Johnson, Mr. Moyers walks quietly. The group turns right into the open walk to the mansion, and the President, without turning, says, "So far so good. Not so busy today."

In the second-floor kitchen, Mrs. Wright has had the broiler on high. Lamb chops go in it, small and pink and curly. The burner under the vegetable soup is turned high. A bowl of tapioca pudding comes out of the refrigerator and is placed on a kitchen table. The kettle has been kept warm; now it is turned up for additional heat. This is for Sanka coffee. Enough for three or four is being cooked, because Zephyr knows that the President doesn't like to eat alone, and she doesn't know who is with him.

The family dining room faces Pennsylvania Avenue. Place settings for seven are on the table. The table looks like a slender slab of mahogany or rosewood. At the President's place is a salt substitute, a large pepper mill, dental floss. The china was bought by the Roosevelt administration. A phone hangs beside the President's chair. In the kitchen, there are some things Mrs. Wright no longer sees. One is a wall sign which says: "Please offer the President second helpings. Mrs. Lyndon B. Johnson."

: 143

Another says: "Please keep all the lights turned out when not in use. Orders from the President. Thank you. Mrs. Wright."

Soft and neutral music comes from a hidden speaker. A message goes up from the ground floor that the President is on the elevator. Sergeant Glynn leaves his station and stands near the lift. In a moment the President and Mr. Moyers are off it, talking. The conversation is about bits of unfinished business. Mr. Johnson asks questions about projects and wants an informal report from his special assistant on their current status. He stops on the left-hand side of the corridor to look in on Mrs. Johnson. As always, he kisses her with boyish joy. The vertical lines in his face break into a dozen horizontal planes in a big proud smile, and as she tries to speak about the boat ride and show him the list of guests, he kisses her again. There are questions about Lynda Bird and Luci, and when the President hears that all hands have had lunch, he puts an arm around Mr. Moyers and presses him toward the dining room.

As he sits, he frowns toward the kitchen. An usher, standing obsequiously in the doorway, turns into the kitchen to tell Mrs. Wright. "All right," she says pleasantly. "I'm fixing it quick as I can." Mr. Johnson pushes the plate back from the edge of the table, puts both his elbows on it, and goes into a confidential discussion with Moyers. Whatever is on the presidential mind comes to the surface when they are alone. Some have said that Mr. Johnson acts toward Bill Moyers as though the young man were his son—a highly intelligent son who could help to lift the weight of a yoke off the President's neck.

3:00 P.M.

The sun gilds the stark white of the mansion with little flecks of gold, and colors a rainbow across the big cascading fountain. The marrow of the day is gone. Within ninety minutes the daily evacuation of the capital will begin—the generals, the admirals, clerks, executives, secretaries, bureau chiefs. Desk tops will be tidied; lipstick will be applied, and the city of Washington will transfer its collective behind from four-legged chairs to four-wheeled automobiles.

The West Wing, where the time of day has little meaning, does not see the sun. The drapes are pulled close, and the artificial lighting makes 7 P.M. look exactly like 7 A.M. The temperature remains the same, and there is no heat of midday nor cool of morning. The inhabitants see the world from Lyndon Johnson's point of view, and this distorts their vision. There are few men in the wing who do not sincerely believe that the thirty-sixth President of the United States is the greatest and most accomplished in history. If this belief represents a form of political myopia, it is difficult to prove, because the presidential assistants are armed with verifying statistics.

"Don't ask me," says Moyers, "just look at the record."

A Day in the Life of President Johnson

"If he was born on the East Side of New York instead of Texas," says Watson, "the sophisticated Easterners would already be calling him the greatest President."

"Greatness must be measured by productivity," says Califano. "Start with George Washington and study the problems in relation to the solutions. Lyndon Johnson is in a class by himself."

"Some of the greatness," says Walt Whitman Rostow, "is the ability to remember a whole series of small unrelated facts, and then, at a proper time, to put them together into a whole so that they point the way . . ."

The balding Rostow is busy working out a draft of tomorrow's work. First there is an agenda for tomorrow's meeting of the staff of the National Security Council: Rusk, McNamara, Fowler, Moyers, Leonard Markel of the U. S. Information Agency, and others.

Mr. Johnson would also like a Rostow report on the meetings of foreign ministers in Brussels—their accomplishments, their attitudes, their dilemmas; another one on the economic and political attitude of Cuba today, with terse reports on Santo Domingo and Viet Nam. For anyone else this would be a week's work. The research is already concluded, and Rostow, armed with dozens of typewritten sheets, encapsulates all of it into terse sentences of statistics and conclusions. He remembers a long White House note under which LBJ wrote in his own hand: "Sorry, I didn't have time for a short one."

Marvin Watson tells his secretary to hold visitors and phone calls in abeyance for a few minutes. This is his time for drawing up the President's schedules. There are phone calls to be made to people in many parts of the country regarding appointments for the next ten days. They usually begin: "The

3:00 P.M.

President has directed me to ask you . . ." or "The President suggests . . ."

The one for tomorrow looks like this:

THE PRESIDENT'S SCHEDULE

11:00 Visit to the Interior Department commemorating the recent acquisition by Interior of the Water Pollution Control Administration.

Scenario Attached.

11:30 Mr. Cy Ching and Secretary Willard Wirtz

Ching, presently the chairman of the Atomic Energy Labor Management Relations Panel, will be ninety years old on Saturday. He has worked with every President since Taft.

This will be a greeting and picture in the President's office.

Briefing paper attached.

12:00 Belgian Foreign Minister Pierre Harmel and U. S. Ambassador to Belgium, Ridgeway Knight.

Briefing paper attached.

12:30 Mrs. Walter H. Glynn, of Des Moines, Iowa, National president of the American Legion Auxiliary, and Miss Doris Anderson and Layton Hurst of the Legion Auxiliary National Office.

Mrs. Glynn will present the President the first official poppy for their annual "Poppy Day" sales.

A *Day in the Life of President Johnson*

This will be in the President's office with photographers brought in.

1:00 Congressman Wright Patman (off the record)

He wants to bring down his portrait which was unveiled at the Committee yesterday.

List of those attending is attached.

1:30 Secretary Fowler and Charles Schultze (off the record)

They want to discuss the increase in the debt limit.

Briefing paper attached.

2:00 Don McBride, newly appointed director of the Tennessee Valley Authority (off the record)

The document is of course incomplete. Watson, the circumspect man, will submit this much to the President early this evening, and the President will order more names tacked onto the late hours and a few squeezed into the early ones. Somewhere between twenty-five and thirty percent of all presidential appointments are hogged by influential time-wasters. The first poppy sale, the first Thanksgiving turkey, the first Red Cross button, the first Warm Springs contribution. In addition, there are the influential Congressmen who want a photo taken with the President for "back home" billboards; the publishers and editors who press for a "word" with the President of the United States; the campaign workers who expect a handshake and a smile; the ranking clerics who expect the President to prove and prove again the neutrality of God by seeing them one at a time; and the handsome little boys and girls who limp in on braces and pose for photos which tug

3:00 P.M.

slightly at the heart and heavily on the pocketbook.

Watson orders the abbreviated calendar for tomorrow published. It will be given to the press after 4 P.M. Here again the press feels left out because the reporters know that President Johnson sees many more persons than are listed on his calendar and they want to know who and why. They accept the handouts suspiciously, asking questions, but finding out little more.

The aura of industry in the West Wing continues as the President eats his lunch. A secretary hurries into Joseph Califano's office to tell him that word from the Hill is that Senator Wayne Morse has just left. Califano, working on labor mediation, nods. In five minutes the small mustached righteous face of the zealot senator will be in the Califano office to discuss legislation to stop crippling strikes such as the one by the airline machinists.

Califano knows that nothing will be done by Congress. So does Senator Morse. David Ginsburgh, a Washington lawyer, will be at the conference. So will Richard Neustadt. All of the conferees know that this is an election year. The result of the meeting will be to give labor the impression that Congress may threaten to pass restrictive strike legislation while doing nothing of the sort.

Understandably, anti-labor legislation is unpopular and runs contrary to all the progressive bills the Democratic party has engineered for the unions over the last thirty years. This, in effect, puts no one on the side of management; indeed, no one on the side of justice. Califano knows that his function, as the White House spokesman on labor, is to settle the issue without

: 149

alienating labor, and the only way in which that can be achieved is to ask labor its minimum terms for peace. Labor, which understands the delicate position of the White House, always asks for slightly more than the President is willing to permit, so that the leadership can go back to the locals with "a package" bigger than the anti-inflation guidelines allow. The rationalization in the unions is that anybody can get what a President recommends; it requires strong leadership to get more.

A secretary comes into the office as Califano tosses a sheaf of papers onto his desk blotter. They depict charts of what airline management is willing to concede to the machinists, and what the machinists demand. The young lady is a step ahead of the senator from Oregon. "Show the senator in," Califano says, but Morse is already in. The others are waiting in an outer office and the solemn conference to hurt nobody is about to begin.

There are other conferences in the wing. Each is important to the welfare of the nation and each represents a "now" problem. The presidential assistants who conduct them are, in effect, the intelligent ears and eyes of Lyndon Johnson, but not the tongues. They may listen or speak, but they cannot make a decision. This, quite properly, is the province of Mr. Johnson, who expects a two-paragraph report on each meeting within an hour or two or its conclusion.

Douglass Cater is at this moment having a conference regarding a speech that Mr. Johnson will make to old people later today. At the age of forty-two, Cater is almost in the ranks of elder statesmen, and his is among the more brilliant intellects in the group. The papers on his desk look as though a nervous burglar frisked them for a hidden wallet, but Mr. Cater's record is one of accomplishment.

In the outer office, as narrow as a library alley, two stenographers and a young man, formerly a reporter, work hard sampling public opinion on legislation for the elderly. He phones people at random, introduces himself, and asks if they have received any benefits from Johnson legislation. He is patient and gentle, and he also listens to personal problems. Each phone call becomes a plus or minus digit in his computation.

Between calls, the young man pecks at a statement later to be issued by the President; he knows that this is merely a first draft, and will be altered by Cater, then McPherson, probably by Moyers, and will reach the desk of the President covered with qualifying phrases and interjectory clauses.

Cater puffs his cigar and asks John Gardner, Secretary of Health, Education and Welfare, and Wilbur Cohen, Under Secretary, in addition to Robert Ball, Commissioner of Social Security, to listen to the speech that the President will make in a few hours and to please cut in if anyone has sensible contributions to make. He reads it aloud, and it turns out to be a friendly, folksy document designed to give hope, as well as help, to the millions of old Americans who live a little longer by virtue of the blessings of medical science.

The few changes suggested by Mr. Cohen are marginal. The conferees agree that the talk, or chat, represents the truth about Medicare, and they are interested in having this speech drawn to the attention of the press. The audience which will listen to it in the Rose Garden will number only a few hundred, but the newspapers can present the government's case to a hundred and twenty-five million Americans within a few hours.

A Day in the Life of President Johnson

*　*　*

Down the hall, Jake Jacobsen uses this hour to make phone calls. He is not interested in the legislative policy conferences under way all over the West Wing; his purpose is to settle personal affairs for the President. The voice is basso and friendly.

A call is placed with Colonel James M. Cross, pilot of *Air Force One*. Jake reaches him at Andrews Air Force Base and tells him that Mr. Johnson will probably leave for the ranch Friday after lunch. The precise time has not been set. Cross says that he and his crew have been running the big Boeing jet through some practice runs, logging airtime, killing an engine halfway down the runway, practicing fire-fighting techniques, and landing problems.

"So far," Jake adds, "he expects sixty-seven persons on the manifest—it may change, as you know—but I'll give you a rundown on the names." He reads them off, and the colonel recognizes some as Texas Congressmen who could not get home this weekend except for an invitation from the President to ride free.

There are more calls. Jake goes down a list, one by one, speaking, listening, saying goodbye, and calling the next number.

Sergeant Glynn is in the bedroom. He draws the drapes. Pajamas come from a chest of drawers. The bedspread and sheets are turned down. The afternoon newspapers are spread on the right side of the bed. The sergeant snaps the bathroom light on and checks the room for orderliness. The wooden valet is placed between the bed and the windows so that the President can hang his clothes. Glynn flicks the lights on and off to make certain that they are functioning. He lifts the all-important telephone from its hook to assure himself that it is working. Then he retreats quietly from the room and assumes his station across the hall.

In the dining room, President Johnson lifts a small bowl of tapioca and holds it under his chin, spooning it slowly. Moyers discusses the morning press conference, recalling questions and answers. The President has several ways of listening. One is to hood his eyes with his lids, so that the speaker, seeing the eyes half closed, is not sure whether he is paying attention or not. Another is to put on a smile and hold it while the speaker talks. A third is to stare hard at the speaker without blinking. A fourth—seldom used—is to permit his eyes to wander around the room. No matter which one is employed, the President's ears are tuned in all the time. He misses nothing.

His eyes are wandering around the room. It is one of the most attractive family dining rooms in America. Each wall is covered with wallpaper depicting a scene in American history. The mahogany sideboard on the left was bought by Daniel Webster, and he burned his initials inside the wood. It is faced with an American eagle and can be converted into a desk. The ornate silver chafing dish and pitchers gleam under views of Boston when three-masters hugged the wharves and of a Washington in which the unfinished White House appears to stand on a hill. All of the silver service in this room—on the Webster sideboard and on a hunt table between the front windows—was bought by Andrew Jackson for $4,308.82.

: 153

A Day in the Life of President Johnson

The plates from which the Johnson family dines are American Lenox; they were bought by Woodrow Wilson and are the least distinguished in the White House. The crystal chandelier over the table hangs in ropes of glass with large teardrops suspended underneath. There is a centerpiece of fresh flowers on almost every table in the White House, and Mrs. Johnson never forgets that her husband's favorite color is yellow. On the table are small yellow mums, relieved by bronze and white wildflowers.

"You see the leads on the Marcos story this morning?" Mr. Johnson asks. He puts the empty bowl down and his spoon beside it. "Most of them," Moyers answers. The President, torn between anger and hurt, says, "I wish somebody could explain to me why all those leads—all of them, mind you—focused on how much money President Marcos is going to leave here with. You know he isn't leaving here with any money. We pledge a billion dollars' worth of food to the starving in India, and the newspapers pay no attention to it. We promise the Philippines twenty or thirty millions in food and they make it look like a give-away program."

Moyers shrugs. "All of them got the official communiqué. They know we agreed to cut our military bases in the Philippines from eighty-five years down to twenty-five. They know the food program was settled. They know that President Marcos expects some compensation for the Philippine war dead, but that matter has not been settled, nor even thoroughly discussed."

"But the story comes out," the President says, "that we're giving Marcos millions of dollars." Moyers nods. "I know. I read it." The President taps the table top with his index finger. "The Philippines are old friends. Marcos isn't here for a hand-

: 154

out; he's a forward-looking, hard-working president. Why must we offend our friends? Practically any chief of state who comes here starts a round of stories by the newspapers about how much we're giving away."

There can be no resolution to the problem of press relations because Bill Moyers doesn't write the newspaper stories; he is a dispenser of information. Mr. Johnson pushes his chair back. Moyers stands. "I'm going to get a little rest," the President says. "We have any further business, Bill?" Moyers shakes his head no and lights a long slender cigar. "Not a thing." He pockets his notes and walks behind the President. In the hall, the two separate. The President flicks a hand in farewell and retires to his bedroom. Moyers goes to the President's elevator. Sergeant Glynn picks up his walkie-talkie and announces the retirement. Again phones buzz all over the White House and no one will call the President unless it is urgent.

Down the hall on the left, Mrs. Johnson sits in Lynda's room with her daughters. This is girl talk, and the subjects range from personal plans for the week, to extended trips, to coiffures and gowns. Lynda, accustomed to a degree of privacy in college, says that she keeps to her room because the White House is too busy. Her mother draws a hearty laugh from both girls by telling about the day she had a meeting with a hundred women to discuss what they could do about helping the Job Corps. Mrs. Johnson needed a room large enough for them. In the Red Room downstairs, there was a conference on the War on Poverty; in the Treaty Room, a civil rights group was hammering out a sensible program; each room had its industrious occupants. "You wouldn't believe it," Mrs. Johnson says, "but we finally had our meeting under a tree near the tennis court, sitting on the grass."

Kintner and Moyers go over a final draft of a speech about Viet Nam. This one is as yet unannounced. The President does not like to be committed to any appearance, any speech, until the last moment. It is possible that if he had his way, all his addresses would come to the audiences as surprises. His assistants feel that Mr. Johnson is gradually being broken to the formal niceties of his office, but the surrender is superficial.

The two men make a few phrasing changes, words which fall easier from the lips than some of the tongue-twisters now there. This particular speech started with the President's announcing that he wanted to discuss Viet Nam. Rostow was summoned for a chat, along with Bob Kintner, who does the initial work on all speeches. The President explained succinctly what he would like to say and what observations he would like to make.

Rostow and Kintner made notes. The next step was to contact Dean Rusk at the State Department and Robert McNamara at Defense, because their departments are involved in Viet Nam. Suggestions and objections were noted; they also supplied factual data and statistics to support the tenor of the speech. This was reduced to writing, and Kintner turned it over to the presidential assistant most involved: Rostow. This man molded the data into words, phrases, and sentences which marched from a premise to a conclusion.

It went to the President, who read it slowly, taking out parts, adding others. Juanita Roberts took the revised version to Moyers, who read it, reworked it, and passed it on to Douglass Cater, Harry McPherson, and Joe Califano. Each man added a thought or two, if he had a pertinent one, or killed a

3:00 P.M.

phrase or paragraph if he had a reason. It went back to Kintner, who restudied it, made a minor change here and there,
and sent it up to the President.

Mr. Johnson went over it again with care, almost muttering
the syllables as he read them. Some words shine in print but
suffer when spoken. The last revisions were made, and Johnson
initialed the copy. It was photocopied, and Mrs. Roberts
placed a stapled sheaf of it in the President's night work. In his
bedroom, he read it aloud to Mrs. Johnson.

Bill Moyers glanced at the document, and was reminded of
how many in the West Wing think of the presidential assistants as a football team. "It isn't," he said to Kintner. "It's more
like the Globetrotters."

The upstairs corridor is quiet. The light which earlier had
filtered in through the east window is now sneaking in small
shafts through the west. The President's elevator is almost
silent. An usher gets off and drops an envelope with a red tag
on it. This means "Right away, or as soon as you can." Paul
Glynn picks it up, and a light flickers on his phone. It is Jake
Jacobsen. "Is the President still awake?" Glynn speaks as softly
as though he were in the bedroom. "I'll see, sir. Hold a
minute."

At the President's bedroom door, the sergeant crouches to
look in the slit of space between door and lintel. He sees a
light, and knocks. The President says, "Come in, Paul." He is
propped up with three pillows, and wears his rimmed glasses.
He looks over the top of a newspaper. "What is it?" Glynn
hands over the envelope and picks up the phone. "Mr. Jacobsen, Mr. President."

A Day in the Life of President Johnson

The President tends to lift his head, like Franklin Roosevelt, when he holds a receiver to his ear. "Yeah, Jake?" He listens a moment, then says, "No, I'll have time for the evening appointments. Plenty of time. Sure. All right, Jake. Any news from the ranch? That's good. We don't have to be down front until eight, so I'll make time for everything."

He hangs up and opens the red-tagged envelope. It's a situation report on Viet Nam. It is scanned swiftly, the eyes hurrying to the bottom of the page to reach the conclusion. The President puts it back in the envelope, and drops it on the floor beside his bed. "Going to be a big night," he says to Glynn. "I'm going to get some sleep." The lights are snapped off. The sergeant tiptoes from the room, knowing that the boss is not to be disturbed any more unless there is a truly urgent matter.

Lyndon Johnson doesn't require a great deal of time to fall asleep. The extra pillows are cast aside, the great head sinks back, the arms are sometimes folded across the top of the sheet; after a few sighs, his mind wanders away from crises and commitments to the pleasant task of recreating happy scenes at the ranch or on the lake; he remembers old friends in Austin, a mixture of political aphorisms from Sam Rayburn and President Roosevelt, the faces of old Congressional cronies, some of them still in the House, others retired—they all flow together in a slowly swirling series of thoughts which fade at the first soft snore.

: 158

THE RANCH

The call is in early on Friday. It's from Jacobsen to Colonel
Cross, a dark handsome man in the pale blue uniform of the
United States Air Force. "The President is going to the ranch
this afternoon. Right after lunchtime." The colonel, sitting in
an office in the East Wing, drops the phone and calls Andrews
Air Force Base. Cross is one of the many men in the White
House who is ready to move on little notice.

He is forty-two, has four children, and was born in Anda-
lusia, Alabama. Like everyone else around the White House,
he wears several hats. He is a colonel; a command pilot;
Armed Forces Aide to the President of the United States; pilot
of *Air Force One*. Cross has a hand-picked team of men on the
plane: Major Paul Thornhill, of Denver; Major Donald L.
Short, of Joplin, Missouri; Lieutenant Colonel Charles F.
Rogers, of Syracuse, N.Y.; Chief Warrant Officer John R. Mc-
Clane of New York; Senior Master Sergeant William J. Chap-
pell, of Wilmington, N.C.; Master Sergeant Joseph Piepoli, of
Scranton, Pennsylvania; Chief Master Sergeant Edward A.
Wight, of Fort Deposit, Alabama; Master Sergeant James A.
Skinner; Technical Sergeant James Brown; Staff Sergeant
Frank Retz; Master Sergeant William Justus.

A Day in the Life of President Johnson

In experience, the crew averages seventeen to twenty-three years of service. They know the man, the plane, the way. *Air Force One* is the designation of any aircraft used by the President, but it is most commonly used to describe the Boeing Intercontinental jet which takes the President on long trips. Built in 1962 for John F. Kennedy, this jet differs from its sister ships in engines and décor. JT-30 fan jets are mounted on the wings and each of the four delivers 18,000 pounds of thrust. The plane weighs 155,000 pounds empty, and carries 150,000 pounds of refined kerosene as fuel. Add 11,250 pounds for passengers today, and 3,000 pounds of luggage, and the weight of *Air Force One* comes to 319,250 pounds; almost 160 tons.

It has flown 2,000 hours and over 800,000 miles. And yet it gleams in its hangar like a brand-new blue and white bird as Colonel Cross phones to have it made ready. Downstairs, Jake is putting a second phone call through to Congress. He says that the President wants the word passed to the Texas delegation that he is going home for the weekend, and if any more of the Congressmen want a lift home, returning probably on Monday, it is theirs for the asking. Lyndon Johnson remembers that his Congressional travel vouchers never quite covered the cost of returning to Texas to see the children and his constituents, so he is generous with the aircraft now at his disposal.

Air Force security men guard the plane every minute of every day. When the kerosene fuel arrives in a huge truck, a sample is taken and tested for purity in a laboratory on the base. Engines are replaced every 1,500 hours and a log is kept on each one.

Within ten minutes of the colonel's phone call, three flight engineers are aboard. The blue and white monster is towed out of the hangar onto the concrete apron. It stands in the sun with a huge "26000" on its rudder. The engineers run the ship

through a series of tests designed to make a malfunction expose itself. Secret Service men board it to examine the closed
spaces and the open ones.

The colonel calls the Pentagon and asks for "Global
Weather." He gets a precise report on cloud formation, visibil-
ity, wind speed and direction, cold fronts, available altitudes to
San Antonio, and traffic. He also asks and makes notes on
alternate routes and alternate landing bases. Two hours before
the President and his party leave the south grounds by helicopter, the engines of *Air Force One* are turned up to be "hot
checked." The whine is heard all over the base, and enlisted
personnel tell each other, "The President is taking off this
afternoon."

A half hour before Mr. Johnson is scheduled to land a few
hundred feet from the big bird, Congressmen and their parties
board and sit in the front section. There, the seats are reversed,
so that everyone sits backward. Secret Service men stand at the
foot of the plane staircase. Others aboard walk through the
front section to the center, which is oak-paneled, and beyond it
to the small "restaurant booth" tables in the rear. Luggage is
already aboard and the hatches are closed.

Mrs. Johnson and Lynda and Luci are waiting at the curving south staircase of the White House. The President is still in
his office. Whatever he does not sign or resolve before he
leaves is packed into a briefcase by Juanita Roberts. When the
helicopter, inbound, is between the Washington Monument
and the fountain on the south grounds, the President is informed. He leaves his desk and walks out through the French
doors, flanked by Secret Service men. He picks up a couple
of beagles and whispers softly as he carries them toward the
noisy helicopter.

In a moment the green whirly-bird lifts itself off a red pad and swings between the big trees back toward the Washington Monument. The pilot announces that helicopter *AF-1* is aloft at 1,000 feet, bound between the White House and Andrews Air Force Base. The controller at Washington International Airport and others keep air traffic away from the President's route. The President not only carries the beagles, but strokes them gently and continually talks to them so that they will not be frightened.

At Andrews Air Force Base, the dogs bound ahead, sniffing, pausing, looking back. He shooes them up the steps of the big jet, and as he reaches the top, behind his ladies, Colonel Cross orders engines three and four—on the side opposite the boarding party—to be started. When Johnson steps inside, the big door with the presidential seal on the outside is slammed and dogged. The President and his family sit in the center section.

Little green lights show up on the instrument panel before pilot, co-pilot, and the flight engineer, and overhead. Engines one and two are started. Cross asks Traffic Control for clearance, and the plane rocks its nose like a happy porpoise as it rumbles along the concrete service strip to the head of the runway. There are no delays; the skies are clear. A white card before Colonel Cross tells him how many knots of speed will be required, at 319,250 pounds of weight and at this particular barometric pressure and temperature, to lift the plane off the runway. On the same card, he reads the exact length of runway he will need to reach that speed.

He moves the throttles up a little. The plane begins to move. The throttles—four of them—are bracketed and move further and further forward. The whine reaches a shriek and *Air Force One* accelerates. Cross's hands are on the yoke. His squinted eyes are on the runway. His co-pilot reads speeds aloud: "Eighty knots, eighty-five, make it ninety, one hundred—V-

one—one hundred and ten, one hundred and twenty . . ."
Cross tugs at the yoke gently, afraid to bruise it, and the jet
lifts her nose, then her main trucks.

She is airborne and tucks her feet into her belly. Warm
thermal currents rising from Virginia farms below lift the
broad flexible wings and let them settle. The silver engines
drink air greedily, heat it instantaneously, and spew it out of
the thrust nozzles at increasing speed. *Air Force One* needs
space, and climbs steadily through the thin white dumplings,
sounding as though her nostrils hurt.

The VIP transponder is on constantly, so that the plane's
radar signal is strong and distinctive and easily tracked by
ground stations. In the main cabin over the wing, the President
sits at a big green crescent desk. His chair is in the middle of
the aisle and he faces a long couch on which his wife and
daughters lounge. Lynda wears a white sailor hat, a black and
white suit, and sunglasses. She thumbs through a fashion
magazine. Mrs. Johnson wears a white wool dress and a
checked waistcoat. Luci tucks her feet under her, a pillow
behind her head, and smoothes her blue shift.

The President moves the telephone to his left. It carries two
red buttons. Then he flicks a remote-control switch and gets
color television on a small set fitted into a corner of the bulk-
head. He studies a shot of Fujiyama and switches to another
channel. There is a children's program of animated cartoons.
He tries another: two smiling women are discussing "mod"
fashions. The President shows a relaxed disinterest.

A steward stands behind him, and Mr. Johnson says, "I want
my dinner." The steward goes aft, silent on the green carpet.
He knows that the President wants to eat now, so that he can
retire for a nap before the plane lands in San Antonio. Congressman Gonzalez is invited to visit the main cabin, and Johnson

beams at his wife and daughters and says, "Haven't I got beautiful women?" The beagles sniff at the rug and find that they have been here before. At once they form a loose circle around the President's feet, and after a little fretting, begin to doze.

Dinner is served as Johnson finds a channel featuring the flight of a Gemini capsule. As he eats he listens to Jules Bergman of ABC. The jet is now at cruising altitude—33,000 feet— with the state of Kentucky rolling under the silver wings at 525 knots, around 600 miles per hour. The imperiously condescending tone of Mr. Bergman begins to fade, and so do his features. Mr. Johnson switches the set off, and devotes himself to the shrimp and rice.

Jake Jacobsen comes in, and Johnson asks one and all if he is the only hungry person on the plane. He is. Mrs. Johnson converses in Spanish with Henry Gonzalez. Jake leans close to the President's ear and discusses the status of the rent supplement bill and a federal security measure. The President whispers, "Everybody wants to steal."

A moment later Johnson is reminded of another matter. It wins no headlines but it is important enough to fight over. The federal government and the state of Utah are litigants over ownership of shoreland along Great Salt Lake. Congress passed a bill designed to keep both parties from each other's throats until the courts decide the issue. President Johnson was prepared to sign it, until White House investigation showed that Utah had been leasing the shoreland. Johnson said he had no objection to temporary leases, but if the courts gave the shoreland to the United States, the federal government should not be bound by state leases. Johnson felt so strongly about it that he told Utah the matter could, in time, become a scandal. He said he would sign the bill only if Senator Moss, Governor Crampton, and holders of the leases gave written assurances that the government would not be bound by the current leases.

The President tells Jake that the bill will become a pocket veto by midnight unless he gets those guarantees. He reminds Jake that there is also a question of magnesium deposits on that land. Jacobsen is ready to get on the phone, but he wants to be certain what to ask for. The President tells him of the written assurances, and he also wants an agreement from Utah not to execute any more leases on that land without the consent of the Secretary of the Interior.

The President nods to Mrs. Johnson. The First Lady, rather than disturb her daughters, crouches easily and comes out from under the desk to have her hand grasped by the President. They go off to the paneled cabin aft of the sitting room, and retire. Both have learned to use travel time for sleep.

The F.A.A. has monitored this flight as it does many others. Cross requires permission for course and altitude changes, and now asks clearance to start descent twenty-five minutes out of San Antonio. Randolph Air Force Base is the nearest airport to the LBJ Ranch (about sixty miles) where the Boeing 707 can find enough room to land. When the aircraft is fifteen minutes off the blocks, the President and First Lady are notified by a knock on their stateroom door, and they begin to dress.

Mr. Johnson emerges smiling. It is a big broad one, the grin of a boy going to the country on vacation. He seeks out Vicki McCammon, the secretary selected for this trip, and as the plane moves onto the concrete, he says, "Now, do we have anything to worry about besides this Mexican thing? We'll do it tonight. Don't let me forget."

Cross taxis up the ramp toward a small Jetstar aircraft and

cuts his engines when he is three hundred feet away. The ramp is lowered and Mr. Johnson says farewell to grateful Congressmen. He is off quickly, nodding to the blue-clad generals who stand at salute. Behind the fence, crowds of Randolph workers wave and yell. The President lowers his head and waves his arm. He walks fast, and his little party moves along with him.

He goes directly to the small jet, finds a seat, and buckles his belt. The President pats the seat facing his for Mrs. Johnson. The beagles are again in his arms, and they kiss him nervously and glance out the window. Colonel Cross and his crew come in and ask for clearance to the 6,200-foot runway at the Johnson ranch. As always, there is no waiting. The engines start, the plane moves slowly to the head of the runway, and with throttles open, scats down the shimmering heat of the runway and lifts high into the sky.

Mr. Johnson excuses himself. When he is happy about something, he just can't wait for it to happen, and he is always happy about going home. So he adjourns to a small dressing room and removes the formal blue suit, the shirt and collar and tie, and comes out in a blue and yellow checked cap, a matching sports shirt worn outside of beige slacks. The change could have waited until he reached the ranch, but the cares of office drop with the clothes; the concealed fatigue is gone, the aches of exalted office too; his spirit is renewed as though, as his wife says, "The ranch is bone of your bone, and blood of your blood."

He is barely sitting again, smiling at everybody over nothing, when the jet banks steeply over the hill country, the white bald boulders, and comes in to land. It touches the runway and runs up black macadam toward the ranch house. "Look at those cows," the President says. "Ain't they pretty?" Mrs. Johnson, with an eye to beauty, says, "The bluebonnets are still out.

I'm glad." Wildflowers line the sides of the runway, blue and yellow and orange; through the windows they look like a blurry coal fire as the jet continues up the runway.

Outside the jet, a golf cart waits, and the President hops in the driver's seat. The back of the main ranch house is a few hundred feet ahead of him, and when everyone is aboard the cart, he honks a horn, calls raucously to some wild peacocks watching from a fence, and they call back. The cart moves silently past a big lean-to and an old fire engine marked "LBJ Ranch" and on toward the kitchen.

Now, for the first time, he sees Dale Malachek, his foreman, and he cannot resist a ranch joke: "Everything working, Dale? Toilet pressure okay?" Mrs. Johnson frowns and says, "Lyndon." He pays no attention, except to the inner joy which keeps mounting. And yet, even in his excitement, he sees everything: the little bungalows out back where the flight crew and the Secret Service live; the ancient oaks and cottonwoods; the creosote bush and the cactus.

The solemn brown eyes are hungry; they drink, they count, they devour. The 6,000-odd acres of hill country which he owns are not land and pasture and stone—they are him. Under a zucca, a pony stands with a mat of mane over his brows and watches the cart suspiciously. Mr. Johnson whistles to him, and he turns his back. When the cart pulls up around the front of the old house, the President is first out, and first into the den, swinging the door wide as though it should never have been closed. The doormat outside says: "All the world is welcome here."

Ahead is a wall of knotty pine; the others are papered in coral and yellow. There is a fireplace with a Salinas painting over it, a green easy chair, a brown carpet, and a small picture of O. Henry with the printed line underneath: "The more wrinkles a woman acquires, the smoother she becomes." It is not a house in the grand manner; rather, it is an old love which was owned by an aunt in the 1890's, and has been repainted, refurnished, had rooms added on opposite ends, as well as a kidney-shaped swimming pool. And yet it has an aura of hurricane lamps, straw bonnets, and a kitchen pump which screeches when it is primed. There is an antler hat rack, a collection of books on birds, and an old-fashioned house blessing:

> O Thou who dwellest in so many homes, possess Thyself of this. Bless the life that is sheltered here. Grant that trust and peace and comfort abide within, and that love and light and usefulness may go out from this home forever.

The President whoops and hollers when he sees Mr. and Mrs. James Davis, Negro housekeepers, in the kitchen. He slouches on the small of his spine on a kitchen chair and they exchange questions and answers so swiftly that an onlooker would hardly notice that Mr. Johnson has now lapsed into the patois of his childhood, that all the stiff and formal language of the Presidency has been left in Washington. He is eager for news, and is happy at their happiness, and he slaps his big hands on his knees, shoves his cap back off his forehead, and demands to know of Mary Davis what nice fattening things she is going to cook for him.

The Davises are young, and the Johnsons appreciate them. They have given the couple a house within walking distance of the ranch. The President chats about small matters, and Mrs. Johnson takes a proprietary tour of the ground floor. In the living room, she notes that a neighbor has sent yellow roses, and will remember to phone her thanks. The piano—well, only Luci plays it. The collection of mounted birds is undisturbed. The fireplace, even in summer, looks friendly because of memories of the children's stockings hanging there at Christmas time, and of the parties when everyone had to recite or perform.

There is no luxury in the old house. Long before Lyndon Johnson aspired to own it, Aunt Frank Barnett Johnson—his father's sister—lived in it, and the young boy walked barefooted down the front lawn and skipped stones in the shallow curving Pedernales River and hunted the hideaways of small animals and birds. There is a hardwood quality to the house now; it gleams with white paint on the outside and varnish inside. However, it is a place where a guest would not be ashamed to walk around in carpet slippers; a home where a man can slouch in the kitchen and speak on friendly terms with the help; a farm building which hides under the hills it owns; a place away from the road, studying its immutable face in a small river.

The dining room has a bare floor. Part of the wall is covered with scenic ranch paper. There is a walnut dining table and eleven place settings. A phone hangs under it at the President's place. His back is to the picture window which opens onto the distant haystacks and the round hills which appear to roll further and further away from the attentive eye; a black cloud which blots the blue sky, bringing rain to a small valley; spoiled peacocks who preen themselves on fences; and the coveys of birds who execute intricate figures of flight, and finding no one watching, sit on a lawn to pick.

Like most housewives, Mrs. Johnson's eyes seldom note the things which are right, singling out only those which are askew. She enters the President's office, a large knotty-pine room with a painting of her husband over the fireplace, and walks around the partition to the desk Jake Jacobsen uses. The gold presidential seal is here, and three desks attest to the fact that this is a workroom. On the right, near the President's desk, is a beautiful mosaic of semiprecious stones, forming North and South America, a present from the citizens of Acapulco.

: 169

A Day in the Life of President Johnson

There is a leather couch and chairs to match, and an ornate saddle, a gift of the President of Mexico, Señor López Mateos. The only photo on Mr. Johnson's desk is one of little Courtenay Valenti with "the poor Prez."

Mrs. Johnson returns to the kitchen. She hasn't examined the master bedroom yet, but she will in a minute. The L-shaped kitchen is almost—not quite—as big as an old-fashioned farm kitchen. The appurtenances are bright and new, but the lingering odor is of fresh sausage, bacon, and eggs. There is a phone with a list of numbers to call in case of fire. The coffee urn holds thirty-six cups. Everything is ample—a red and white Formica-topped table with chairs for six; two large freezers; shelves of pungent spices; a double sink with a dishwasher. Behind it, the utility room holds a washing machine, a dryer, an ironing board, a vacuum cleaner, and, on the floor, a big green watermelon awaiting surgery.

The main ranch house has thirteen rooms, including guest bedrooms on the second floor. The master bedroom is simply furnished, with a double bed, a double dresser, a rocking chair, night tables, and a walk-in closet shared by husband and wife. There is a portable table for rubdowns, and, mounted in the wall, three color television sets.

The richness is in the land, but it isn't "Texas rich." The Johnsons are cattle breeders, not oil barons. The original property consists of 400 acres, situated thirteen miles west of Johnson City, Texas. Mrs. Johnson, who would have done well in business whether she married Lyndon or not, has since bought 1,800 adjoining acres, and, from time to time, has bought craggy hills and valleys between the ranch and Lake Lyndon Johnson, ten miles away.

But even with all these holdings, a radio and television station in Austin, and a portfolio of stocks and bonds, the President says, "I still owe money to the banks." Owing money to anyone bothers the Johnsons considerably, because both are frugal. It amused the sophisticates of Washington when the President walked through the White House at night turning lights off; it is even more amusing to note that at Texas political rallies, he had a habit of tossing his tawny Stetson out into the crowd, but had prepaid a little boy $1 to retrieve it. The Stetson cost $25.

Not far from the ranch is an old stone fence which corrals a group of stately oaks. Inside are the graves of the Johnsons. Red granite headstones expose the inner sentimentality of Lyndon Baines Johnson. The legends on the graves of his parents say:

Sam Ealy Johnson, of purest gold from the Master's hand, a man who loved his fellow man. 1887–1937.

Rebekah Baines Johnson, none knew thee but to love thee, none named thee but to praise. 1881–1958.

The President visits the graves as though his parents were still almost within reach of his voice. He removes his big beige hat, and notes the fresh flowers on the mounds. He points to an empty spot next to the graves. "This is reserved for me," he says. "The oldest child should go next to the parents . . ."

It is morning and the zest of spiritual release is still with the President. He sits in a den chair too small for his body and flaps his Stetson hat against his knee. The listener sitting opposite is Dale Malachek. Out on the front lawn, the President's standard now flies below the American flag. Luci and Mrs. Johnson

: 171

sit on chaise lounges beside the swimming pool. It is early, but Mr. Johnson has already been out on part of the ranch in his Lincoln, bumping over rocky trails, stopping the wheels before gates so that the automatic treadle will open them, honking his cow horn and looking as happy as a boy who has just won a huckleberry pie-eating contest no hands.

He stopped to study a white-faced cow with calf. "Isn't she pretty?" he said to Mrs. Johnson. "She's so fat she can hardly walk." He looked at others with a critical eye. Near a hilltop he found a dozen black-faced cattle and picked up his dashboard microphone. "This is Volunteer," he said. "Put Dale on." When the foreman answered, the President told him where he was, and said, "There's a dozen head of Black Angus up here. We never had anything like these. You know who owns them?" Malachek said "No." "Then find out who owns 'em and get them back on their own property. We're not going to let them graze for nothing."

Now and then he stopped the car, got out, and sifted dry soil between his fingers. From under the brim of the big hat, he squinted at the sky—the slitted eyes of the man who knows the goodness that comes from sun and rain; a man who had learned, over the years, that the world lives off the top eight inches of soil, that a steak is no more than good grass converted into tasty proteins, that a field of bluebonnets is more than pretty, it holds the soil on a slope when the spring freshets come.

None of it was first-rate ranch land. Long ago Lyndon told Lady Bird that the best fertilizer is the footprint of the owner. This is why the President gets back to the LBJ Ranch as often as possible. He must see and feel and know, because he and his wife worked hard to make the place as good as it is. Frequently he sticks his hands into his trouser pockets, scuffs the earth with his shoe, and says, "What should we do here, Bird?"

He had said it while looking at wildflowers beside the landing strip. "You should put a mower over this in about three weeks," she said. "That's when the seeds will drop. Take the mowings—stalks, leaves and all—cart them off and drop them on a hillside. Next year you'll have a new field of Indian blankets and coreopsis." The President listened and grunted.

It is possible that Lyndon Johnson's political career was a diversion from the interest closest to his heart. His father was in politics and he gave all he could to his constituents, and then he started to give himself and he went broke. Some of Johnson's earlier forebears were in politics too. They were sharp and energetic Texans—half Southerners and half Westerners. None of them aspired to go as far as Rebekah's boy. The loftiest honor in the land, as far as he was concerned, was to be a United States senator from Texas. It is doubtful that any man worked as hard to achieve it; certainly no one has ever put in so many hours of unremitting labor to make himself worthy of it. Having achieved it, the accolade of being elected the youngest majority leader in Senate history added little to what he already had. It meant that the Democratic party had confidence in and respect for Johnson, and his colleagues had no hesitancy in dumping all of the work in his lap.

Selection as a vice-presidential nominee by John F. Kennedy was a political expediency, not a love affair. On the day that it happened, Senator Jackson of Washington sat near a barrel of apples waiting for a phone call from Kennedy, naming him as the choice for Vice-President. When the call came, he listened to the junior senator from Massachusetts and said, "Yes, Jack. Sure. Certainly I understand. No, no. I'll stop over later." Jackson had been dropped, and Lyndon Johnson selected, because Kennedy was going to need all the southern and southwestern votes he could get. Lyndon Johnson could pull his weight on a campaign team, but Kennedy was elected by the narrowest of margins.

Johnson was too realistic ever to envision himself as the Democratic party nominee. The moment tragedy handed it to him, he began to work harder than ever in the new position. If anything, he was moving further and further away from the Pedernales, and politics had already taken the prime part of his life from him. He always gave Washington all he had, and maybe a bit more than he should, but all along the route he was aiming for home, for the ranch. He had come to Washington at the age of twenty-three, and now he saw himself in that magnifying shaving mirror in the White House with a face approaching sixty years of wear and tear. And he still was not home. Nor would he turn his face from the work in the White House until he had wrung it dry of whatever substance it had. And the triumphs and the trials which lay hidden along the path of all those years affected Lady Bird as well as her husband. His initial desire for this ranch was a whim of the heart not of the head, and if some notion lies close to his heart, even though Mrs. Johnson does not agree with it, she will acquiesce. They had just bought a new home in Texas when in 1951 he said he wanted to buy Aunt Frank's old place, a mile and a half from where he had been born.

Lady Bird knew the place, and she could assess the work which would have to be done to make it a ranch house. She was opposed to the idea, but took a long look at what was in her husband's eyes, and said yes.

On another occasion, when he was offered the Vice-Presidency, Lyndon Johnson looked at his wife and said, "Well, Bird, what do you think?" She was again opposed. "His personality and temperament are not exactly suited to being a number-two man; besides, we thought that being a senator from the state of Texas was just about as big a job as there is in the whole world." Still, she saw that he was intrigued by the challenge—the one additional step in a long climb—and she knew that he wanted to do it. So again she said yes. But she was not happy with it, and she wondered if he would be, win or lose. She fought as hard for election as Johnson did.

Johnson's sudden yearning for a ranch won sympathy from Lady Bird, not because it was wise or sensible, but because she recognized he wanted roots where he once had them. He was so happy when Lady Bird agreed that he hurried to Mr. Brigham at the Blanco Bank and asked to borrow the money to buy the old place. A small-town Texas banker can be snobbish even in the presence of a young senator, and Mr. Brigham asked questions about how many head of cattle, and what kind, and how many acres and how much money and how would it be paid off. Lyndon Johnson gave him the answers.

"Well, boy," Mr. Brigham said, "I'll lend you the money. You don't have to hurry to pay it back. I'll give it to you. You better not expect to do it off cattle. Now, if you're going to play cowboy and stomp in boots around the post office on Saturday, I'm not going to interfere." Lyndon Johnson winced at the lashing, but he took the money. Later, he earned enough to pay it back. Brigham was still in no hurry, and seemed surprised that the "boy" had the $3,000. "I put that money on deposit in his bank," the President said, "right to the penny." Mr. Brigham became a resident of an old folks' home and died refusing to recall the transaction, in effect bracing himself against believing that anyone could make money on cows out of those rocky hills.

The President sets his hat on one knee as he and Malachek talk. "We worked seven days a week in those days," Mr. Johnson says. "We do now too. No playboys in our family. Never spent much time at baseball or football games. Nor cocktail parties and the social circuit." He grins and slaps the hat again. "People ask me if I have a hobby. Dale, if everything ran as well as I would like it to, I could go horseback riding, or even swimming. But I can't depend on anyone else to do things."

The men sit in silence for a moment. The President is in a reverie. Then he arouses himself with an expression like a man swallowing a whole persimmon, and he stands. "Now, Dale," he says, "we have a small house empty over on that hill and I just got it painted. I wish you would go over the roster of ranch hands and pick out a good ambitious Mexican or Negro and put him in there with his wife and children. We've got to prove to these young fellows that there is more to a job than a salary. It's up to you, Dale. You know them.

"Now, another thing. I don't like the look of some of the cattle. A few of them just don't look right. Healthy enough, but the heads are mottled. I want you to breed them out, Dale. Pick the best-looking cows for those bulls. Understand?" Mr. Malachek does.

On Sunday the breeze comes up the high banks of the river without marring the surface of the water. A buck and two white-tailed does stand transfixed on the macadam runway. The sun throws strong blue shadows behind the ranch house. The Secret Service men, front and back, stand like the deer. Mr. Johnson emerges from the back entrance buttoning his blue jacket. The door slams, and the deer and Secret Service men come to life.

The agents get in their car. The President holds the door open for Lady Bird, and the deer race off the face of a hill with a sound like a gambler shuffling a deck of cards. Mr.

Johnson slips into the driver's seat and presses the horn button. He rolls down the electric window and yells, "Vicki, you got thirty seconds." In less time than that, Miss McCammon, young and dark and attractive, emerges from the back door with hands up, pushing a final bobbie pin in a little further, dusting powder from the yoke of a blouse with Kleenex.

The President backs out, and moves off to church. The Secret Service car follows down the service road between the ranch and the river, crossing closely behind the President to Route 290. The switchboard has already announced that the Johnsons are on their way to Johnson City, fifteen miles away. The President applies himself as vigorously to driving as he does to any other job. He rolls fast, and Mrs. Johnson watches the speedometer. When it inches past seventy, she looks up at him, and though he does not acknowledge her glance, the big foot comes up off the accelerator a little. "Could have been in Fredericksburg by the time you get in the car," he says to Miss McCammon. Mrs. Johnson laughs. Vicki shrugs. "It takes a girl time to get ready, Mr. President." He nods glumly, leaning over the wheel. "I know," he mumbles. "How well I know."

His brown eyes scan the countryside left and right as the Lincoln pours over the concrete. This is all part of the Edwards Plateau and in midsummer it shimmers with color. There are fields of buttercups, phlox, verbena, black-eyed Susans, and carpets of firewheels. Signs proclaim this as the country of tangy peaches, but it is also an area noted for cattle, sheep, and wheat. In the mirror, Johnson sees the Secret Service car behind him, and he knows that additional agents from the office in Austin are already at the church.

On the high power lines, the President notes his skimpy audience: mockingbirds, scissor-tails, shrikes and meadowlarks. They see his car coming; they watch it go. He knows that there are wild turkeys in the hills to the left, but he sees none this morning. Two roadrunners chase a lizard across the highway, but they are gone before the President has a chance to watch. He glances at a scrub forest on the right. The trees are dwarfed and starved; the soil is weak and gives barely enough to sustain life. Texans call these areas shinnery. The land has been burned, beaten, and frozen. A century ago many of the German settlers in the hill country had nothing to offer a guest except friendship and laughter.

The tougher the land became, the tougher the settlers. Sam Ealy Johnson defied the soil, the Comanches, the rattlesnakes, and bitter winters. He built his own stone fort with gun slits, and invited his neighbors to shelter when Indian raids were in progress. Some of the Johnsons died, and so did some of the von Meusebachs and Solms and Schmidts. If the Indians could not reach them inside the fort, malnutrition could. It was not a forgiving land.

Sam Ealy Johnson and his brother Tom never ran from trouble. They couldn't afford to look for it, but when it came, they were impelled to face it. They raised cattle, and in the late autumn they drove herds through the whipping snows north to the Kansas market. They sold those that survived, took their money, and rode back South to the stone fort.

Once when the Indians raided the settlement, Sam and Tom waited until it was over, then led a group of men in search of the war party. The Comanches knew the hill country better than the Johnsons. They doubled back to raid the unprotected village. When Eliza Bunton Johnson, a young wife of two years with an infant, saw the Indians coming back up the Fredericksburg trail, she hurried into the little house, still carrying a bucket of spring water.

She picked her baby up and grabbed an extra diaper.

Quickly she ran halfway down a flight of steps into a storage cellar, then turned, lowered a trap door, and with her fingers inched a small carpet over it. The diaper was stuffed into the baby's mouth, and the infant, in protest, tried to cry through it. In the chilly cellar, Eliza, crouched in a corner behind barrels, heard the Indians enter the house and stomp across the floor boards. The emptiness angered them, and they ransacked the place, destroying whatever they could not carry. Mrs. Johnson held her baby close to her breast and wept because those wedding presents had been carried all the way from Colorado by wagon. Eliza was there when Sam and Tom returned that night, the diaper still in the baby's mouth.

The little stone fort still exists, and as the President's car slows down going into Johnson City, he glances at it, says nothing, and pops a stick of gum in his mouth. He passes a stream of water, low and clear between sandy banks, and looks in the "mirror." He had been a tall skinny kid who couldn't be filled out no matter how well he was fed. "When I was growing up," he says, "we sat by that creek and ate pork and beans."

Johnson City is a stone bead on the necklace of Highway 290. It is a dozen streets running north and south, east and west, and is held together by a stone courthouse, a church, a jail, and a few silent men in cowboy hats leaning against the hardware store. The neat old-fashioned house in which the President grew up is a block to the south of Route 290. Social life wasn't much, then or now.

During his high school years, when Lyndon was allowed out after supper, a boy could spend the evening with the fellows at O. Y. Fawcett's drugstore, or he might be invited to a girl's house, where the refreshment was a frosty pitcher of fresh lemonade and the game was dominoes. On Saturday evenings he might go to the movie, where the silence of the drama was shattered by the playing of a single Victrola record over and over. An ambitious boy might do as young Johnson did—pick cotton at seventy-five cents per hundred pounds, or set up a five-cent shoeshine stand in front of Roy Scofield's barbershop.

The President drives the car through the streets slowly, drinking deeply of the past, thinking of how he helped to build Route 290 with a pick and shovel, the sweat tickling his back; of how he ran away to California and came home tired and depressed and hungry, and his mother forgave all because he said he was ready to go to Southwest Texas State Teachers College if she still wanted him to go.

He taught school at Cotulla, and the Mexican students taught the teacher something too. He learned that some people are not welcome because their skin is not fair enough, or their conversation is cluttered with foreign sounds. He wanted the children to remember what he taught them; they wanted him to remember too.

There is no conversation in the car as it moves at funereal pace up and down the streets. The President leans over the wheel as though hugging it, and his eyes encompass old and dear places and faces: a few buildings which he now owns, tracts of sod where he and other boys kicked cans, the porch where he made his first speech in a run for Congress.

Lyndon Johnson has attained almost all that a man can aspire to. The thrill of fighting for success was his when he won the Presidency in his own right by the largest vote ever given a candidate. Once painful memories have been sweetened by time, but they are still imprisoned in his mind. He learned to hide them within himself years ago, when old friends began to act deferential; when neighbors wanted him to visit—and he wanted to go—but they were afraid to ask.

The car turns left to the First Christian Church. Com-

municants are outside, holding cameras not Bibles: the Glid-
dons, the Bushnells, the Schultzes, the Summys. A few knew
him away-back-when, and they wear the knowledge as a dec-
oration. As the President of the United States gets out of the
car, closing the door slowly, the flashbulbs wink and he nods
good morning to certain faces in the crowd. The ladies are in
bright summer finery and the men stand back a little, waiting
for his recognition before trading theirs.

The church is small and white, bright with morning sun.
Pastor Aiken waits at the front door to shake hands. The President follows Mrs. Johnson and Vicki. He selects the third pew
on the right side, and the Secret Service agents find places
across the aisle. The windows are slung open, and the breeze
cools a trifle as it comes indoors. There is an upright piano
against the right wall and a choir behind the altar railing. The
pews are full of couples who try not to stare at the President
and the First Lady. Their eyes are on hymn books.

Lyndon Johnson has the aisle seat and he kneels at once and
bows his head. Here he has no august position. The distinction
between him and the others is that they pray for themselves,
and ask guidance for the President. He asks for guidance for
himself, and prays for all. When the President concludes his
prayer, he sits, and for the first time notices the faces of children everywhere.

This is children's Sunday. Boys will preach; boys will conduct the Psalms; boys will sing. All of them have scrubbed
skin, rebellious hair whacked into a reasonable slick; bow ties
which might light up and spin, and Sunday suits. Tim Terry,
who has been taking piano lessons, spreads his young fingers so
that they span an octave of keys, and he plays a solemn
prelude to the services. The final chord is still in the ears when
Scott Haley stands behind the pulpit and in a childish treble

enunciates words of old wisdom: "'He said it with kindness, He said it with love, the blessed Lord Jesus who came from above . . . Suffer little children, and forbid them not, to come unto Me; for of such is the Kingdom of Heaven . . .'"

The choir sings "Good Morning to You" and the President sees, for the first time, that there is a little girl in the group. She is Marcia Gliddon. Her face is small and pixyish. Her blond hair has been pampered into place, and she yanks the hem of the starched dress over bony knees. Her eyes are on the President of the United States but the flirtation is marked with shyness. She looks at him, singing well through the gaps in teeth, until she sees him look at her. Then the lids lower, and she squirms on the chair, again tugging at her dress.

Boys pass the silver plates which hold the symbolic bread and the little glasses of grape juice. Some speak their words firmly; others have the treble lisp of kindergarten. " 'Even a child maketh himself known by his doings whether his work be pure, and whether it be right. Train up a child in the way he should go, and even when he is old he will not depart from it.' " The President says "Amen" and joins in the singing of "Onward Christian Soldiers." Mrs. Johnson shares her hymnal with her husband, and he sings loud and flat, his lower lip out and fluted, his voice rising in intensity as it approaches the proper key.

Greg Haley, Scott's brother, preaches the sermon and he speaks sternly of Sunday Christians who do not remember His teachings on other days. There is an offering, and President Johnson has a bill folded so that no one can detect the denomination. As Brent Schultze intones the benediction, Marcia Gliddon's blue eyes are still on the President. When the communicants leave their pews, Mr. Johnson sees that she is taking a farewell glance at him, and without altering the neutral repose of his features, he lowers one lid in a solemn wink. Once he had little girls like this.

Outside, a larger crowd waits and cameras do the winking. The sun is brighter and hotter, and his protectors, in sunglasses, face away from him and study the people. He waits patiently, his hand on the car door, and then he ducks in and starts off for the ranch. Halfway up the street a stout woman stands alone with a camera. Mr. Johnson sees that she is moving the film from one number to the next, and is not ready. He stops the car beside her, and she says, "Oh, I'm so nervous I'm all fingers."

The electric window is rolled down and Mr. Johnson's face is framed in it. "Take your time," he says. "No hurry. I'll wait." He does. The woman, grimacing, at last reaches the next number, and aims the camera at the President. He paints his smile swiftly. The camera clicks. "Any more?" he says. The lady shakes her head no. "That will do. Thank you. Thank you for waiting for me."

He drives up the street and points to a corner. "That used to sell for five dollars a front foot. Now it's sixty-five." Mrs. Johnson studies a small park with trees, bought for Johnson City with money she earned writing an article for *Life* magazine. "Lyndon," she says, "I wish you would consider a good name for that park." But his mind is away again, dwelling on the homely philosophies to which he has subscribed almost all his life.

"Old folks should have a great deal more comfort than they have. And better surroundings too." The voice is slightly exuberant. "Children should have their teeth and eyes checked more frequently." He glances at his wife. "I've seen children with terrible teeth." Mrs. Johnson is watching the buildings of the small town go by, and she nods and smiles at neighborly pedestrians. "I have heard of tests," the President says in a soft growl, "which can detect mental retardation at birth. If we could spot this, and do something to correct it, and maybe have checkups again at ages three and four . . ." The voice trails off. "There should always be follow-ups on children before things have a chance to take root."

He swings to the right on Route 290, and begins to build up speed. "We talk a lot about older people, and we do as much as we can, but who speaks for older people who are still young enough to be educated? Between the young and the old, there are millions of people who want to learn new skills."

The car is moving swiftly when it passes the easterly part of the LBJ Ranch. Across a small valley is a little house near the edge of a hill. The Johnsons hope that Luci will live there. Mrs. Johnson watches it glide by, and smiles. "I can just picture Marshal Dillon riding up to that place."

The President is lost in his thoughts. A phone call comes in for "Volunteer" and Mr. Johnson picks up the receiver. It is Mr. Jacobsen, who says he is making up a pouch for delivery to the White House by courier. The President's assistant wants to know if he should include the Utah tidelands bill. (It must be signed by midnight or it will die as a pocket veto.) Jake assures the President that the federal government has all the Utah guarantees on leases, present and future, to insure government freedom if the courts decided to give this shoreland to Uncle Sam.

"Send it," the President says. "Get it off as quickly as you can." He hangs up. Mrs. Johnson is still looking at the hilly land on the right side. "How about a ride in the boat this afternoon?" he asks.

4:00 P.M.

The First Lady gets off the White House elevator. "Is he awake?" Glynn gets to his feet. "Not yet." "Let him sleep, Paul," she says, blowing a kiss at the bedroom door. In five minutes Bill Moyers phones Glynn. "Is he awake?" "Not yet, sir. I'm going to awaken the President in five minutes. He had a five o'clock appointment."

In the West Wing, fourteen students and their teacher are shepherded into the Cabinet Room. They are from the Cotulla school where the President once taught. They are frozen into immobility as they stand, looking across the gleaming surface of the table to the lectern with the seal of the President. The blond teacher has an obviously new hairdo and is wearing a two-piece fuchsia suit.

This trip to Washington has cost them $1,000, and they mowed lawns and baked cakes for a year to try to earn it. But they were still a little short, so their parents—mostly Mexican Americans—contributed the rest. Some of their fathers and mothers had studied under Lyndon Johnson.

A pretty girl named Orfalinda Garcia has shoulder-length dark hair which falls over a white dress, and she tosses her head nervously. "If I have to present anything to the President," she murmurs, "I'm just going to topple over." She fans her face with her hand. She remembers what her father told her many times: Lyndon Johnson was a good teacher and a strict one; once he caught young Garcia mimicking the teacher, and he took the student out back and spanked him hard.

Sergeant Glynn opens the bedroom door softly. The room is dark. He snaps the foyer light on, tiptoes into the bedroom, and says, "Mr. President? Mr. President." Johnson stirs in his sleep, swallows, opens his eyes and says, "Paul? Is it that time already?" He gets up quickly, the bedroom lights go on, and he walks to the bathroom, pausing only to look at the little bedside clock, which points to 4:45.

The President talks through the towel as he dries his face. "Paul, why don't you go home? There's going to be nothing doing here. A few appointments, then the state dinner." The sergeant demurs, but permits himself to be outranked. At Andrews Air Force Base, he has a wife and three children and there is still time to spend the evening with them. He hurries to get the President fresh clothing, and they talk back and forth in terse syllables.

At one minute to five the tie is knotted and Mr. Johnson leaves the bedroom as Glynn says, "Goodnight, Mr. President." The President replies, "You do as I say. Go on home," and gets on the elevator as the word is flashed around the White House.

5:00 P.M.

In another minute the President is walking with the Secret Service along the edge of the Rose Garden, glancing at the late afternoon sky as he heads for his office. He walks in, and Juanita Roberts is waiting for him. He nods and takes a look at his desk. There are some more letters to sign, some new deliveries of mail, a couple of sealed envelopes from assistants, and a half dozen phone messages.

"The children from Cotulla inside?" Mrs. Roberts says they are waiting. He pulls his tie down, and walks straight through her office. As he bursts into the Cabinet Room, the students, whispering and moving about, are caught by surprise. There was no advance notice, no blaring of trumpets, no roll of drums. They were alone, worrying about what to say, what to do, and then he stood among them. Orfalinda Garcia is caught with her mouth open, and it remains open.

At once the President walks to her side and murmurs, "Don't be scared. They're not going to get you." He assesses them one by one, and must be pleased with what he sees because he approaches the lectern with a smile. He has a special tone for these children. It is soft, almost confidential. He says that

A Day in the Life of President Johnson

Washington appears strange and alien to the innocent visitor, but a student can learn a great deal here. He grasps the sides of the lectern and speaks extemporaneously.

"Anyway, government isn't a place. It's people. Your President, as you know, was a schoolteacher in Texas. Your Vice-President was a druggist in Minnesota." The theme is that ambition should be boundless. Study is important; application of knowledge is just as important. He tells them how he taught school for $125 a month, lived in a room over a garage, swept floors and "I sold Real Silk Sox on the side."

A year ago, he says, he wanted to go back to Cotulla to sign a college scholarship bill. "This was because when I taught at your school, not one of my students was eligible to go to college." The children listen, transfixed. It is as though they know that they will be asked at home, "What did he say?" and each one is trying to commit the words to memory. The talk is short. When it is over, Mr. Johnson walks briskly around the table and shakes hands with each student and the teacher.

A boy presents a drawing of the Cotulla school. He doesn't mention it, but it required two days of work, not counting the time spent looking for a frame. Miss Garcia's fears come true. She has been given a memento to present in the name of the school, and the President puts an arm around her and bends his head low to hear her weak tones. He finds out that she is a Garcia, and he grins and shakes his head. He knows that it was her father that he once spanked, but he does not mention it to the child because he thinks he's upholding the dignity of the parent. He hands a memento of the White House to each student and to the teacher.

"Let's go outside," he says. "I have an old picture of my class when I taught at your school. Now I'd like to have my picture taken with you." The tension of speeches and presentations is broken, and they follow Lyndon Johnson outdoors, as their parents once did.

The lady stares at a tank of fish. The work is done, and Bess Abell can hardly believe it. A state dinner is a most important function and entails weeks of preparation and mountains of mail. It requires a superior knowledge of protocol—and red tape. It necessitates the ordering of flowers, cars, menu, engraved invitations. Now, for better or for worse—and it had better be better—Mrs. Abell has finished her exacting schedule for the White House dinner in honor of President Ferdinand Marcos and Mrs. Marcos of the Philippines.

Mrs. Abell's office is on the second floor of the East Wing, an area of females of Amazonian wills, referred to as the "Dogs, Daughters and Delphinium Department." The social secretary requires a secretary and, at this time, additional help to insure the smooth-functioning of the state dinner.

There are other women behind other doors. Liz Carpenter, gay and gray, the First Lady's press secretary and staff director of the distaff wing, is short and round and gifted, a woman of hearty laughter who uses her gestures to polish her words. At one time Mrs. Carpenter and her husband Leslie ran a Washington news service for publications in the East and South. Today Mr. Carpenter runs it by himself while Liz dominates the East Wing ("where the action is") to such an extent that the men who have offices on the extreme ends of the second floor—Secret Service and military aids—tiptoe on their way in and out.

Mail is important here, and it gets to the First Lady quickly. The reason for this is that when Mrs. Johnson was young, she wrote a letter to a United States senator and received a form-letter reply: "Write to your Congressman." The First Lady now insists that all letters be answered personally. When Luci's engagement was announced, she began to receive 3,000 letters a week, largely from teen-agers wishing her happiness and offering advice.

When a beagle named Him died, Mrs. Christine Stugard, who is in charge of family mail, was inundated with 9,000 sympathy cards. She is a slender, gray and spectacled woman, who finally sent a note to Liz Carpenter which said: "If we get any more mail to Him, will you please send us a beagle who can type?"

In the East Wing, there are plants and couches and settees. The telephones appear to be grafted to ears. Sharon Francis, in charge of the unofficial Office for Beautification, corresponds with mayors, governors, and garden clubs.

There is no law to assist Mrs. Johnson and her staff in this work. It is a volunteer program. The only notice the federal government has given to the matter is the Highway Beautification Act of 1965, the Housing and Urban Development Act of 1965, and an indirect interest on the part of the Department of the Interior, with its Department of National Parks.

Sharon Francis has thousands of boxes of flower seeds contributed by women's garden clubs. They are all properly filed in a cabinet, but if the East Wing develops a leak, Sharon Francis expects that the second floor will become instant jungle. The First Lady has exhorted the states and the cities to assist in this work because she knows that she cannot do it alone. She wrote to fifty governors and 950 mayors asking them to count on whatever personal assistance she can give. However, she realizes that it is far better to clean one corner of a room thoroughly than to do a whole house shoddily, so she confines most of her work to Washington, D.C. She knows, better than her husband, that this is a city of contrasts between majestic beauty and moldy slums; between the neat and snobbish antiquities of Georgetown and the peeled paint and dead ivy of the Negro section. Of course, Mrs. Johnson's influence is felt in many other areas. Sixty industries in the meadow section of New Jersey between Elizabeth and Jersey City have notified Mrs. Johnson that they have begun a "competition" to beautify the factory sections. Lynda Johnson gave a check from McCall's for a magazine article to a Washington public school for landscaping and flowers. The wives of members of the Cabinet as well as wives of U.S. senators have volunteered their time and efforts to help in this program.

The White House had a small blight of its own. The Associated Press phoned Liz Carpenter one morning and said, "We have a tip that the White House grass has cancer." Mrs. Carpenter clutched her throat and whispered that she would call right back. She dialed the ground-floor office of Irving Williams, a tall slender man who serves as gardener. She asked the question. Mr. Williams said, "Yes. We have a patch on the south lawn. There's a better name for it than cancer, and there is also a cure."

Mrs. Carpenter sits behind her desk, looking across the room at stand-up sketches of Mrs. Johnson in formal gowns. She looks, makes a face, rocks her head from side to side, and hurries down the hall. As she passes the calligraphy office, she comes to an abrupt stop. Inside, four or five men, skilled in script, are hunched over magnifying glasses and cards of invitation.

"You're not working on invitations for tonight?" she asks. One man looks up. "These are invitations for a function next month." "Ahhh," says Mrs. Carpenter. "Well," she continues gaily, "we try to keep you fellows straight. If it wasn't for us, most of you would turn to counterfeiting." The men inside also write the script for presidential acceptances or regrets; they do the covers for publicity releases and press kits too.

In a moment she is on her way, too fast to wait for an elevator, too slow for the marble stairway. On the ground floor, she waves to Joseph Bruno, in charge of the East Wing reception office. Mr. Bruno has completed his day's work, which is to herd the visiting American public through the White House in an orderly fashion, make sure his assistants have put up the plush ropes in the public rooms, see that the loudspeakers inform the people about the appointments of "their house," and get them out on Pennsylvania Avenue again. The White House averages about 6,000 visitors a day. Two million Americans troop through it each year. This is one percent of the population, a high figure for one house. As a result of Mrs. John F. Kennedy's television tour of the premises, suddenly Joseph Bruno had to contend with 26,000 visitors a day. When the weather is good, the average is 8,000 to 10,000 each weekday.

Before the turn of the century, White House guards had to watch out for souvenir snippers, a group of ladies who arrived armed with shears, prepared to cut pieces out of the drapes and corners off upholstered chairs, and who dropped rare snuff boxes and ashtrays into copious purses.

There is little vandalism now and the Johnsons encourage Americans to see the White House. The family attitude is: "It is as much theirs as ours." And the America which shows up outside the east gate, magnetizing itself in a long queue all the way around the White House fence to the south lawn, is not always a well-dressed group. In the summer men arrive in loud sports shirts flapping outside of casual slacks; women often wear tight jeans and cheap cotton dresses; children are in

5:00 P.M.

shirts stenciled: "Superman" and "Batman" and they wander
under the guiding ropes to finger rare treasures. A special detail must clean up the litter when they leave. Some visitors
accord less respect to the White House than they would the
home of a neighbor. Recently, a descendant of Abraham Lincoln took the tour. He was rare. He removed his hat.

The hum of soft exhaust fans mixes with the sharp clatter of
dinnerware in the big White House kitchen. A good-looking
young man in a puffy white hat stands watching from stage
center, surrounded by the hanging pots and pans, the stainless
steel cabinets of the big white room. Henry Haller is the Swiss
chef who cooks for state occasions; just as Zephyr Wright cooks
upstairs for small family dinners; and just as the U.S. Navy
runs the kitchen in the West Wing mess. The chef pats his
aproned stomach. "I had my dinner already." He grimaces. "It
was not of the best." His work today is to execute a menu—a
fairly simple menu—for the Marcos dinner tonight. The small
stiff card which will lie beside every plate this evening says:

Dinner

Inglenook   Crabmeat Chesapeake
Pinot Chardonnay

Beaulieu
Cabernet Sauvignon   Roast Sirloin of Beef
                                          Creamed Spinach

                                          Garden Salad
                                          Trappist Cheese

Almadén
Blanc de Blancs   Glace Imelda

        The White House

            : 193

Mr. Haller is not a temperamental chef. He requires neither a mood nor a flash from heaven to decide what to do about state functions. The guest list numbers one hundred eighty-five persons, so seven bushels of spinach have already been cooked. The roasts are all simmering in their juices. The crabmeat is a problem, because the chef knows that the President does not like mayonnaise, and a crabmeat cocktail must have something to bind it together. He makes a special sauce, with a dash of this and a smidge of that, and emerges with a sherbet glass of crabmeat which has the tantalizing odor of the sea, but none of the eggy taste of mayonnaise.

The creamed spinach had the green field-flavor of the vegetable, but with subtle overtones of spices and cream. The beef will be cut generously in the usual well-done, medium, and rare choices. It is prime beef, nicely marbleized throughout but not fatty. The salad is the least artistic, consisting of lettuce, quarters of small tomatoes, escarole, and small diced bits of vegetables, drenched in the dressing of the diner's choice.

The dessert is named for Mrs. Marcos—Glace Imelda—and is especially molded to look like a ring cake. It is iced lime sherbet enclosing a mound of fresh blueberries, and each diner will cut his own wedge and cover it with the tight-skinned berries.

The chef can cook fancy or plain, depending upon the wishes of the hosts. Some of his own favorites are from recipes of his mother who still lives in Switzerland, and they are not difficult recipes. Now that he and his staff of twelve have finished most of the work, Henry Haller leans on a stainless steel table. He glances around his odoriferous "office." The electric steel cutters have been cleaned and the mixers are spotless. The counters gleam, except for the one on which a field of crabmeat sits in orderly rows. This reminds him of the time,

5:00 P.M.

not long ago, when Lyndon Johnson tasted crabmeat, pushed it away, and said, "Take the rest of it home to your wife." Tonight, Mr. Haller vows, the President will ask for seconds.

Mr. Johnson is still chatting with Congressman Tom Curtis as he walks the legislator to the door. The subject of their conversation remains their secret and the President is back to his office in time to sign the remainder of the mail. Marvin Watson comes in to say that a group of senior citizens is now assembled in the Rose Garden. Mr. Johnson's face automatically lights up at the sight of the very old or the very young; his basest suspicions are reserved for those between.

He won't keep the old people waiting. The pen is dropped, and the President hurries out through the French doors to sunshine and applause. Mrs. Roberts just has time to remind him that his remarks are on the outdoor lectern. His aim is to discuss Medicare, and in a philosophical monologue, he will not only be talking to this small group of people, but to the nineteen million Americans who are eligible for medical and hospital care. Beyond them lies a great mass of Americans who, he feels, must look kindly on governmental efforts to shoulder the economic responsibility of taking care of their parents. It is, he feels, not only a noble, progressive measure, but also a vote-getter.

Two hundred chairs have been set up in rows on the grass of the Rose Garden. The United States Marine band, in red coats, plays "Hail to the Chief." When it is played, all Chief Executives must stand still and listen, and the stirring strains of homage, repeated a few times each day, finally take on the irritating qualities of a cracked record.

A Day in the Life of President Johnson

The television cameras aim at the President from diagonal positions, in order not to obscure the President from the audience. The radio networks have four tapes spinning silently. A White House stenographer sits behind a stenotype, straining to get the exact words of Mr. Johnson, especially where he digresses from the prepared text. The late sun casts a long shadow across the audience, so that some are in cool shade and others hold conical newspapers over their heads to protect them from the sun. The old ladies are in their best hats and smiles; the men, largely bald, fold their arms to sit like an unofficial jury.

Secret Service men surround the President; some are in the back of the garden; others crouch in front, studying the faces of the audience. There is a slight fragrance in the early evening air. At the window behind Mr. Johnson, Walt Whitman Rostrow parts the filmy beige drapes. He is a moment too late to catch the President, but as he looks at the broad, blue-jacketed back and the expectant faces, he recalls something he once said to a writer: "Don't sell the President short on sensitivity toward people. It was sharpened by his father's business failure. At age sixty, Sam Johnson had to take a job as a bus foreman. It didn't hurt him, but it scarred Lyndon Johnson."

Mr. Johnson speaks slowly, conscious that these people must understand that the government of the United States is assuming the role of the dutiful son and daughter for their sake. Uncle Sam is not to be construed as a nebulous figure grinding out dollars automatically, but rather as a vigorous government according assistance, respect, and maybe even affection to those too old to produce and earn.

The President, who can make a good speech when he elects to speak his mind without notes, now permits himself to fall into the burnished-generalities clichés served up by his staff.

5:00 P.M.

"Never again," he says portentously, "will any older American need to go without basic medical care because he can't afford it. Never again will children and grandchildren have to sacrifice their future to pay the medical bills of older family relatives. Never again will our aged be threatened with economic ruin whenever illness strikes."

It is a triumph of age over insecurity, and the audience likes the "never again" and bursts into applause at almost every sentence. He asks the help of the aged in bringing government and medicine together to fight the infirmities of age. "Together we will make this program work. Together we will guarantee older Americans the care they need and deserve. Together we can quicken the race and add to the number of those successes already achieved."

The accomplishment is great and enduring; it is demeaned by hackneyed words. The "never again" and "together we will" attempt to set up a partnership between the President and the people; it tells these people nothing they could not learn from reading the Medicare bulletins sent out by the Department of Health, Education and Welfare.

The cameras stare with unblinking eyes at the hopeful faces, the old American Legion overseas caps, the whoops of joy. The President says that this is not all. He wants older people to have more adequate housing. Also he would like to create a more "meaningful retirement." The old people not only understand this premise; they anticipate it.

"Some of our senior citizens want to work. They should be given that right. Some want to go back to school. They should be given that right. Some want to develop new skills and hobbies. They should be given that right. And some want to volunteer their services in community programs. They should certainly be given that right."

: 197

A Day in the Life of President Johnson

Many of the older people get to their feet to applaud; some to whistle. With his words the President has shored up their pride. They want the money; they ache for the security; but in the unproductive years, they want to produce. The only way in which they can expunge the feeling of charity is to be given an opportunity to contribute, and the President of the United States has just promised to give them that chance.

The old, who have time, press the President to continue. They want to hear more, but he smiles and waves and says, "I thank you for standing beside us over the years. And I count on your support in the exciting and challenging months to come." He is gone while they look forlornly at the four buses which carried them to his presence, to what may have been the supreme moment in their lives.

A Secret Service man holds the door open and Mr. Johnson, without a nod, is back in his office, striding toward the desk, speaking by intercom to Watson: "I got Schultze and Hughes at six o'clock. If they get here a little early, send 'em in." Watson starts to say, "Yes, Mr. President," but the button is released and Johnson is back at work before he hears more than the word "Yes . . ."

He signs documents and glances at his watch. It is 5:48 P.M. and his day has a distance to go, but he knows that the West Wing, like an hourglass, is slowly emptying itself. If the President has any business with these people, he had better communicate it. The personnel leave in inverse ratio to their importance—the typists and stenographers first, walking out slowly in groups of two or three to find a bus; the male clerks and statisticians; the ladies of the East Wing; the uniformed policemen and agents whose replacements have arrived; researchers and phone operators; the key secretaries; the assistants themselves. The emigration to suburbia, to concrete flats and hotels, requires hours of filtering and will not be complete until late in the evening.

Although Congress has just adjourned, Mr. Jacobsen has already typed a short report for the President, who knows the things it has accomplished, and the things which have been left undone. He monitors their work, and the work of the Supreme Court, minutely, even though he has no responsibility for it. Mr. Johnson "feels" a responsibility because much of what he accomplishes—or doesn't—depends upon the action of the Congress and the acquiescence of the Supreme Court. They can slow him up; they can sometimes stop him. He frets about this because he hasn't the time to placate, to appease, to plead.

The man who designed the "Great Society" is trapped by time, because even with the co-operation of the two other wings of government, the goals are multitudinous; the balance between private enterprise and the welfare state must be maintained, but the moral debt to the aged comes high in cost as does the attempt to bring a good education to the young; the lifting of the economic status of the poor and unwanted can only be achieved by the taxing of the rich, so that America compresses its classes upward from the bottom and downward from the top.

If Lyndon Johnson is nothing else, he is a leader with vision who knows enough not to run too far ahead of Congress, the Supreme Court, and the electorate. Whereas John Kennedy dreamed of tomorrow's sunrise, Lyndon Johnson is content with today's sunset. The one was a poet, standing on the edge of space dreaming of far-off stars; the other sifts soil with his fingers, or feels a problem with his mind, asking what can be done right now.

6:00 P.M.

The second-floor corridor is empty. The lavish protraits stare down at the fading sunlight on the rug and the increasing brightness of the table lamps up and down the hall. In her room, the tall and graceful Lynda Bird completes a small parcel of personal notes, each postponed until conscience forces a pen into hand. She pauses only long enough to pick up the phone and ask Zephyr to fix a tray. They discuss what would be nice to eat, and agree that a cup of soup, a couple of chops and some creamed carrots, a little toast, a pot of tea, and some peppermint ice cream will do.

Lynda is not going to attend the state ball this evening, but will use the time to wrestle with personal chores. In a room across a foyer, Luci the dynamic writes thank-you notes for wedding gifts already received, and phones her intended husband to see if he would like to watch a movie tonight. What movie? he asks, but Luci doesn't know. The White House has its own little theatre and projectionist and she doesn't know the names of films on hand. If Pat can get back to the White House quickly, they might have a quick snack and find out about it.

6:00 P.M.

He is sorry, but business is going to hold him for a while. He will get a sandwich and a cup of coffee and join her on the second floor about 7 P.M. Then they can decide where to go, what to do. Like most serious young ladies, Luci tries to analyze the man of her choice, and one of the things she most admires about Pat is that he does not agree to everything she proposes. The eternal feminine desire to be dominated—in an affectionate way—is strong within Luci. And yet outwardly she appears to be almost belligerently independent.

The big studios send feature films to the White House on request. They are shown in an old storeroom on the ground floor near the East Wing. It has been converted into a theatre of sorts, neither attractive nor utilitarian. It is about twenty feet wide and sixty feet long. At the back is a projection booth. In front is a silver oxide screen on which can be shown sixteen-millimeter and thirty-five-millimeter movies. There are four big overstuffed chairs down front with standing ashtrays; sixteen chairs behind. The tastes of the family vary with movies as they do in food. The President finds precious little time to look at a motion picture, unless it is something involving one of his world interests. Then he studies it for a while, and falls asleep.

By this time the First Lady has completed her calisthenics in her room. Except for the ball, and the late night work, her day is nearly complete. She expects to lie on the bed and nap until it is time to dress.

On other evenings at this time, when there is no state occasion, the President sometimes phones and says, "Honey, why don't we invite some people over?" Until the Johnson administration, few Presidents so casually invited anyone to the private quarters of the mansion, except perhaps Dwight Eisenhower when he and Mrs. Eisenhower wanted to play bridge with Walter Bedell Smith or Alfred Gruenther. The Kennedys were saddened to feel that they were separated from old friends in Georgetown, but on occasion were informal enough in their attitudes to send out casual invitations.

The Johnson invitations are spontaneous and instantaneous. Many a friend had a roast in the oven when the voice of Lady Bird was on the phone, saying, "Lyndon and I would be delighted if you could make it about eight-thirty. We expect to have three or four couples, and we'll eat whatever Zephyr has on hand and sit around and talk." An invitation to the White House is so highly prized that almost any housewife is happy to turn the kitchen burners off, call in a sitter for the children, and start dressing.

The invitation list for these events consists of Cabinet members and their wives, staff members, and sometimes senators. The number varies from six to twelve, and has never exceeded fourteen. The First Lady favors these impromptu dinners because "The President needs the balm, the velvet of relaxing with friends. Sometimes I do."

On other occasions at this hour, Mrs. Johnson tries to get her husband to walk across the street for an hour and bowl in the Executive Office Building. He will do it, but he counts it as time wasted. There is no impulse within him to compete in a game. The President gets out of bowling what he puts into it: very little. His average is about 125.

The President has two and a half minutes with nothing to do. The next appointment has not arrived, and Mr. Johnson finds himself with no letters to sign, no orders to give, no dictation waiting, no one asking for a quick decision, no groups sitting patiently in the Cabinet Room and the Fish

Room for guidance and an accolade—nothing. One hundred and fifty seconds begin to tick off, dragging their feet for a man of action.

He sticks his hands into his trouser pockets and walks out to look at the south lawn. General Eisenhower's putting green is close by, but Lyndon Johnson never uses it. The swings and trampolines of the Kennedy administration are gone. He watches workmen removing the chairs on which the elderly sat. The last of the Marine Corps instrumentalists packs a tuba in a black case, snapping the catches, oblivious to the presence of the President behind him. Mr. Johnson looks at the sky. The blue is deeper; there are peach and gray crevasses in the clouds, and yet it is more of an afternoon scene than evening. Mrs. Roberts joins the President. He looks down at her and says, "It's just warm enough for a boat ride." Her eyes make little beaded crescents when she smiles. "But not tonight, Mr. President."

He nods and goes back in. "I know," he says. "This is a busy night. Maybe tomorrow if it's nice." The President thinks of the yacht when the air is soft and balmy and a moon is promised. He has no seafaring background, except for a wartime hitch in the Navy, but he feels an affinity for the water. The pungent salt spray, the silvery immobility of the moon, the far-off lights on the shores of Virginia and Maryland do much to ease the tension of the day, even when the President denies that there is any tension. It is doubtful that the President comprehends the dangers which are concomitant with working at peak speed for long periods of time. He knows only that when he gets in a boat, or arrives at his ranch, he feels relaxed and at ease.

The yacht, christened the *Honey Fitz* by President Kennedy, retains the name even though Presidents have, by habit and fiat, been renaming theirs as far back as the first presidential craft. Eisenhower called it the *Barbara Anne*, in honor of a granddaughter. There is a smaller presidential boat which Kennedy called the *Patrick J.* Under Johnson, this too will retain its name.

The cruise seldom lasts longer than two and a half hours, and is always the same trip—east on the Potomac to Mount Vernon and back to the Navy dock at Anacostia. It is an old 92-foot steamer with narrow walkways, an open quarter-deck aft, a narrow glassed-in salon, a few cabins below, and a good-sized bridge and small forward cabin.

The U. S. Navy requires at least an hour's notice to get up steam and put a working party aboard. Guests, who do not require much more notice than the yacht, arrive at the White House at 8 P.M. while the President concludes his work. Lem Johns puts one Secret Service detail aboard, and another aboard a thirty-foot cabin cruiser which will follow the *Honey Fitz* and keep other boats off. The cabin cruiser is so overloaded with communications equipment that its natural trim is bow down; it looks like a midget submarine about to take a dive.

The party arrives at the dock in a fleet of White House cars. Sailors line the rails of Navy and Coast Guard ships to watch the boarding. The captain of the *Honey Fitz*, Commander Worth Hobbs, waits in whites near the gangway. Sailors in whites stand at salute as the President boards. On the sundeck, canned music plays "Hail to the Chief." On the bridge, Commander Delbert Barbee watches the last of the party come aboard, and calls, "Single up those lines."

The crew consists of five sailors, an engineer, the commanders on the bridge, and eight stewards from the White House. Lem Johns takes a position forward, on the forepeak; two

other Secret Service agents with walkie-talkies are already out
patrolling the river. Commander Barbee calls for casting off all
lines and slow astern on the the starboard engine. Soft music
filters through the loudspeakers.

The guests represent a broad spectrum of Washington, offi-
cial and unofficial. This night, besides Mr. and Mrs. Johnson,
Lynda Bird is aboard. So are the Rostows; secretary Yolanda
Boozer and husband; Victoria McCammon and her fiancé,
Simon McHugh; Emmet Riordan and his wife; Hearst Washington correspondent Marianne Means; the Jack Valentis
(Mrs. Valenti was Lyndon Johnson's secretary when her name
was Mary-Margaret Wiley)—Courtenay Valenti has received
a special dispensation to remain up late with her doll Lisa. Dr.
Young is aboard; so is Juanita Roberts. Often the Clinton An-
dersons of New Mexico are included; also the Robert McNa-
maras and the Paul Glynns.

The President likes the boat party to be in pairs. He insists
that secretaries and stenographers bring their fiancés. Once
aboard, the President pre-empts a big wicker chair at the stern,
almost under the American flag. The *Honey Fitz* cruises at
nine knots, enough to stir a breeze but not a big wake. The
music is sweet; the shipboard conversation breaks up into
small groups. The President dons a peaked cap and folds his
arms across his middle.

His half-sleepy eyes are on Courtenay, who occupies herself
with ordering Lisa to be a good girl. When an adult speaks,
Mr. Johnson pays half-attention, and if possible, responds with
a word. Now he awaits a propitious moment, then yells at the
top of a mournful voice that nobody loves "the poor Prez." The
little girl with the dark ringlets pauses in her duty of wrapping
the doll in a small pink blanket to pout and yell, "I do." He
demands the kiss, the hug and the grunt, and she hurries to his

side to be assisted to his lap. The kiss and the hug are acceptable, but the President insists that the grunt is not up to standard.

Courtenay Valenti slides off his lap and tells him that he is not going to get another grunt. "All right," he says sadly, "if that's the way it has to be." She leaves her doll on a chair along the open deck to find a comb for Lisa's hairdo. While she is gone, the President of the United States kidnaps the doll and hides it on the seat behind him. Miss Valenti returns with a comb, looks at the empty chair, then looks underneath.

"Lisa loves the Prez," Johnson says. "I'll bet she would give him a good grunt." The little girl understands the implication. She hurries over to the President, hugs him and grunts loudly. The ransom is paid and the kidnaper returns the child. As the boat glides eastward, the molten lava of headlights on shore slides down the highways. Small boats coming upstream veer toward the *Honey Fitz,* and Lem Johns orders the cabin cruiser to come forward between the offenders and the presidential yacht.

Mrs. Johnson and Lynda pass bowls of popcorn and hors d'oeuvres. The stewards prepare fold-away tables and set them before the guests. The President permits himself one drink of Scotch. He walks forward to the salon and makes a few phone calls to the White House. Lynda curls up in a deck chair to pen notes in a diary. The President, undoubtedly with the future in mind, has a secretary who keeps a daily diary of events. He may become the only President who is his own historian.

Dinner is served; it consists of a salad, lamb chops, wild rice, a glass of wine, and ice cream. Afterward the President tries a nap in his chair, but the breeze is fresh, so he goes into the cabin, stretches out on an easy chair, and pulls the cap over his eyes. Others gather in the salon, and the conversation is incessant. Twenty minutes later the President is awake, squinting around the cabin. Whatever he is looking for is not there, so he gets to his feet and walks aft. Only Walt Whitman Rostow and his wife sit braving the breeze.

The President looks along the narrow companionway on the port side and sees Mrs. Johnson, elbows on rail, watching the foamy water glide past the cabin lights. He tiptoes up behind her, grabs her around the waist, and spins her to him. The kiss, even after so many years of marriage, is hardly perfunctory. He joins her at the rail and they watch the water together, conversing in low tones.

At Mount Vernon, the engines of the *Honey Fitz* are cut in power, and the lonely notes of "Taps" are heard echoing from the sun deck, to the bluffs of Virginia, and back again. Everyone aboard stands at attention, except Courtenay. Someone points out that the President insists that this be done for George Washington on every trip. Mrs. Johnson says, "He thinks it's the least we can do for the father of our country."

Slowly the *Honey Fitz* swings in the channel. Commander Barbee has lookouts posted fore and aft, and the Secret Service cruiser falls in behind the yacht for the homeward trip. When the ship is aimed west, Barbee calls for standard speed and the trip back begins. The aft deck is now without a breeze, and those in the salon are soon out on deck. At 10:58 P.M. the yacht is back at the dock. The gleaming limousines are waiting. The President wants to see the 11 P.M. news, so he hurries forward to the cabin behind the bridge.

The television set is a small portable, and Mr. Johnson turns it from one network to another, digesting each version of national and international news, switching to another when a commercial is on, or when a station is relating local matters.

The rest of the party waits aft. When the news is over, the President comes down the walkway to the gangway, and says, "Well, let's go home." Sailors in double lines stand on the dock at salute, and the phrases of appreciation and the good-nights are said here.

At 11:20 P.M. the cars move off toward the Anacostia gates; the President and his family head for the White House and the night work; the others for home and bed. The Secret Service car follows the President, and the news is flashed to the White House that the President has just left Anacostia for the mansion.

The President stands talking with Juanita Roberts. Then, hearing noise behind, he returns to shake hands with his final "on the record" appointment, Charles Schultze and Sam Hughes. "Been waiting for you fellows," he says. "Sit down." The men draw up chairs, and, on their laps, open briefcases. The subject this evening will be the United States budget.

The President switches to the problem of economics. Johnson is in the unhappy position of being personally thrifty, yet his budgets are the biggest in American history. In 1966 the war in Viet Nam was costing over fifteen billion, ten percent of the budget; and the poverty program, the slow spiral of inflation, and urban renewal were digesting billions to support the Great Society.

In nonessential areas, the President trimmed $3,000,000,000 so that expenditures would not run completely out of hand. And yet the budget is, to him, a chronic toothache with no relief in sight. In Johnson's administration, employment has reached an all-time high, not only in millions employed but in percentages of the labor pool. Unemployment was so low that for the first time in American history, political opponents complained that Johnson had dried up the labor market. This, in turn, led to a higher return in income and corporation taxes, and the country flourished. It could afford the Great Society as Lyndon Johnson saw it; it could afford to rebuild slum cities and toss billions of dollars toward educating American youth. But it could not afford it in addition to $15,000,000,000 in Viet Nam.

Add to this the three-percent decline in the value of the dollar each year, and a balanced budget becomes a nightmare. The budget for the current year comes to an estimate of $145,000,000,000 in expenditures and $145,500,000,000 in receipts. A surplus of $500,000,000 is indicated, an index of health in the national body. However, as the President knows better than anyone, three percent of it represents increased cost of services and goods, and this comes to $4,350,000,000. About $10,000,000,000 more is invested in the containment of Communist forces in Southeast Asia. If these two items—and no others—could be eliminated, almost $15,000,000,000 could be saved, and the Johnson administration would be rated the most prosperous in history.

Therein lies the presidential dilemma. The monolithic-socialist society of Asia has no hope of winning the war in Viet Nam, or anywhere else. The economic blood-letting of the United States is sufficient for their purposes. Their "small" actions in Korea, South Viet Nam, and the earlier threats to Berlin, to Matsu and Quemoy, average about seven percent of the national budget in cost. Force in a far-off outpost must be met by force, or America must resign its post as leader of the West. The theoreticians of the West agree that if at some future date the United States decides to permit the Communist to overwhelm weaker neighbors on the Asiatic mainland, it can expect the Reds to colonize nations closer to the United States. To state it simply, America is faced with the ugly problem of pouring men and treasure into containment of the forces of communism far away, or husbanding its men and money and wait for communism to come to American shores.

A country which genuinely seeks peace loses the initiative at once. The United States, and President Johnson in particular, has sought peace on any terms which might be called just. These overtures have been rebuffed every time because it is not in the interest of communism to have peace. They fight at minimal strength in their front yard. The United States must escalate or lose at a distance of 7,000 miles. The opportunity to erase a surplus and create a deficit in the United States budget lies not with Johnson and the American Congress, but with Hanoi and Peking and Moscow.

So the President sits with two executives of the Bureau of the Budget and they talk of the breakdown, department by department. Johnson has repeatedly admonished his Cabinet secretaries to pare every dollar they can, and to get a dollar's worth of goods and services for every dollar spent. This is not a gesture; Johnson realizes that he must face ever-higher budgets, and they must be supported by comparable income and a frugal economy.

The items of expenditure run to hundreds of thousands of carefully enumerated goods and services. Each one is weighed several times: by the department of economists; by the Cabinet secretaries and bureau heads; by the Budget Department functionaries; by Mr. Schultze and Mr. Hughes, and now, after it is pared to its essentials, it comes to the President for a department-by-department examination.

As the nation's housekeeper, the President likes to consider

6:00 P.M.

each figure in relation to the cost last year. He nods approvingly when he hears a smaller sum for fiscal 1967 than for fiscal 1966. When one is higher than the previous year, he expects the department head involved to justify it. A man who will not permit a few stray cattle to graze on his grass is averse to spending a dollar more than necessary in government.

He is also aware—as Schultze and Hughes are—that these are estimates projected into next year, that some of them may exceed the figure now before him; on the other hand, they are conscious that judicious spending may allow some of the departments to complete the year below their estimated expenditures. Economics is the only subject known to man which can be dull and horrifying at the same time.

The President wanted to discuss broad outlines of the budget. As the talk progressed, he found himself getting deeper and deeper into the small figures. Often he wrote estimates on a pad and worked out the percentages himself. Mr. Johnson knows that the American people expect the finest of living, the most secure force to protect them, and the greatest advances in the sciences, but the one thing they do not want is an addition to their taxes. Trying to reconcile these conflicting hopes constitutes an almost insurmountable presidential problem.

7:00 P.M.

The White House empties as it fills, slowly. For two hours secretaries and clerks have been leaving. Now, one by one, the second echelon packs briefcases, switches off lights, and says goodnight to policemen in the sentry boxes at the west and the south gates. Mr. Kintner, still in his plush dungeon, dictates a memorandum to the President:

> I thought you handled the Cabinet meeting extremely well and within the time period. I felt that the presentations—particularly those of Secretary Gardner and Administrator Bell—were extremely good. Several Cabinet members and several of your assistants who were present mentioned how effective they thought you were and the meeting was.

An apple for teacher. Kintner is enthused because Mr. Johnson administers these meetings in the manner of a locomotive engineer running a crack train—everything and everyone on time and green lights all the way. The aim is to jam as much constructive work as possible into each waking moment; therefore the President does not encourage the frippery and goodfellowship which were part of other administrations. The President assumes that each member is efficient and that each one trusts all the others, and he would be shocked if this were not so.

As employees leave, others arrive. At the south gate, ushers who will wait on tables at the reception have been arriving for an hour. They don their uniforms downstairs and report to the kitchen for duty. J. Bernard West, chief usher in several administrations, establishes his headquarters in a small office between the first and second floors of the mansion. He checks with kitchen, State Dining Room, and Liz Carpenter in the East Wing. He is a confident man who never panics—and wouldn't even if soup slipped and congealed around a guest's pearl necklace.

A bus comes in the southwest gate, and after inspection, follows the oval road to the diplomatic reception room. The bus carries the orchestra section of the United States Marine band, plus a group of U. S. Army violinists. Secret Service men stand under the canopy and in the ornate reception room watching and checking people.

For the President, the hour is still part of a workday, even though he must dress for the state dinner. He is at his desk, and he picks up the *Evening Star* and scans the first few pages. He calls Juanita Roberts on the intercom and asks for a cable which has just arrived from Ambassador Henry Cabot Lodge in Viet Nam. Yolanda Boozer hurries down to the Situation Room to get it. The President phones Congressman Robert Jones and then places a call to Harry McPherson.

The people around the President look for signs of fatigue, but there are none. He is fifty-seven years of age, a time of life when most men husband their energies and talk of retirement or are already retired. Mr. Johnson acts as though life began when he assumed the Presidency. Today, for example, his off-the-record performance—quick telephone calls, impromptu visits—is close to the edge of incredibility. Among the items not listed on the official record are these:

Received a phone call from Ben Heineman, the chairman of the Council to the White House Conference "To Fulfill These Rights"; they discussed the pros and cons of the President's attendance at the White House conference. Later the President phoned Mr. Heineman at the Sheraton Park Hotel. He phoned Walt Rostow about the morning situation abroad. This was followed by a call to Bill Moyers.

Nicholas Katzenbach phoned the President. There was a short meeting with Dean Acheson, former Secretary of State, Under Secretary George Ball, Bill Moyers and Walt Rostow, Clark Clifford and Bob Kintner. Mr. Clifford is the chairman of the President's Foreign Intelligence Advisory Board. There was also a visit from Hubert Humphrey, a short chat with Bob Pierpoint and Bob Fleming, and a two-minute conference with Marvin Watson and Fleming.

When the President was having his afternoon rest, a phone call from United Nations Ambassador Arthur Goldberg and George Ball was put through from the State Department. The President ordered Walt Whitman Rostow to handle it, and to determine the urgency of the call. After his nap the President was paid a short visit from Cyrus Sulzberger of the *New York Times,* followed by two phone calls: one from George Meany of the American Federation of Labor; another from Bill Moyers. The President then heard from Kintner and called Joe Califano.

A note from Juanita Roberts told of the boy who executed the drawing of the Cotulla school and who is being aided by the Poverty Program. His mother had been killed in an automobile accident and his stepfather was permanently injured.

7:00 P.M.

He has lived with his grandparents and an aunt and uncle most of his life. "The chaperone reports that because of the training this boy is getting under the Poverty Program, they feel that he will have a bright future."

Senator Clinton Anderson brought Senator J. William Fulbright to the White House for a discussion on Viet Nam with the President. Mr. Anderson waited in Marvin Watson's office while Fulbright and Rostow joined the President. All possible options opened to the United States in Viet Nam were discussed. Senator Fulbright listened politely, and as one opposed to the administration course, offered no advice but said he wished he could share the administration's confidence; in any case, he promised to keep in touch.

Marvin Watson brought the Lodge cable to the President, who read it at once, and sent a reply. The President called Mr. Moyers and said, "Come in and see me." For a while the President sat with Yolanda Boozer and dictated notes and letters. He asked Marvin Watson to bring in a summary of the President's remarks for the dinner tonight. He sent flowers to Senator Carl Hayden at Bethesda Naval Hospital, with a card: "Carl, I know you will be back with us in the next five days. We hope all will go well. L.B.J."

Flowers and a note were also sent to Congressman Rogers Morton, who is ill. Also to Congressman William J. Randall of Independence, Missouri. The President signed three nominations for U. S. Marshal and sent them to the Senate. He placed phone calls to Congressmen Brooks and Pickle, Senator Mansfield, Senator Bayh, Senator Harris, and Senator McGee. Instinctively the President saves money in placing calls by saying, "Try him at the office and at home. I don't want him if he's out of town."

In the late hours he calls or sees from twelve to twenty

: 215

persons. The President's tendency is to settle matters as they arise. The phone calls, the summons to come to the White House office, are matters to which all superiors in the Executive Branch of government have become adjusted. At first they chafed; a few dropped hints that a man is entitled to some time with his family. In this, the President is pitiless: "I drive myself harder than I drive you, and you're a lot younger."

Too often America thinks of the Presidency in terms of a popularity contest. In 1927, when a young man named Charles A. Lindbergh lent himself to a stunt—flying a single-engine plane from New York nonstop to Paris—he came back such a hero that there was serious talk about running him for President of the United States. Dwight D. Eisenhower, with no experience in economics other than requisitioning material for the Army, was urged to run for President even though no one knew whether he was a Democrat or a Republican, whether he was a liberal or a conservative. General Ulysees S. Grant attained the office in the same way.

Fitness and experience in government appear to have little to do with the possibility of victory. The more popular the man, the better his chances. John F. Kennedy, as a junior senator from Massachusetts, could not match the governmental experience of Vice-President Richard Nixon, but Kennedy had charm and wit and won a close race. His most noteworthy aphorism was taken from the words of a headmaster at a school Kennedy attended: "Ask not what your school can do for you; ask what you can do for your school."

Kennedy was not truly popular until after his death. He worried about the impending election of 1964 and began campaigning in Texas in November of 1963. When he died the national conscience was crushed, and citizens who said they loved him and voted for him covered his memory with lovely lies. Kennedy's position was akin to that of Woodrow Wilson and Harry Truman, neither of whom was nationally appreciated until they left the White House.

It is doubtful that Lyndon Johnson could win a popularity contest. He is too stern, too caustic, too businesslike, too busy running to meet events to become an idol. In the autumn of 1966 he made a speech in New York in which he declared that he had picked up the torch from John F. Kennedy's lifeless fingers and had passed into law the dreams of his young confrere and the aspirations of others before Kennedy.

This was passed off by the newspapers in favor of other, brighter events, but it is what history will show. Kennedy dreamed great programs; Johnson signed them into law. Kennedy fought his Congress so that it split into four wings: liberal Democratic, conservative Democratic, liberal Republican, conservative Republican. He won some battles, and lost others. When his assistants counted up the "sure" votes in Congress, John F. Kennedy became a minority President because there were not enough to give him command of the House of Representatives and the Senate.

Lyndon Johnson, the professional politician, and John F. Kennedy, the realistic idealist, managed a working relationship. It had to be so, because when there was disagreement, Johnson deferred to his President. Kennedy, who fancied himself a littérateur, was not above reading a Johnson speech before delivery and blue-penciling it. This did not set well with Johnson, but he did not complain. Nor was it always appreciated by the Kennedy cronies when Johnson proved that he had "done his homework" before staff meetings and was able to supply Mr. Kennedy with answers to baffling questions. It is even possible that President Kennedy did not have a proper appreciation of Johnson's capacity for hard work when he asked the Texan to be his Vice-President. The sophisticated Kennedy had a social life; Johnson had none.

And yet history already begins to appreciate that these two were a good combination for the early 1960's. Johnson felt himself not only bound and pledged to every Kennedy aspiration, but did not try to break the bonds after the Dallas assassination. He not only picked up the torch; he carried it high and far. And as the Kennedy clan dropped one by one from the Johnson administration, politicians kept an eye on Lawrence F. O'Brien, the Boston redhead who was as much of a professional politician as Lyndon Johnson. If O'Brien quit, the pros reasoned that Johnson would be his own liaison man with Congress, as well as Chief Executive.

O'Brien stayed on, and reached Cabinet status when President Johnson named him Postmaster General. There was a natural wariness on both sides at first, because Kennedy loyalty is a personal matter, difficult to transfer even after death. "Laddy" O'Brien became convinced that Mr. Johnson wanted him to stay, and needed him, and he transferred his devotion to the new man with the same honor he accorded to the old. As a mark of affection, President Johnson took O'Brien to a small post office near the LBJ Ranch to swear him in.

The President and his Postmaster General make a formidable team. Each has a background of precinct politics—Johnson under his father in Johnson City, Texas; O'Brien under Mayor Jim Curley of Boston, Massachusetts—and neither is so remote in attitude as to ignore the smallest Congressional campaign. When Johnson asked O'Brien to call him in the middle of the night—"Because I want to bleed with you"—he meant it. Politics, the raw vote cadging and counting, is the lifestream of both men and it is possible that they work in closer harmony than O'Brien and Kennedy.

The President sets the policy and the measures. O'Brien hefts them and assesses the probability of fruition. Throughout the multitudinous daily phone calls and impromptu visits between the two, it seems as though there is always a chronic need for a few more votes than they have. Nor is the President too busy to ask a wavering senator or representative to stop in for a sales talk. O'Brien ticks off the Congressional campaigns, and tells the President which ones he feels are "sure" but require additional Democratic party insurance, and still others where the Democrat is in trouble.

Johnson's accomplishments in the field of legislation are unparalleled, but Congress too had a large share in this record. At one point, October 7, 1965, President Johnson surprised both houses by taking the lectern to thank them publicly for their achievements:

"There haven't been many times in our history," he said, "when the President could stand before Congress, at the end of a session, and express the gratitude and the pride that I feel tonight. . . . All too often the relations between the Executive and the Legislative branches have been marred by bitterness. George Washington warned that his legislature would 'form the worst government on earth' if some means were not found to stem its corruption.

"A great Republican, President Theodore Roosevelt, once wished he could turn loose sixteen lions on his Congress. When someone pointed out that the lions might make a mistake, he replied, 'Not if they stay there long enough.' We all remember the time Harry Truman named the 80th Congress 'the second worst Congress in the history of the United States.' I can bring this up without fear of hurting anyone's feelings here tonight, because I too was a member of that Congress.

"Now we are going to balance the ledger. Tonight the President of the United States is going on record as naming this session of Congress the greatest in American history. And I am well aware of what that statement means. . . ."

Taking the laurel from his brow to place it on the head of Congress is adroit political science, but it does not alter the truth that the arithmetic of legislative accomplishment favors Mr. Johnson. The formula is that the President asks a continuous stream of fresh ideas from his assistants, sifts them carefully, draws up most of the legislation in the White House, broaches it to Democratic leaders at weekly breakfasts, finds sponsors for it, engineers it in and out of committees, and searches for sufficient votes to bring passage in both houses. This is not to say that Lyndon Johnson is, in effect, Chief Executive *and* Congress; the thing he does personally, which was not done by his predecessors, is to wheedle, cajole, and convince the leaders that his measures are in the best interests of the United States and that time is of the essence. No historic honeymoon between the Executive and the Legislative branches has lasted as long as this one.

The Elementary and Secondary Education Act—designed to cost $1,300,000,000 a year—was judged impossible of passage because this bill, and similar measures, had made enemies in Congress. The lobbies were full of special pleaders who desired aid for private and parochial schools, new school construction, and salary raises for all teachers. The Congress was worried about how much of the money would eventually filter to hard-pressed students.

Johnson's bill was specific in detail, and after passage, enabled fifteen thousand local school districts to develop special programs for seven million underprivileged boys and girls. It also provided new textbooks for forty-nine million children and nearly two million teachers. It started twelve regional educational laboratories where teachers and scholars could concentrate on research in new methods of imparting knowledge to students.

Although intent may be noble, application can be base. Medicare, for example, had a history of defeats until Lyndon Johnson pressed it into enactment over the opposition of the American Medical Association and the Republican party. Nineteen million Americans were enrolled, and the President saw a burden being lifted from the shoulders of those with the least strength. However, the AMA, having lost its long fight, suddenly joined Medicare with glee, and many physicians began to raise their fees. Other doctors maintained the line on fees, but for the first six months there were hikes in daily hospital rates, a bonanza of new nursing homes, strikes by nurses and interns for higher wages, in addition to gouging by some pharmacists. But the overall good far outweighed the bad, and Medicare, which had been sidetracked for twenty years, became a boon to those most prone to illness and least able to afford it.

When President Johnson fought for passage of the 1964 civil rights measure, reasonable men were ready to admit that the law was overdue by one hundred years. Yet civil rights was such a political yo-yo that for two years no man could accurately assess "the most good for the greatest number" against the abuses.

The man who proposed to right the wrongs had two grandfathers who fought for the Confederacy. He also had a keen knowledge of how hard President Kennedy had fought for civil rights, and what it had cost him in prestige and electoral votes. Still Lyndon Johnson moved stubbornly ahead, and the Congress passed it into law. It guaranteed Negroes access to public accommodations; authorized the government to sue school systems and public facilities where discrimination was practiced; provided that federal funds could be cut in cases of nonobservance of the law; and demanded that corporations and unions grant equal employment opportunity to all.

To achieve this, the Johnson administration had to fight not only the white supremacy groups, which envisioned a mongrel culture, but also the new fanatical Negro groups which fomented urban riots and pillage, and sometimes, sudden death. It seemed as though, by some dark alchemy, the white supremists and the black haters were on the same side, and that the aspiration of true equality of all men had become a dirty phrase.

In the newspapers, Lyndon Johnson appeared to be standing alone in his battle, but he won it. This also applies to the voting rights measure—perhaps more so, because Congress was in no mood to interfere with archaic state laws governing the right of suffrage. Most Congressmen were happy to point with pride to the fact that the Legislature had passed no notable voting law in ninety-five years. They did not want to interfere with the states, and said that states rights had been abrogated sufficiently in recent years.

Again President Johnson exercised the magic of hard-boiled persuasion, and on August 6, 1965, signed into law a bill which suspended the use of state literacy tests and other devices designed to "qualify" voters to use polling booths. It also authorized the use of federal agents to register voters in those states which dragged their heels in complying with the new law. To bring the lesson home, federal registrars signed up 400,000

7:00 P.M.

Negroes in five southern states before the bill was one year old.

The Rent Supplement Bill was tricky. Mr. Johnson pointed out that in almost thirty years, only 590,000 units of low-rent housing had been erected. The population of the country was approaching 200,000,000 persons and a good percentage of these could not afford high city rents. The President proposed that low-interest government loans would provide an incentive for nonprofit groups to build 375,000 units of housing in four years. He also suggested that low-income families be placed in existing private housing with government rent subsidies. "This," he said, "is the most crucial new instrument in our effort to improve the American city."

The Republican party decided to kill it at once with a roll-call vote. In the House, the Johnson group won by the narrow margin of 208 votes to 202. They prevailed in the Senate by seven votes. The fight was bitter and long. When Johnson won, and signed the bill into law, the opposition blocked the passage of funds to implement it. He has the law; Congress has the money. Knowing Johnson, tacticians on both sides of the legislative aisle are certain that he will continue the fight until rent supplements become a reality.

Johnson was at his ranch in December, 1963, when he devised the War on Poverty. There is something about all grand designs which excites the politically innocent and elicits derision from the sophisticates. So it was with this measure. The proposal received world attention. The chronically poor of this country—numbering about 35,000,000 persons—looked toward Washington with hope.

Most of these were isolated from work by economic geography. In the Appalachia area, men sat on creaky unpainted porches because the mines and the mills had been worked out. In Massachusetts, textile factories and shoe manufactories were cold and empty, but the people who had once worked in them remained. Parts of Kentucky had towns with no work and no bread.

Jaded politicians—and many of the realists too—were opposed to the program before President Johnson spelled out the details. Many editors and columnists reminded the President that Jesus had said, "The poor ye shall always have with you." . . . Some called it a gigantic dole, but others who were products of poverty were eager to make it work.

Those who opposed Johnson on this measure took the words "war" and "poverty" and announced that the government was about to spend itself into prosperity, as it had done before. To the contrary, the President is a firm believer in the axiom: "What will work for me will work for others." He was not being condescending when he told the Cotulla schoolchildren that their President had been a teacher; their Vice-President had been a druggist.

He knew that poverty could not be defeated by money. The goal was to fight it with education and opportunity—to transplant families in worked-out areas to greener grounds, and to teach them skills which can be sold at a good price in the labor market. "Through all these years," he said, "I have sought, asked, and been given the opportunity to make some effort in the field of fighting a war on poverty, illiteracy, ignorance and disease. . . ."

The measure, called the Economic Opportunity Act of 1964, was fought in Congress. If any bill may be singled out as a test of strength between the President and the Congress, this was it. For a while it appeared that Johnson could not depend on his "sure" stalwarts in the cold marble halls of the Capitol.

7:00 P.M.

Still, the President and his Larry O'Briens fought it until the War on Poverty became the law of the land.

Perhaps no accomplishment has given Johnson more pleasure than this. It was a personal triumph against odds. For the first year he asked and received $947,500,000 to implement the struggle. The President did not expect to eradicate poverty at once, nor even in his term of office, but he desired to start the fight. This involved locating the areas of economic blight on a map of the United States and sending teams of experts to these sections to examine the current and future status of towns, villages, and farm areas.

In the bill was a Job Corps "to give young people work experience and training in conservation camps and residential centers." It also established a domestic "Peace Corps" and proposed community action programs to stimulate local economic effort. Once it was launched, the politicians and the press held the President responsible for each individual lapse in the program, and ridiculed the Job Corps when some of its recruits turned out to be burglars or rapists.

Possibly the greatest miscalculation that the nation has made about Lyndon Johnson is that nothing is too small to gain his attention and his will to fight. It had been thought that merchandising was up to the merchants, and that a poor product would in time fall of its own weight. Certainly the federal government could not stoop to tell manufacturers what to build and how to build it.

In 1956, in the Senate, Johnson stood up to speak about the related problem of increasing highway deaths and the lack of safety devices in automobiles. He heard no answering cry; no one was in a mood to fight General Motors, Ford, Chrysler, and the other giants of the automobile business. For a number of years it appeared that he had forgotten the notion. How-

: 225

ever, in 1966, President Johnson became caustic and told the automobile industry to "stop fighting the small print" and help devise a bill for a safe car which would save American lives.

Instead, the industry fought it. Hearings were held, but it appeared that this measure was doomed. But Lyndon Johnson won, and on September 9, 1966, signed the Auto Safety Act into law. The industry was given two years in which to produce cars with safety features built into steering wheels, windshields, dashboards, automatic door locks, and tires.

There were other victories, and some defeats. Johnson won his fight for a Higher Education Act; a Cabinet-rank Department of Housing and Urban Development and another for transportation.

His enemies call him a wheeler-dealer; his proponents call him a clever politician; his assistants regard Lyndon Johnson as one of the greatest statesmen in American history. No assessment is valid because all the returns are not in. History cannot subtract from Johnson's enormous accomplishments in the first thousand days in office. He arrived with a will to get things done, and time has not diminished his energy or his will to fight for what he feels is right. Certainly it can be said that up to the early days of 1967, no President in history has run the course of achievement so swiftly.

Juanita Roberts looks at her watch. The time is 7:30 P.M. and she is ready to leave. She peeks through a partly open door. The President is chatting with an off-the-record visitor. She says nothing, not even "goodnight," but Mr. Johnson sees her and glances at his watch. He must leave to dress.

Kintner is leaving too. He carries a bulky briefcase, which

swings with his stride. As Mr. Johnson picks up his "night reading," the news that he is leaving for the mansion is flashed to the nearly empty offices. In a few, lawyers work over the phrasing of a new bill; otherwise, the West Wing is ready for the night cleaning women. White House policemen sit behind desks in the curving corridors; some peer into offices and snap lights off.

In the big reception hall, a handful of reporters sit reading the late afternoon newspapers. This is the night watch of the nation's press. Most of the time there is little to do, but if a crisis develops in the late hours, they are ready. The wire services will cover the Marcos reception, so these men do not concern themselves with it.

The doors to the President's big office are open. The only sound is the soft clack of Yolanda Boozer's typewriter. She is at work and will remain until much later. The file cabinets, mute and green, are locked. In the main hall of the Executive Mansion, Dr. George Burkley makes arrangements for an assistant physician to be in the office in case medical aid is needed. He leaves, nodding goodnight to the Secret Service men in the corridor outside his office.

Upstairs the First Lady is beginning to dress. The President is in his bedroom, and his tuxedo and studs and black tie are laid out for him. The Johnsons do not require much time to dress, even when the occasion is formal. The President switches the television on and undresses. In a moment he is in the bathroom. He doesn't need a second shave, but he runs the electric gadget over his face while his mind flicks through the events of the day—the things done; the things still to be done.

The invitations are marked for 8 P.M. but he knows that he is not expected to appear with Mrs. Johnson until twenty minutes after that. The President of the Philippines will leave Blair

House a few minutes after eight, and Mr. Johnson wants to be alerted to the time of arrival at the White House because he plans to greet him in the Oval Room.

Thankfully, all the details have been left to Mrs. Johnson and Mrs. Carpenter, and this leaves the President free to concentrate on other matters. In fact, all he has to do throughout the evening is to await word from his wife about what to do next. Formal occasions do not sit lightly with Lyndon Johnson, because he is not a formal man and sees no joy in high-blown social affairs. However, he has learned to accept it as part of the job. It is work, just as the daily office tasks are.

This evening, he knows, has posed a delicate problem because due to prior appointments, the Johnsons will not be present tomorrow when the Tom Lea portrait of Samuel Rayburn is hung in the new House Office Building. Therefore, the artist and old friends will be in the Yellow Oval Room at a late hour, and Mr. and Mrs. Johnson must end the formal reception at a reasonable time so that they can greet the Texas group with whom they share so many memories.

The chief of the Secret Service, James Rowley, drives up near the southwest gate and parks his car. He watches the arrival and checking of guests. Actual supervision is in the capable hands of Lem Johns, but Rowley, who worked the White House detail many years ago, is in the habit of driving up to one of the gates in the evening and watching the coming and going of employees and guests. Often he will drive through the west gate and park his car between two others, sitting behind the wheel and watching.

His hair has grown whiter, but this is more a matter of

7:00 P.M.

inheritance than anxiety. The smile is gentle and Irish; the voice is soft and unobtrusive, but there is a Dallas nightmare in his head and he will live with it, as his agents will, through all the days that remain. It is not a concern of the conscience— or guilt—because no one could have foreseen that in one window out of thousands, a young man would stand waiting. No amount of preparation could have divined the event, but Rowley and his agents live with the event as though by mentally replaying it, they will devise a system so that it will not happen again.

The cars line up at the southwest gate. Representative Patsy Mink of Hawaii presents her invitation; Senator and Mrs. Frank Lausche of Ohio are followed by Justice and Mrs. Hugo Black, and behind them are General and Mrs. Harold Johnson. Mr. and Mrs. Bill Moyers arrive early because he wants to confer with the young and handsome press secretary to the President of the Philippines, Señor José D. Aspiras.

Two short and gray men are passed through the gates quickly. One is Vice-Admiral Hyman G. Rickover; the other is His Eminence Francis Cardinal Spellman, who was a favorite guest of the Roosevelts and Trumans. A Hollywood actor, Richard Egan, arrives with a square-toothed grin; James A. Farley, who was the Larry O'Brien of the Roosevelt administration, nods his tall bald head as he proceeds alone. Mr. and Mrs. Steve Parker present credentials; the guards smile because they recognize the lady as actress Shirley MacLaine.

The James W. Symingtons are already in the diplomatic reception room. He is the chief of protocol, and he asks the young U.S. Army captains, attired in white dress, to please escort the guests up to the East Room. They chat and move slowly, in twos and fours, to the elevator or stairwells. The evening has commenced.

8:00 P.M.

Dusk, trapped between daylight and night, hesitates as though it could outwit both. It now waits over the Custis-Lee mansion across the Potomac River, with barely enough strength to silhouette the long cascading lawns and the sentinel headstones of Arlington National Cemetery. A flash of lightning near Fort Myer blots dusk into darkness and the applause of thunder is faint and far away, as though done with gloves on.

On cue, Washington comes to life. Necklaces of topaz street lights burst into brightness. Along the edge of the river, the bronze and melancholy figure of Abraham Lincoln stares perpetually up the Mall to the majesty of the illuminated Capitol. Classrooms light up at George Washington University and Georgetown, and the cold shaft of Washington Monument is bathed in the warmth of white light. The best tables at smart restaurants along Pennsylvania Avenue and up Connecticut are already taken. The modish windows of fashionable stores are lit and the waxen faces of models stare haughtily at pedestrians. Movie marquees mesmerize eyes with flashing lights. Tired tourists drive in low gear and children lean from car windows, shouting, "What's that place, Daddy?"

8:00 P.M.

The White House, imposing by day, becomes regal at night-fall. The well of light behind the white columns and the sparkling water tossed skyward from the fountain gives the Executive Mansion an aura of silent nobility. Big lights crouching in the grass expose the flat whiteness through the dark trees. In any era, in any place, it would be an edifice of importance. This building offers triumph and tragedy in separate measures, as though the pale stone can, at times, lift itself into moods of national ecstasy, and fall suddenly to the depths when the only sound is the pulse of a muffled drum.

Guests are still arriving, but they seem slightly harassed. The invitation reads: ". . . will present this card at the southwest gate, The White House, at eight o'clock." Most hostesses regard guests who arrive on time as social nuisances, but at the White House, eight o'clock means eight o'clock. Thus the latest group, held up by traffic, or baby-sitters, or a zipper which refused to function, tries to hurry through the gate. The officers still take their time examining invitations and faces in cars. The speed around the oval must be maintained at five miles per hour, and the latecomers draw up to the canopy outside the reception hall without time to permit ushers to open the automobile doors.

They pop out, and the ladies hurry inside in long tight gowns which permit only the tiniest steps, and on up to the East Room. To some, a presidential reception is an old story; to others, it is a glimpse into a world glittering with pomp; to all, there is the tickle of unusual excitement. No one attends a White House gala casually. Even Merriman Smith, dean of the White House press corps, a man who has earned the respect and confidence of several administrations, feels the aura of the occasion.

It is an opportunity to dine with the President of the United

States, and it is more. The guests are gentlemen and ladies of note, and the conversation is bound to be rewarding. For the eyes, there is a bevy of women beautifully gowned and coiffed and jeweled; a clutch of men in white shirts and dinner jackets. The setting is as rich as a wedding cake; the atmosphere is calculated informality. Here the society of birthright is replaced by the society of accomplishment.

The East Room has been partitioned so that only the south half is used. The big crystal chandelier hangs like a fruit cup of diamonds; the old parquet floor, laid down in 1902, gleams with long paths of reflected light; pale satin drapes hang in the tall windows, screened by a gold valance and long pleated tiebacks. Gold benches hug the walls, waiting for those too tired to stand. President James Monroe's ornate candelabra— gilt ladies on orbs holding the candlesticks over their heads —decorate the long mantel. A full-length portrait of Martha Washington, hands limply at her sides, hangs only an archway away from one of her husband painted by Gilbert Stuart.

The room is imposing. The majesty of the United States is here. And yet it is neither as large nor as august as some of the rooms in Schönbrunn Palace in Vienna, not as stiffly formal as the great reception hall of Buckingham Palace in London. It has been referred to as a "lofty, dignified salon, associated with splendid and solemn events. Levees and receptions, weddings and funerals have taken place here; today it is the first state room seen by the public visitor on a tour of the White House, and the room where guests gather before a state dinner."

It is all of this. The room has encompassed part of the his-

tory of the United States. The solemn baritone notes of Pablo
Casals' cello were heard here; so were the shrieks of Mary
Lincoln as she looked upon the waxen face of her husband on
Easter Sunday, 1865. The room was an unfurnished barn to
Thomas Jefferson; a wedding scene for Glover Cleveland; a
place of many mirrors and eye-tiring carpet for President
Ulysses S. Grant; a refuge where when no one was present
Harry Truman could sit at a gilt Steinway piano, one with
eagles on its legs, and tap out an old ragtime tune. It is also the
place to which John F. Kennedy's body was brought at 4:05
A.M. on November 23, 1963.

The President lifts his chin to adjust his bow tie. A light
flickers on the bedside phone and the tie is pressed flat against
the collar as he lifts the phone. "Yes," he says. "All right." The
Marcos party is en route. They are expected at the Pennsylvania Avenue gate in eight minutes. The President hangs up.
He is ready. The jacket is pulled down and he joins Mrs.
Johnson in her room.

She is dressed. Her habit, in common with her husband, is to
be on time. She is wearing a plain alabaster-white gown with a
beaded sleeveless jacket. Her dark hair is coiffed bouffant. The
make-up is artful, because it is applied subtly, to give the
impression that Mrs. Johnson is not wearing any. She sits at
her dressing table, flicking the final strands of hair into place,
and Helen Williams stands back, clasping her hands and
watching.

"My, don't you look pretty," the President says. She does.
Mrs. Johnson stands, and the total effect of sheath and coiffure
is to add height to her diminutive stature and make her look

much younger than her husband. He touches his lips to her cheek, and Helen Williams holds the bedroom door open.

The Secret Service man in the corridor uses his walkie-talkie to tell headquarters in the East Wing that the Johnsons are proceeding to the Oval Room on the main floor to meet the Philippine President and First Lady. More Secret Service men are with the Marcos party; a few others stand on the porte-cochere waiting, watching.

In the East Room people have gathered in groups close to the walls; the only motion is by those who are crossing the room to greet others. Tall ushers carry silver trays laden with daiquiris, Scotch and soda, orange juice; whiskey; they buck the tide of personages slowly, holding the trays high one moment, low the next. The conversation is animated, and from the hall there is a sustained sibilation of sound as the groups form, melt, and re-form into fresh groups. In the main hall off the East Room, the red-coated orchestra swings into a lively fox trot and tapered feet begin to tap. The young Army captains stand in the foyer, directing guests, or taking part in the conversations when solicited.

Outside, a group of dark gleaming cars pulls to a stop under the amber effusion of hanging lights, and the Marcos party steps out to be escorted in to the White House. Part of the entourage consists of the Secretary for Foreign Affairs; the Secretary of Finance; Señor Benjamin T. Romualdez, a special envoy to the United States with the rank of ambassador; Press Secretary Aspiras; Brigadier General Hans Menzi, a middle-aged pilot who is senior presidential aide, and the Speaker of the House of Representatives of the Philippines and the Under Secretary of Agriculture.

All of them speak excellent English; President Ferdinand E. Marcos, for example, was a solider in the United States Army in World War II and was decorated in battle. He has come a long way in twenty years; but so has Commander Lyndon Johnson, U.S.N.R. The Filipino ladies are all attractive. They seem never to grow old, or if they do, it must occur in the late years, and it drops them from youth to age overnight.

They have creamy skin, and they wear gossamer gowns of Filipino fashion with shoulders puffed like small wings. They hold the sides of their long dresses between pinched fingers, and they bow to greetings as they follow Mr. Symington to the Oval Room.

The faces around the East Room are familiar to newspaper readers. The Vice-President and Mrs. Humphrey are good mixers, and keep moving, shaking hands, saying hello, exchanging pleasantries and going to the next cluster. Senator Philip Hart of Michigan bends an ear to a whisperer, and smiles. Leonard Marks, the director of the United States Information Agency, takes his wife by the hand and exchanges greetings with William M. Blair, Jr., Ambassador to the Philippines, and William P. Bundy, Assistant Secretary of State.

The superintendent of the Air Force Academy, Lieutenant General Thomas S. Moorman, is in brilliant uniform; Major General Philip deWitt Ginder is outranked by his wife tonight; she is Jean Dalrymple, and will direct the entertainment after the dinner. In a sense, everyone is lost in rank. The room is alive with Cabinet members, senators, representatives, members of the Council of Economic Advisers, admirals, generals, and presidential assistants. Dr. Claude A. Buss, professor of history of Stanford University, stands for a moment in the center of history. Walter Reuther, union leader, has a boyish grin and a handshake, and stands close to the big fireplace.

The astronaut Walter Schirra, Jr., studies the faces around the room one by one, trying to fit names to them. Howard K. Smith, of the American Broadcasting Company, inclines his head to hear a question from a woman. Jack Valenti stands beside his wife, but keeps an eye on all the groups and is one of the few who knows them all.

There is time for a second drink. It promotes conversation and the buzz is a decibel higher when the band stops in mid-waltz to strike up "Hail to the Chief." All around the room words die on lips, and the young captains make gentle motions with their gloves for the guests to form into a reception line. President Johnson approaches the door with the gloved hand of Mrs. Marcos in the crook of his arm. He pauses to wait for President Marcos and Mrs. Johnson to draw abreast, then he enters the room. The applause of the guests can be heard over the last strains of the march. The two Presidents bow, and they nod to personal friends. It is a hand-holding foursome, and the sophisticated guests detect the camaraderie between the two Presidents.

Marcos has a handsome dark face, a façade behind which lies intensity of purpose and a stubbornness which almost matches that of his host. Ferdinand Edralain Marcos at the age of forty-nine is not satisfied with being the leader of thirty-three million Filipinos on seven thousand islands; he wants to be a leader in Southeast Asia, from Formosa to Sumatra.

Nor does he want to alter his thinking eastward to the United States. Marcos prefers to school the United States to turn its eyes westward. The world's dawn is coming up in the wrong direction—a dawn with strong red bands of light. The

8:00 P.M.

ambitious leader wants the United States to turn away from its traditional orientation toward Europe to a posture which faces Asia.

He stands next to Lyndon Johnson in the receiving line, and his face is animated with boyish delight. Third in line is Mrs. Johnson, who addresses herself to Mrs. Marcos, on her right. A uniformed officer stands ten feet from the arch, to introduce in booming tones the guests who form a loose line around the room. The keynote is not formality, in spite of the tendency of a few women to compromise between a formal bow and a curtsy. The President of the United States introduces each guest as though he were a personal friend, and his handshake is warm and firm. "Mr. President," he says, passing the guest onward, "this is our distinguished senator from . . ." "This is one of the prettiest ladies in the Southwest, where we grow a lot of pretty ones." "Mr. President, this is the Governor of New Mexico and Mrs. Campbell . . ."

Mr. Marcos acknowledges each one with enthusiasm. The guests move on to Mrs. Johnson, who wears a big smile and helps to reintroduce each guest to the First Lady of the Philippines. It is a prescribed chore, not always relished by the hosts but borne with a minimum of stiffness. The guests leave the room for numbered and assigned tables in the State Dining Room and the Blue Room. The dinner is a little too big for one room, especially since the Johnsons abandoned the old U-shaped table at which guests had to sit according to rank, in favor of round tables seating eight, where protocol gives way to informality.

The guests are in no hurry. Some wander through the public rooms to study familiar portraits and furnishings. Others lounge in the main lobby, with jewels flashing yellow and blue and red, listening to the orchestra play familiar tunes. With the

: 237

A *Day in the Life of President Johnson*

onset of night, the lighting seems brighter. The scene is, in itself, a painting. The black and white of starched men stands boldly against the marble and granite of the center hall, and the red-jacketed musicians sway to the old waltzes and new fox trots.

Mr. Marcos misses no detail. Through the energetic smile he absorbs everything and everyone. He has been in Washington only thirty hours, but he has already met many of these men; he has been in ideological conflict with some of them. He had expected a $250,000,000 stabilization loan, and when he detected no enthusiasm for it, at once began to discuss a Southeast Asia conference to be held in Manila. Attendance by the President of the United States would make a big man of Marcos, the host, and would at the same time bring the free nations of Southeast Asia together in a cohesive group.

President Johnson saw in Marcos a man of nerve and decision, and permitted himself to be talked into making the flight to Asia. The agreement amounted to more than an endorsement of Mr. Marcos as a true amigo; it turned American attention one hundred and eighty degrees east. Most chiefs of state get a pretty thorough briefing on each other before meeting, and Marcos and Johnson saw something of the other in himself.

Marcos averages fifteen to sixteen hours of work each day. His strong suit is a determination to work with the Free World without becoming a lackey to it. He grew up on a ranch. His father, a local politician, was a stern man who passed on the fundamentals of good politics to his son. At the University of the Philippines, he picked up a neglected education and won a scholarship. In school, he debated the political questions of the time. Twice he felt that his political party passed over him in favor of a less worthy man. In his flight toward the sun,

8:00 P.M.

Marcos had encountered storms personal as well as political. When he saw the pretty Imelda Romualdez sitting in the House of Representatives, he walked to her side, asked her to stand up, and stood back-to-back to find that he was one inch taller. "I'm getting married," he said, and eleven days later Miss Romualdez became Mrs. Marcos. She campaigns at his side. His most difficult internal problem is poverty.

On this night he is standing beside the President of the United States as an equal. He is neither the tool of America nor its listening post. Marcos wants to lead, as well as to be led. He and Johnson see Asia eye-to-eye and watch the same dangerous dawn.

When the last of the guests has been presented, the Johnsons and the Marcos relax. They chat in the big, now almost empty room as the guests move by degrees through the corridor, enjoying the music and the banter. Among the distinguished personages, the petty confusion of "which-room, which-table" begins. This is a game in which the wife says, "You have the invitation in your pocket," and the husband says, "You put it in your bag before we left." The young Army captains assist, and having received a signal to seat the guests, look like so many collies around a herd of expensive sheep.

9:00 P.M.

The cast-iron dignity of the state reception vanishes as the diners sit. The President comes into the room with his glasses on, holding Mrs. Marcos by the arm and steering the graceful and willowy lady to the head table under the white mantel. There is a polite patter of palms; the guests stand and Mr. Johnson beams happily as he holds a chair out for his dinner companion.

Before being seated, he looks around the big room at the white tables, each with eight persons, and then, having assured himself that all is in order, extends his hand again to Francis Cardinal Spellman and Sylvia Porter, financial columnist. An usher in the far doorway nods, and waiters begin to serve the crabmeat cocktail.

From all over the room, eyes furtively scan the President, and when he appears to be in animated conversation, the buzz of table introductions begins. Each table has a host; couples are split, not only so far as tables are concerned, but rooms too. President Marcos is seated in the Blue Room with Mrs. Johnson. A system of loudspeakers connects the rooms.

The place settings are elaborate, with Truman gold dinner-

9:00 P.M.

ware and wine goblets. There is a mixture of cut and wild flowers on each table. The lighting is soft, coming from electric candles overhead and from wall clusters. The waiters glide in silence, passing trays of crabmeat in molds. Wine stewards pour. The buzz of conversation lifts, and the President leans across his plate to be heard by his guests. His attitude is "at home," and his head and eyes turn from one to the other at his table. He finishes his crabmeat, laughing at a joke and wiping his mouth.

He catches the eye of a waiter and nods. In a moment Mr. Johnson has a second helping of crabmeat. He and the Cardinal conspire to keep the conversation on a sparkling anecdotal level. At another table, Bill Moyers is monopolized by a gray-haired woman in red. Jack Valenti, puffing on a cigar, crosses his legs in the aisle. A general who was a Japanese prisoner for over three years notices wryly that there is rice on the menu.

The music is soft and pleasantly archaic. The tunes are humable, and the notes barely intrude on the conversation. The walls are of natural oak, set between pilasters and painted off-white. Over the mantel behind President Johnson, Lincoln sits pensively, with crossed knees and hand under chin. This portrait was painted four years after he died.

In the Blue Room, Mr. Marcos sits under a center chandelier, chatting with Mrs. Johnson. When James Hoban designed the White House, he thought of the elliptical Blue Room as the most elegant area in the building. It is not as big as the State Dining Room, but bears the imprint of dainty design and exquisite furnishing. The walls are hung in two tones of cream-white satin. At the top of the wall a royal-blue valance hangs in folds, tipped with gold fringe. The center chandelier appears, when lighted, to be draped in diamonds. The small armchairs are seated and backed with blue satin decorated

: 241

with gold stars and the seal of the President.

Like a pretty child, it is a room one longs to decorate. Many Presidents and their First Ladies have tried it. On the south side, huge French doors once opened onto the President's Park. These are now windows. The room has, at times, been flamboyant with clusters of gas lamps and pier glasses. At others, it has appeared severe. Monroe's pier table still reposes beneath a painting of George Washington. The chairs and center table were ordered by Buchanan. President Arthur's Tiffany glass screen stands outside a door. President Madison ordered specially designed low sofas with Greek fluting on the ends. Most of it was burned in the fire of 1814. It was President Van Buren who first saw the room as "blue." The last person to redecorate it was Mrs. John F. Kennedy, in the autumn of 1962.

Hubert Humphrey is at a side table. A guest asks happily, "Why was I invited?" and no one can answer. The topics at another table range from generals who play golf at Burning Tree, to freedom of the press and concomitant abuses, to the beauty of Mrs. Marcos. Adele Simpson, the designer, at another table, tosses a flower to Senator Lausche. He tries wearing it between his teeth, but switches it to a position over his ear.

On the ground floor, near the flower shop, several workmen have finished their dinner, and under lights, move heavy objects off the garden walk into a sheltered corner of the vestibule. These are the gifts which the two Presidents have exchanged. The first family of the Philippines brought the Johnsons a set of carved mahogany furniture. There is also a nine-

9:00 P.M.

foot credenza, a big semicircular desk, also made of Philippine mahogany, and six armchairs.

All of these are heavy, but must be handled with care. There is also a big wood screen with Filipino figures embossed on both sides. In addition, there are large paintings of Mr. and Mrs. Johnson, done on black velvet and framed. There are gifts for the children: for Luci, place mats and napkins made of pineapple cloth. For Lynda, dessert plates which seem to have been made from shells.

The Johnsons gave their guests several gifts, but the one which captured the attention of the Marcos was a silver box with handles, bearing the seal of the President, replete with etched quotes from both men. The one from Mr. Johnson reads: "We dream of a world where all are fed and charged with hope. And we will help to make it so." On the other side, a quotation from Mr. Marcos reads: "Come then, let us march together toward the dream of greatness."

The family gifts exchanged between chiefs of state almost always include the children. For the young Marcoses there was a doll house completely furnished, a doll with a wardrobe, and a slot car racing set.

As the workmen tidy the gifts, they realize that there will be a new order, probably in the morning, to crate the assortment. Some will go to Manila; others will head for Johnson City, Texas.

The diners are well into the salad and Trappist cheese when strolling musicians appear at the head of each aisle. There are nine Army violinists and cellists in red jackets, and against a wall, an accordionist. The diners return their forks to their plates to applaud as the group begins a rendition—in harmonic thirds—of "The Shadow of Your Smile." The violinists move individually from table to table, and a stout man half rises in his chair to see the musicians.

As he sits, the whole back of the chair falls to the floor. But he has savoir-faire; he doesn't turn to see what happened. He digs into his salad. Bill Moyers, puffing on a slender cigar, turns gravely to his opposite number, Señor Aspiras, and murmurs, "When I say we have antiques in the White House, I mean antiques." The chairs, Queen Anne style, were built by McKim, Meade and White in 1902. Two ushers remove the debris from the floor; another carries a fresh chair down the aisle. The diner lifts himself an inch or two and permits the chair to be slid under his hips.

Mrs. Marcos lifts her radiant face suddenly as the instrumentalists begin to play a Filipino folk song called "Planting Rice." "Planting rice is never fun, bent from morning to the set of sun . . ." Her features gladden. She begins to sing softly with the musicians. A few Americans who have seen duty in the Philippines join in. The lady applauds vigorously when the song is complete.

They break into "I Could Have Danced All Night" and the sound of the strings is so pleasant that the diners appear to be captivated. Obviously, no one wants the dinner to end; the retired general is eating the rice on his plate. The President digs into his salad, and his head nods to the rhythm of the great songs of yesterday. The ladies begin to breathe a little deeper, and eat a little less. Some disavow dessert, then look at it a second time and decide yes.

The musicians begin to retreat, and the diners emit a disappointed "Ohhh." They are still playing a musical comedy hit as they back out the door into the great center hall. An usher tells

the President that those in the Blue Room are nearly finished
dinner. Demitasse is being served. The gentlemen have a
choice from boxes of cigars.

In the big kitchen, ushers carry trays laden with soiled
dishes. Women group them for washing. No work will be left
until morning. When the chef leaves tonight, his place of work
will be gleaming. Some of the ushers repeat the compliments
of diners on the succulent quality of the beef. The head man
merely nods.

The waiters pause a moment, breathing hard, and pick up
freshly laden trays. One grins at Mr. Haller. "The President,"
he said, "had a second crabmeat." The chef looks surprised.
"Did he say anything?" The waiter shoulders a tray of demitasse cups. "Yes, sir. He said, 'This one is different.'"

The chef has little interest in the other compliments. His
night is complete.

In the East Room, the sectional wall has been removed and
a stage has been set up midway in the room. In front of it, two
hundred chairs are placed in rows. There is a curtain. A stage
director tests it. There is a proscenium and footlights. A group
of singers comes onstage. Some are in heavy make-up. Others
are adjusting costumes.

The director of the Marine band uses the little stairway on
the left side and walks onstage to go over the order of entertainment. The actors group around him to get the final word
once more. Every number has been rehearsed and timed. Still

there are questions. "Do I leave stage right?" "How about an encore? Any encores?" "Where will the President sit? Will I be able to see him through the footlights?" "Each one of us finishes his number, waits for applause, takes one bow, and goes off. Right?" "Do we use microphones or just sing straight out?" "How about the cues? Do I look at you for the introduction?"

The orchestra again sits outside the door to the East Room. On the racks and on the floor are sheets of music, enough to last all night. There are plenty of Strauss waltzes, and one musician is reminded of a wife in the arms of her husband. "You'll have to waltz a little faster, dear," she said. "They're playing a rhumba."

When the Army violinists come out into the hall, the director of the band knows that the dinner is nearly over. He is ready.

10:00 P.M.

A state visit, no matter how broad the smiles of its guests, can be a chore and often a bore. This is especially true when two Presidents meet. Long before the confrontation, the foreign departments have met and have decided what can be discussed by their chiefs and what cannot. Even the address of welcome is carefully screened for the precise tone of cordiality. And at supposedly informal luncheons, discussions become iron-clad, with technical assistance at the table in the form of generals, specialists in trade, State Department experts, and presidential assistants.

Ad libs and off-the-record opinions are discouraged as dangerous. Commitments are never made before being weighed by both countries, with judicious note being taken of the internal effect on both sides, including press interpretation. The reciprocal receptions staged by the Presidents entail a carefully balanced guest list—and is studied by both sides, by the Presidents, their wives, their press and social secretaries, the state and security groups, before invitations are sent. To seat a few hundred guests without offense is almost impossible. To include one person who may be anathema to the guest of honor is a grave discourtesy.

This reception is different. President Johnson wants the world to know that this is a meeting of comrades-in-arms; that the friendship of the United States for the nation it spawned is warm and deep; that he and Ferdinand Marcos can be careless of speech and can reach agreements without the aid of the "specialists." There is an air of mutual trust, and on Lyndon Johnson's face is a rare unstudied smile.

He sips a little of his Sanka, and stands at his table to vociferous applause. The feeling of friends-among-friends has permeated the tables. The President half raises a hand and the guests sit back. There will be no formal speech. He is going to be his most effective—speaking informally and saying what is on his mind.

"Mr. President," he says crisply, "Mrs. Marcos, ladies and gentlemen—Mr. Valenti: For some time I have wanted to get to know the President of the Philippines and talk over matters of mutual interest." His eyebrows begin to lift as Mr. Johnson recounts that as each of his men returned from a visit to Manila (Vice-President Humphrey, Secretary of State Rusk, Special Assistant Valenti), they made identical reports: "The Philippines are on the march; President Marcos is a great man. He sure has a beautiful wife."

The President joins in the laughter, now emanating from two rooms. Mrs. Marcos inclines her head and covers her face with one hand. "When I invited President Marcos to visit us here in Washington, my assistants said, 'We hope you invited Mrs. Marcos.'" He is sure that both Presidents are lucky to have such charming and popular wives. Casually he traces his career and that of President Marcos, showing that militarily and politically they met the same hardships and overcame

10:00 P.M.

them. As an added aside on American politics, Mr. Johnson draws a big laugh when he says that "the difference between the Democratic and Republican parties is that the Republican party has its splits between elections, and the Democrats have theirs on election eve."

The talk becomes serious for a moment or two, when the President proposes a new partnership between the United States and the Philippines. "Our talks were good. We looked honestly and thoroughly at the problems that face us. We both understand that if free nations that are small are to be the architects and the guardians of their own destiny, they must be willing and able to discourage intruders. . . . As old comrades-in-arms, we have made plans to join in a new alliance. This time the enemy is hunger, the enemy is disease, the enemy is ignorance. . . .

"A man of courage is almost always a man of faith. Tonight we are proud to honor such a man."

Mr. Johnson raises a goblet of wine. "Ladies and gentlemen, I ask you to join me in saluting a hero in war and peace—join me in a toast to the President of the Republic of the Philippines." The audience is on its feet. Some raise their champagne high. Some toast the guest of honor with coffee. Before he sits, the President says, "I look forward to the time when we can explore the stars together."

As the applause dies, the crisp, slightly accented voice of President Marcos comes through the speakers. He thanks the President of the United States and makes a witty response to lovely First Ladies as vote-getters. He refers to his wife as "the reason why I won." In discussing the problems of his country, he enunciates an aphorism: "A man who does not look back to his origins cannot reach his destiny."

Mr. Marcos refers to the United States as "the most powerful

: 249

democracy the world has ever known. In Asia," he says, "the Philippine nation is an *experiment* in democracy." He thinks it will work. He feels that it has worked. Before he left Manila, he said that the most important thing that has happened in the Viet Nam war was the holding of free elections in South Viet Nam. He proposes a toast to his friend and the friend of his nation: "President of the United States, Lyndon Johnson."

Outside the White House, the summer lightning has traveled from Virginia to Washington without loss of strength. The crayon-dark clouds touch the tip of the Washington Monument, and a scattered peal of thunder seems to echo the applause in the Executive Mansion. Winks of blue-white flashes touch the faces of buildings and monuments, but the rain holds off. The birds are hushed in trees; the petals of flowers tremble alone in darkness.

Passing the White House, a cab driver sticks his hand out. "No rain," he says to his passenger. "Just a lot of noise." The passenger is looking the other way. "The White House sure is lit up," he says. "Wonder what's going on?" The driver sees that the light ahead is glowing orange, and he begins to tap his brake. "I read it in the paper," he says. "Now I forget. Some high muckety-muck is getting the royal treatment."

This is not strange. The majority of Americans are poorly informed because they choose to be. The citizen can discuss Luci Johnson's coming marriage with authority, but many cannot and will not lend eye or ear to the reason why her father wants the country to have a necklace of friendly nations stretching off the Asian mainland, from Japan through Formosa to the Philippines.

10:00 P.M.

The Marcos visit is not only front-page news, but a field for speculative punditry as well. And yet, because the United States and the Philippines found themselves in accord, the press coverage fell off from the high plane of foreign affairs to the level of social events. Almost ignoring the American-Philippine rapport, tomorrow's *Evening Star* will publish a page of political columns with these headlines: "Crosby S. Noyes: Vietnamese Really No Strangers to Democracy"; "Doris Fleeson: Primaries Fail to Show New Paths"; "David Lawrence: Marcos' Visit a Dramatic Reminder"; "James J. Kilpatrick: Johnson Lets the Feel of His Lasso Slip."

Good news is not news. It has always been so. This is not an error on the part of the newspapers; it is pandering to the readers' requirements. Good news sells no newspapers. Any editor or columnist who tries to tell his readers that all is serene at home and abroad—if it were so—is headed for oblivion.

When the President of the Philippines concludes his visit, less than ten percent of the population will be able to recall his name.

The eyes of President Johnson flick across the array of tables. He wants to conclude the dinner, but not before the diners have an opportunity to finish dessert, puff on imported cigars, and enjoy some conversation. His head hangs low, his forehead is puckered with thought, and after a glance, he decides to give everyone a few more minutes. From the Blue Room, he gets the whispered word that dessert dishes are now being picked up by the ushers.

Softly Mrs. Marcos compliments the President on the dinner

music. She says that she is surprised that the American musicians learned the native Philippine songs, especially "Planting Rice." Mr. Johnson grins. The small boy in him relishes surprises. He likes to engineer the unexpected. He studies her pale yellow gown. "You people must have a pretty good CIA yourselves," he says. "That yellow is my favorite color." Mrs. Marcos denies friendly espionage. "It is my favorite color too," she says.

Normally, state dinners hobble President Johnson's conversation. He is naturally gregarious and opinionated, and if he is permitted to be himself, can discuss a wide range of subjects with authority. However, state receptions are hives of gossip. A casual opinion on the part of the American Chief of State, or the distinguished visitor, sets up a hum of confidential phone calls in foreign offices and the State Department. The offhand remark is often expanded into a revelation of foreign policy. It is interpreted and reinterpreted until the value of an idle jest is exalted to the status of a "planned leak."

Herein lies the difference between the Marcos dinner and most of the others. Both Presidents were disarmingly candid; both First Ladies felt "at home" with each other. If there was any surprise in the meeting, it was Johnson's astonishment that the President of a small and poor oriental nation could plan philosophically so far into the future. He had not expected much more than the renewal of friendship between two countries willing to fight for freedom. On the other hand, Johnson was a surprise to Marcos. The Filipino expected that Johnson would be well briefed about the Philippines, but was impressed to find, in conversation, that the President of the United States could quote "chapter and verse" of the complex interrelation of foreign affairs. Later Marcos said to an aide, "He knew even the smallest details—even the subtleties of our problems." At times in their discussions, Johnson seemed to anticipate the next point and cut through the spidery web of diplomacy to say "Yes" or "No" at once.

It would not be dollar diplomacy, he said. An agreement of Asian friends would have to go beyond loans and the pooling of resources in an export-import bank. Nor could it be a military alliance, Mr. Johnson said. The first would be too cheap, the second expensive. A meeting of national friends implies an equality of governments large and small, and if Mr. Marcos envisioned a meeting in Manila in which Mr. Johnson would be regarded as a representative of one of the members, then he would be in favor of it. Even more, he would attend it. But he would not dominate it.

There is nothing that Johnson has achieved in the field of diplomacy which better epitomizes his personal views than this sudden, almost blunt, agreement to fly to Manila. The open-hearted Texas handclasp is in it; the lack of subtlety, suspicion, and bargaining runs contrary to the wheeler-dealer image which has been dealt to the American people, but is much closer to the real Lyndon Johnson.

Mr. Johnson stands and helps Mrs. Marcos with her chair. The guests come to their feet to thank the President with their hands for a cordial evening. He nods and offers his arm to his guest, and they lead the way into the great center hall. Walking across the plain red rug, they meet President Marcos and Mrs. Johnson emerging from the Blue Room. The band leader raps his baton, halts the music for a moment, and the orchestra swings into Mr. Johnson's favorite: "Hello, Dolly." The President taps his foot, and says, "Let's dance before we go inside."

He walks with Mrs. Marcos to the pale marble of the north portico, enfolds her in his arms, and begins his sedate dance. Gallantly, President Marcos invites Mrs. Johnson to dance, and the two couples swing slowly around the marble floor.

Vice-President Humphrey watches, smiling and nodding in tempo, and asks his wife to dance, but she declines. The two couples may want to dance alone, she feels. The great glass lantern in the portico casts a gleam on the faces of the dancers; the orchestra concludes "Hello, Dolly" and starts on a medley of waltzes by Johann Strauss. Many of the dinner guests pause behind the white columns to watch, but some continue on to the East Room to get seats for the entertainment.

The duet-dance of the two presidential couples is a rare scene. Some older ladies watching from the center hall smile approvingly and tell each other that no President within their memory would cut away from the formal decorum of the evening to "skitter around the hall" in an impromptu dance. Another woman says, "Two Presidents are doing it." One says moodily that it is good to have a President who is unafraid to follow his impulse.

President Johnson seems to sense all the eyes, and he stops dancing to chat with Mrs. Marcos as the remaining guests move to the East Room. The few still in the hall applaud, and President Marcos stops dancing. The four engage in conversation, and a moment later step into the East Room to join their guests. The center of the front row has been reserved and President Johnson supervises the seating, placing President Marcos and Mrs. Johnson on his right, and Mrs. Marcos to his left.

On each chair is a green and white program, embossed with a presidential gold seal and inscribed: "Moments from Great American Musicals." Mr. Johnson presses his glasses tight against the bridge of his nose and flips the page. The White House learned from Jean Dalrymple that this is the one hundredth anniversary of the American musical comedy, which some believe began with a production called *The Black Crook* in New York. Miss Dalrymple, director of the New York City Center Light Opera Company, agreed to honor the anniversary with singing members of her troupe, and popular hits from fairly recent extravaganzas.

Mr. Johnson sits. The lights in the East Room dim. The footlights brighten, and the Marine orchestra comes up, loud and lusty, with a medley from *Oklahoma!*

The Situation Room is so deep in the White House that the lighting casts the same neutral glow at night as it does by day. There are only two ways to tell dark from light. One is to carry a calendar watch; the other is to note the size of the staff on duty. The night staff, working under Arthur McCafferty, is small and busy. The stenographers' fingers hit the rubber heels of the electric typewriters and watch the keys tiptoe across a line; the Army clerks attend the teleprinters—reading, ripping, and reporting. McCafferty and his assistant assort, assess, and assemble.

The Situation Room is alert at all times. It is peopled twenty-four hours a day, and along with its counterpart in the Pentagon, is the eyes and ears of the nation. It is the one department which can command the attention of the President at any time, whether he is awake or asleep. The electronic intelligence never stops chattering the news of the world, great and small. The Army ratings move from one machine to another. They must know at all times what is coming in, because the machines are gaited to announce events almost simultaneously with their occurrence, and this would be pointless if there were no men to monitor the chatter.

Arthur McCafferty, as calm as a windless pond, fingers a roll of paper coming out of a machine on the lower landing. This is the morning report from Viet Nam—*tomorrow's* report. He reads it as the keys punch the words. If any of it is new, unusual, or alarming, he will page Mr. Rostow in the East Room with an oral digest.

If Rostow thinks the matter requires no immediate reaction, Mr. Johnson will not be disturbed. On the other hand, if Rostow is not available, Mr. McCafferty can make the decision himself. The news tonight is of small actions near Da Nang, a plastic bomb exploding in a native market place, and a routine analysis of North Viet Nam military intentions in the monsoon season.

Mr. McCafferty reads it through, and when it is complete, rips it out of the machine and reads it again. None of it will require attention from the President. However, the night boss sits at a desk, marks up a copy, and sends it upstairs to Walt Whitman Rostow. It comes back marked "Hold."

Onstage in the East Room, Karen Morrow, young and vibrant, brings a wise grin to the faces out front as she sings "I Cain't Say No." She wears a dirndl and fills the room with the Rogers and Hammerstein lyrics.

Miss Morrow takes her bow, her shadowed eyes studying the applauding Presidents and First Ladies. She has been rehearsing for this for a long time, but the actual performance comes to four minutes on a White House stage. The curtain swings down, the ends swaying an inch above the floor, and the music starts again. This time it is a selection from *The Pajama Game.*

The President crosses his legs and composes his hands on his lap. His expression shows appreciation of the performers, but it is as nothing compared to the understanding of Mrs. Johnson, a true aficionado of musical comedy. She loves music and the legitimate theatre. This is one of the few occasions when she has managed to corral her husband for an evening of music.

11:00 P.M.

The reaction of the audience is in itself entertainment. The applause is loud and prolonged after each song. Luba Lisa sings "Steam Heat" with a syncopated yearning for additional warmth; Robert Lu Pone and Tony Salatino crouch and swing in a dance. The sophisticates laugh at the double-entendres; women in rich gowns and flashing jewels nod with the beat of the music. It is a surprise to find such brightness and color in a house whose mood is historically solemn. The guests hold their enthusiasm just short of whistling.

President Marcos places his ankle on the opposite knee and murmurs some of the words to the music. His wife, who is a singer, studies the costumes and settings eagerly, and looks like a bright-eyed teen-ager watching her first show.

Admiral Hyman Rickover, lean and pale, adds extra furrows to his normal frown. Robert McNamara wears a faint grin. Francis Cardinal Spellman finds Jack De Lon amusing. Mr. De Lon plays the part of Nicely Nicely Johnson of *Guys and Dolls*, and sings "Sit Down, You're Rockin' the Boat." He does so well that the audience continues its applause after the curtain has closed, but there are no encores this evening. As one performer

: 258

11:00 P.M.

concluded his work, the musicians drop the sheet music to the floor in the hall and begin the eight-bar introduction to the next number.

This one is from *Carousel*—"If I Loved You"—and brings De Lon back onstage with Louise O'Brien. This is followed by a second song from the same show: "Mister Snow." It is doubtful that the singers ever had a better audience.

In another part of the building, the White House ushers are escorting couples to the President's elevator. They are taken to the quiet of the second-floor corridor, where the squeak of a loose board underfoot is heard all the way to the cathedral windows, and on to the Yellow Oval Room. Most of them are late arrivals from Texas. A few, who are members of Congress, worked late. Several are house guests, with small suites on the third floor. They greet each other with loud huzzahs and open arms. All of these people were political confreres, and personal friends, of the Johnsons back in the 1930's. This is the Texas delegation, or a good part of it, as it stood in the administration of Franklin D. Roosevelt.

Some have retired. A few are still at their posts in Washington. Each has a high regard for all the others. They had hoped that the President and the First Lady could be in the House Building for the unveiling of the portrait of Sam Rayburn. The Johnsons, unwilling to forgo the occasion entirely, asked "Sam's boys" and their wives, in addition to artist Tom Lea, to share a few minutes with them at this late hour.

They do not have long to wait, but none would mind, because they know that Mr. Johnson and Lady Bird will get there as quickly as they can. Besides, all of them have a lot of time to bridge, and as the waiters pass among them with trays of drinks, the wry tongue of Texas needling is heard among the men, and the women join in the laughter.

Ordinarily, the Johnsons retire to their rooms at this time. Or they may adjourn to his. In either case, the President carries his "night reading" under his arm. Mrs. Johnson carries a portfolio of mail, reminders, and suggestions in her hand. He flicks on the ceiling light, turns the television sets on, and undresses. The President hangs his clothes carefully in the closet.

After the ablutions, he dons his pajamas and sometimes a robe, and fluffs a couple of pillows on the outside of the bed. He wears his metal-rimmed glasses and reads the first sheet of paper, lifting his chin to get the focus on the top of the page, rubbing his ear sometimes, lifting a pen from the night table to make a notation, turning the digested pages downward neatly. He listens to news on the networks. If Mrs. Johnson sits in the room with the President, they hold a now-and-then conversation while both work.

Should he get through his work early enough, he will make a few calls involving the material he has just read. Or the President will cinch the belt of his robe and stroll out into the corridor in his slippers, and say, "Any news?" The night man sometimes has an envelope. Sometimes he says, "No, Mr. President."

Back in the room, Mr. Johnson phones the office of the White House physician and says, "Send one of the chiefs up." There is a fold-up rubbing table in his room, and one in the First Lady's. The Navy chief petty officer lugs a small bag with rubbing unguents. The President strips off the pajamas and

11:00 P.M.

eases his big frame onto the table, stomach down.

Strong hands moisten tired muscles with ointment, and the kneading of neck and shoulders commences. The President, still wearing his glasses, holds a paper before him, and as his body jiggles, manages to read it. When he wants to write a note on one of the sheets, he murmurs, "Hold it a minute."

Mr. Johnson has convinced Mrs. Johnson of the efficacy of the rubdown, and sometimes, when the ardor of the day brings on fatigue or tenseness, she puts on a bathing suit and submits to the relaxation of neck massage. Mrs. Johnson likes to have the table turned so that she can watch television, even though the net effect of the rubdown is to induce a sweet drowsiness, the advance agent of sleep.

Altogether, the musicale embraces six hit productions. The East Room echoes to the triumphant strains of "I'm in Love with a Wonderful Guy," from *South Pacific*. For the closing number, a woman and a man harmonize in a Lyndon Johnson favorite—"Big D," the hit song of *The Most Happy Fella*. The two actors sing it Texas style, loud and swift, accenting the joy of two citizens of Dallas meeting for the first time.

As the curtain closes, part of the audience gets to its feet to applaud. The President confers in a whisper with Mrs. Johnson. The Marcoses and the Johnsons arise and walk to stage left. The curtain is parted again and the entire cast is onstage. The Presidents and their wives, backs to the audience, walk across stage, shaking hands with each singer and dancer, expressing appreciation for a lovely evening of music.

The actors stand straight, listening as though these words must be engraved on the mind forever. Then President Johnson leads the party back to the others. He shakes hands with some guests, who want to say thank you. In the reception hall, the President beams happily on one and all, and puts an arm around his wife to dance as the orchestra reverts to familiar waltzes.

The Vice-President waits until a fox trot is heard, then dances a modified frug with Mrs. Marcos. Between dances Mr. Johnson leads the lovely young Mrs. Marcos from guest to guest, talking over the noise from the band, insisting that she is the prettiest woman in the White House, with one exception. He points to a long-haired blonde, wife of a writer, and says, "I think it's a tie between you as to who is the prettiest." The two women smile a secret acknowledgment at each other.

Mr. Johnson is ready to dance with anyone who wants to try a chorus or so, but the women hang back, and he contents himself with small conversation with one group after another. President Marcos says he thinks he will return to Blair House. It has been a tiring day. Mr. Johnson is polite. He asks his opposite number not to hurry. But Mr. Marcos knows that tomorrow will be another arduous day in Washington, and before he returns to the Philippines, there will be a half dozen more in various cities around the United States. Both men have found that fighting a war is less enervating than fighting the social whirl.

Many of the guests leave, departing by the south entrance, where chauffeurs have been waiting beside dark cars in the night. Others stand chatting, with perimeter vision on the hosts and the guests of honor. The President and Mrs. Johnson escort the Marcoses out on the colonnaded porch. There the goodnights are said. President Marcos reminds President Johnson that there will be a reception in honor of the Johnsons at the Shoreham tomorrow.

11:00 P.M.

Johnson goes to the foot of the steps to help the Marcoses into their car. Again the goodnights are said, the gratitude is profuse. The President waits until the car crunches around the circular drive, then returns to Mrs. Johnson. The smile, momentarily, has left her face. "Some old Texas friends, you remember, are upstairs. Let's say goodnight and go up there. These people have been waiting, I'd guess."

The President nods. He takes her arm and says goodnight to the remnants of the diners and goes upstairs to the Yellow Oval Room.

The impulse of old and cherished friends may be to whoop and holler a greeting, but White House guests are conscious of the august barrier around the Presidency. The entrance of the Johnsons evokes polite applause. The President walks around the big bright room, shaking hands, swapping sectional jests, and relaxing like "one of the boys." Mrs. Johnson greets the ladies by first names and is kissed on the check. The consciousness of rank lies with the Texas delegation; the Johnsons chat animatedly and, in effect, try to fan the flame of old affections to a momentary brightness.

President Johnson, always deferential to his elders, addresses Judge Ewing Thomason and his wife as a freshman Congressman might the Speaker of the House. Still the glow of pride is in the eyes of the guests. This is most obvious when the President is not looking. He is one of their own; he is the first native son of Texas—born and raised in the state—to become the Chief Executive of the country. Behind the sparkle of masked pride is another thing: not one of them saw Lyndon Johnson as a future President. They appreciated his arduous labors in the House and Senate, but as Texans, they knew that most conventions were dominated by the bosses of the populous East and Middle West. Judge and Ann Worley spend a few minutes with the President as he sits heavily on a couch. Everybody recalls old times; other days; the era when everybody was nobody and all would crowd into a small apartment for talk and ham and cheese sandwiches.

The men, somehow, always managed to isolate themselves to discuss political tactics and legislative measures; the women staked claims to the settee and the kitchen, reciting the latest news from back home, the progress of children, the impossibility of maintaining a home in Texas and one in Washington. All of them were like young birds then, flying in an exclusive covey, making political turns in unison, pecking and chirping, building nests almost as bright as their hopes.

Each of the men has made his proper mark in life. There are no failures. Marvin Jones, who rode the political train with the rest in Congress, is now a judge, cloaked in the dark robes of dignity. George Mahon is still a member of Congress, outlasting all of his old cronies. Mrs. Tom Connally, widow of the snowy-haired senator, gets extra attention from the men because her husband was their peer in the Capitol when they were too young to know how to keep their mouths shut.

Cocktails and coffee and canapés are served. Neither the President nor Mrs. Johnson will permit a sign of fatigue in themselves. If they feel tired, they move around the room a little faster, and trade old jokes and chuckles with these people. They honor the painter of the Rayburn portrait and recollect old stories about the sainted "Mr. Sam." Nor will they tolerate any diplomatic maneuvers to cut this part of the evening short.

The faces around the room are older. Many of the fierce old

11:00 P.M.

fires are banked. Once upon a time any of these men, in from the prairies and the hills, would have fought valiantly—even to the political death—for a principle. The fight would have entailed the use of Texas yells and epithets. That was a decade ago, maybe two. The fierce fight died with the taut smooth skin. The features now are almost patrician; shaggy brows have whitened; eyes are deeper and less certain; wisdom has usurped will; the world of compromise is not only palatable, it is preferable to the youthful option of winning all or losing all.

None of them realize it, but they are now the Tom Connallys and the Sam Rayburns of Texas. In the aging faces the Johnsons see their own advancing years. Each member—wife as well as husband—is aware of the early years of struggle and the fat prime years of success, but no one is sure which he would choose, or even why.

Mrs. Johnson walks to a little table near the fireplace and adjusts her glasses and raps for attention. The President, who is sitting deep on a soft gold couch, stops talking. The others turn, and the First Lady, glancing at notes on a sheet of paper, lifts her voice a little and says:

"We of the Texas Delegation—and it's hard for Lyndon and me to think of ourselves any other way—we who are Texans and are in Washington temporarily—are so glad to be with you, our dear friends, tonight. It's a homecoming in a way." This is the keynote. Mrs. Johnson, who extends friendliness and dignity in equal measure, folds her notes and removes he glasses and rambles on with no formality, talking of "dear Abby and Ewing," presenting gifts, including a gold bracelet with the presidential seal for Judge Thomason's wife, and, as a surprise, tells the guests that this is the wedding anniversary of Ann and Gene Worley.

A Day in the Life of President Johnson

This, she says, means cake and champagne. The most surprised persons in the room are the Worleys. A little later the President stands with a knee leaning on the couch, to say a few words to these people who mean so much to him now, and who will mean more when he moves back to Texas. He speaks softly, *en famille,* with one hand in a trouser pocket. Sometimes he looks at the couch: sometimes his eyes raise to select one face for address.

"When I was a little boy, the principal source of pleasure was when someone could come and stay all night with us." He grins at the Thomasons, who are house guests at the White House. "Ewing and Abby have been staying up all night with us here." Before the next thought his face becomes solemn again. "One of the greatest blessings a man can have is to have his father's friend as his friend. Ewing was my father's friend. That friendship has passed over to me."

His knee shoves against the cushion on the couch and there is a long silence. No one speaks. No one munches a piece of cake, or sips a little wine. The President wants to say something about the United States, but he doesn't want to pontificate before his friends. He wants to say what he has to say simply, as though instead of standing here in this room in the White House, all of them were in his den in Texas.

"I don't guess that there are any people anywhere who don't want what we have got," he says. "That's natural. But we only have two hundred million people, a small percentage of the total." The guests stand immobile, a mirage of faces on a desert of time. "It isn't much of a percentage, but we produce more and we earn more than the others."

The President looks up, and now the dark brown eyes move across the still faces. "Big or small, we are going to have to help the others, especially those who aren't eating well." He snaps the thread of thought, as though his long-range hopes for his country should not be a part of what started out to be a jolly visit. He begins to speak of people in general, and friends in particular. There is nostalgia in the sentences; a carefully hidden sentiment bubbles to the surface. But he doesn't want to be mawkish either. "Everyone in this room has a special meaning for us."

This is a Lyndon Johnson the President hides. This is what lies under the surface of the master politician; this is what is hidden by the stern, tough features of the boss who rammed cactus words down the throat of Congress when he pointed a finger at the members in joint session and said, "This time I'm not going to give you eight months to think about it [civil rights]. I want you to get it out of committee and bring it to the floor and debate it and, I hope, pass it."

The President talks on, ruminating, and he mentions how deep he thought he was in friends in one campaign when it appeared that he had won election to Congress by eighty-seven votes, but how lonely he felt when the full count disclosed that he had lost by about the same number. The huzzahs, the handshakes, the back-slapping died in empty echoes. No one stood at his side. No one said, "Better luck next time." No one could spare a word to direct him to the bus home.

These people understand. The President does not have to be diplomatic. He is free to say whatever is in his heart, just as he once felt free to talk to them when they were all young and ambitious and full of plans to save the world. He wants to end the talk, so he imparts his ultimate dream to them, and only to them.

"When they pull down the curtain on my life, I will be satisfied if they say I did something for my fellow man—for education." He nods to himself. "I'll be satisfied."

12:00 MIDNIGHT

Tomorrow begins, and there is more work to be done. The old friends, who do not see the President and Lady Bird as frequently as in other days, are loath to leave, and they look for signs from their hosts. There are none. Mrs. Johnson stands near a window, talking to the Worleys. The President leans back on the couch facing the fireplace, looking up at a group which stands before him. Each can think of an amusing memory. The President is able to respond to each one with laughter, and he can think of another one.

A man mentions that he must leave. Tomorrow is another workday. He looks at his watch. Midnight has passed, and the slow swing eastward of the earth places the city of Washington at 12:29 midnight. Others pick up the cue: "We musn't stay any longer." At the moment when the men begin their farewells, the women remember all the little things they wanted to inquire about, or to relate. The chatter becomes loud and fast; sometimes it sounds as though all the women were talking at the same time.

The ushers, dark and tall, stand ready to show the guests to their cars or to their rooms upstairs. Husbands leave the side of the President to prod wives into saying goodbye. In a few minutes the room is empty. Bits of cake stand on plates. A cup of coffee, now cold, glistens like onyx under the lights. Mrs. Johnson's do-not-forget-to-mention notes are still on the end table.

Down the corridor, the last of the visitors is on the elevator. The President puts his arm around his wife's shoulder. There are no words to say. He nods goodnight to the guard on duty at the desk. Across the hall, where the seal shines on the rose-wood door, he turns the knob, and they disappear.

Inside, the Johnsons chat a minute about the day. Lady Bird is tired. "I'm going to do a little work," she says, "and I hope you will do the same and go to sleep. It has been a long day." The President removes his tie. "No," he says, "it has been a nice day. I enjoyed myself tonight. I'm going to make a few calls, look over the work, and go to sleep."

He kisses Lady Bird at the door between their rooms. He enfolds her in his arms and says goodnight as he says everything else, with authority. When he is alone, the President undresses. In the bathroom, he steps on the scale and learns that he is picking up weight slowly. It isn't much because of his diet, but the little extras now and then, the little tastes of forbidden food, are not noticed on his big frame until he steps on this contraption.

The pillows are fluffed; the sheets turned down. Mr. Johnson slips into bed, turning the ceiling light off and leaving the bed lamp on. His glasses are on, the night reading is at hand. He picks up the phone and talks to Joe Califano at home. The question concerns purchase of government bonds by government employees. "Have you been in touch with Larry O'Brien?" he says. "All right. Yes. I'll take it up in the morning. Good-night."

The second call is in. The President discusses surplus stockpiles of goods. "We have $485,000,000 in warehouses," he says. "Well, it costs money to store, and from these reports, I gather we don't need it. We should sell it when there is a pinch in copper and steel and other merchandise. It is going to help the economy and relieve the pressure on the consumer. At the same time it will help to keep prices down. This applies to aluminum and lead and bauxite and a lot of minerals. Yes. That's it. Remember, we held down the price of butter and bread and lumber by selling government stockpiles."

He phones Jake Jacobsen. There is no late news, nothing which requires the President to "bleed" with an assistant at this hour. The phone is set in its cradle. The work of reading and making decisions continues.

The White House is quiet. Here and there a policeman paces a hall slowly; a guard reads under a desk light; outside, men patrol the dark grounds. The threatening storm has passed. The stars are dimmed by the effulgent glow of street lights. A restaurant worker hoses a sidewalk. Students sing lustily in an old car. Rows of lights in government buildings flick on and off as platoons of cleaning women sweep tons of wastepaper into hampers and move on to the next floor.

It is almost—not quite—1 A.M. Washington is asleep. But not all of it. The night sentries man their posts in many buildings. The rest of the capital, from Silver Springs to Falls Church, from Bethesda to Capitol Heights, is storing energy for tomorrow. By day the city is bright and awesome rather than beautiful. In the late hours a dark gossamer veil is drawn across the pale stone, as though night were mourning. Only the trees maintain a stiff dignity. The reflection of a red light on a slow-cruising taxicab can be seen in the black macadam as a long exclamation point.

This is the home of the artificial smile, the rigor-mortis handshake, the temporary apartment, a city where the hunter flushes a lame duck, a settlement where even the streets are at odds with each other. The smart policitians struggle for office; the brilliant ones become lobbyists. It is where democracy induces biennial convulsion. It is cathedrals and slums and embassies and hotels and movies and students and military men and monuments and quaint homes. The temporary officeholders rule the natives; the arts are discussed but seldom seen; most of all, this is a city of rank—perhaps the only place in the world where a two-star general might deliver a message.

At the pinnacle of it all is the office of President of the United States. It was always the most powerful office in a magnificent democracy, but power begets power and the weight of it today crushes the man who has it. He has become the dispenser of all good and all evil. The quality of these adjectives is determined by the people, who decide what is good and what is evil. They may withhold applause when his work is good, but they never fail to hiss his blunders. Public scrutiny of the office, and every act of the President, is what makes the position impossible today. An intelligent patriot is not enough for this job; he must be without stain past and present and be desensitized to criticism.

Since 1920 it has been considered a triumph for a President to leave office with his honor intact. He cannot hope to augment it. Since 1946 it has been considered an accomplishment if a President does not precipitate a world conflict. Tension is the daily state of existence; weaponry squares its own strength year by year and potential casualties are estimated in the hundreds of millions. The ultimate in sophisticated resignation was reached in 1962, when bomb shelters went out of style.

The salary is poor; the hours are long; there are no true vacations. And yet the incumbent always wants to stay one more year, as though the governments of the world—in that time—might renounce greed as a goal. As though, as Lyndon Baines Johnson has said, "And man shall say to man: 'There, on this earth as in the eyes of God, walks my brother.'" For this, a man could be condemned as a naïve Christian.

It is barely one hundred years since a brother lifted a rifle and drew a bead on his brother in the United States. Man may have to creep another millennium or two to attain the stars.

The glasses are removed and placed on the night table. The drapes have been drawn. President Johnson rubs the sides of his nose, where the spectacles rested. The night reading is placed near the bed. Far off, a church bell tolls a single solemn note. The night light is turned off. The sheets and a bedspread are drawn up over the chest. The President of the United States emits a short sigh.

His day is done.

ACKNOWLEDGMENTS

The foregoing is a result of eleven days spent in the company of the First Family—eight at the White House; three at the LBJ Ranch. Most of the material came from seeing and hearing the events. A smaller percentage is from interviews. I feel grateful to the following:

President and Mrs. Lyndon Baines Johnson.
Their daughters, Lynda and Luci.
Mr. Jack Valenti.
Mrs. Elizabeth Carpenter.
The Messrs. Bill Moyers, Jake Jacobsen, Marvin Watson; in fact all of the assistants to the President, and especially to Walt Whitman Rostow.
Mrs. Juanita Roberts and the young ladies who work in her office.
Colonel James Cross, Mrs. Zephyr Wright, Mrs. Helen Williams, Mr. Lem Johns, Sergeant Paul Glynn, Mr. Jim Jones, and last, but by no means least, to my wife Kelly, who as usual was a competent researcher and assistant.

A Day in the Life of President Johnson

Books which were read and annotated include the following:

My Hope for America, by Lyndon B. Johnson (Random House).

Lyndon B. Johnson, Man and President, by Henry A. Zeiger (Popular Library).

A Family Album, by Rebekah Baines Johnson (McGraw-Hill).

The White House, published by the White House Historical Association.

The United States Government Organization Manual.

Washington Exposé, by Jack Anderson (Public Affairs Press).

President's Country, edited by Jack Maguire (Alcalde Press).

Lyndon B. Johnson and the World, by Philip L. Geyelin (Praeger).

Lyndon's Legacy, by Frank L. Kluckhohn (Monarch Books).

A Texan Looks at Lyndon, by Evetts Haley (Palo Duro Press).

Mrs. L.B.J., by Ruth Montgomery (Holt, Rinehart).

Also pertinent copies of *Life* magazine, *Newsweek, Parade* magazine, *Time* magazine.

Jim Bishop

ABOUT THE AUTHOR

JIM BISHOP created the "day in the life" books, most of which have been national best sellers. *The Day Lincoln Was Shot, The Day Christ Died,* and *A Day in the Life of President Kennedy* were read by millions, and his newspaper column is widely syndicated. Mr. Bishop and his wife Kelly now live in Florida.